D0049609

Alien Wars

Alien Wars

The Soviet Union's Agressions Against the World, 1919 to 1989

General Oleg Sarin
Colonel Lev Dvoretsky

PRESIDIO

Copyright © 1996 Oleg Sarin and Lev Dvoretsky

Published by Presidio Press
505 B San Marin Dr., Suite 300
Novato, CA 94945-1340

Library of Congress Cataloging-in-Publication Data

Sarin, O. L. (Oleg Leonidovich)
    Alien wars : the Soviet Union's aggressions against the world,
1919 to 1989 / Oleg Sarin, Lev Dvoretsky.
    p. cm.
    Includes bibliographical references.
    ISBN 0-89141-421-5 (hbk)
    1. Soviet Union—History, Military. 2. Soviet Union—Foreign
relations. I. Dvoretskii, L. S. (Lev Semenovich) II. Title.
DK54.S27   1996
947.084—dc20   96-14223
                                     CIP

Printed in the United States of America

Contents

Foreword

It all started with Lenin and became holy writ with Stalin and his successors: worldwide Communist revolution with the involvement of the peoples of the world pointing to the destruction of the capitalist system. Failure to fulfill this goal was considered outside the realm of possibility. The leaders of the Soviet Union would stoop to any kind of illegality, using deception, lies, and hollow promises, even the force of arms, to pursue their dreams.

In this book we present, we think for the first time, the story of the various military interventions attempted by the Soviet Union against neighbors to either gain territory or to bring whole countries under Soviet influence under the sacred religion of Communism.

In our previous book, *The Afghan Syndrome*, we told the story of Soviet adventurism in that poor country, Afghanistan. As disastrous as the attack on the Afghan resistance fighters proved to be to both countries, it unfortunately was only the last of many such aggressions. This book, therefore, deals with foreign wars, wars conducted by the Soviet Union for the benefit of irrational politicians and their equally crazy plans.

The Soviet state became an empire after the civil war following the 1917 Revolution against the tsar and the then-existing order. It survived World War II, but it was not a typical empire understood by politicians of past centuries. And it was not a simple continuation of the tsarist system of amalgamated states. To understand this, we must turn to the past.

The Russian empire was a relatively young political formation. What had emerged by the time of the early twentieth century was a very different animal from what the ancients had known. The emerging country of Russia was influenced by a variety of aggressors in both Europe and Asia. It was not until the time of Peter the Great in the eighteenth century that Russia could be characterized, under the Romanov dynasty, as an empire, developing over the centuries in all directions, incorporating principally lands from which previous aggressions had come.

Pretexts for expansion were found quite easily in the spirit of the time, sounding similar to the excuses for aggrandizement by other countries such as England and France. Expansion of Russian territory was necessary to secure greater space and to provide for the security of caravan routes. Russian wars in Turkestan were required to save those peoples from British domination. Wars in the Caucasus became necessary to save Christian inhabitants, peoples of Georgia and Armenia for example, from Muslim enslavement by Turkey and Persia. Wars in the Balkans were to save Slavic brothers from the same Muslim intruders.

After the revolution Lenin gave tsarist territorial expansion great credit as stated by his colleague, Academician Pokrovsky[1], who saw Russia as the historic "gendarme" of Europe starting with Catherine the Great. Pokrovsky wrote a revisionist short history of Russia[2] very much appreciated by Lenin, who wrote an introduction to it and ordered it to be used by schools throughout the country. After Stalin's accession to power, he ordered the book to be revised, omitting Lenin's introduction. Lenin was never against the concept of a Russian empire, only the tsarist aspect. He stood for even a larger expansion to include the entire world. He wrote into the foreword of the new Soviet constitution, "The new Soviet state will become . . . the first resolute step on the way of uniting the laboring people of all nations in the *Worldwide Soviet Socialist Republic*[3]."

Lenin immediately got to work, taking many "resolute" steps. Previous tsarist invasions were virtual child's play compared with Lenin's. The first victims were the closest: Ukraine, Byelorussia, the Caucasus, and various provinces in middle Asia.

The example of Ukraine is interesting. During the years 1917 to 1920, the country was invaded five times by foreigners: first by the Germans, next by Denikin's White Army, and three times by the Red Army. At the start Lenin hoped to subvert the new

Ukrainian Republic during the talks with the Central Rada (parliament) or by armed rebellion from inside. The Rada rejected his ultimatum, citing its right of self-determination as acknowledged by the Bolshevik government itself. Lenin's attempts to organize armed rebellion also failed, so in December 1917 he sent the Red Army to occupy Kiev. This first occupation of Ukraine lasted only two months, as Ukrainian troops in March ousted the Soviets from their land. In February 1919 they tried again with the same result. But in June 1920 the Red Army again occupied Kiev, and at last Ukraine became a part of the new Soviet empire with the false status of a sovereign Soviet republic.

The Bolsheviks could not imagine Soviet Russia without the Caucasus. Russia had always had interest in those lands. The first Russian tsar (Grosny) was married to the daughter of a Cabardine knight. Her name was Maria Temryukova. The wedding took place in 1561 after Ivan Grosny occupied Kasan (1552) and Astrakhan (1556). At this time Russian borders advanced along the Terek River, but further attempts in the sixteenth through the eighteenth centuries were futile, both because of resistance of the Caucasian people and the interests of powerful neighbors like Persia and Turkey. A massive invasion at the beginning of the nineteenth century, featuring Russian armies comprising some 200,000 troops, did not end for about fifty-five years, persisting through the reigns of three tsars. This invasion cost Russia more than any other attempted by the tsars, but finally was successful in incorporating the Caucasus into the Russian empire.

In 1917 the people of the Caucasus were placed in a terrible situation, literally caught between Lenin's Bolsheviks and the White Army of General Kolchak. Since Kolchak wanted to preserve the old empire, the Caucasian people allied themselves with the Bolsheviks who had declared that non-Russian people would be free to dissociate from Russia and establish their own independent states. But in 1920, after defeating Denikin and Kolchak, the Red Army immediately began to conquer the Caucasus and Turkestan, lured by the immense space, rich natural resources, and a large population.

Turkestan and other Muslim areas posed special problems, and final domination of that region did not occur until 1926. At first the Soviets did as little as possible to disturb the religious character of the regions with strong Muslim heritage. Gradually, however, Lenin was able to virtually stamp out religious practice in those lands. Finally it even became a criminal act to use the words "Muslim people." Beautiful examples of Muslim architecture of the thirteenth and fourteenth centuries were turned into anti-Islamic museums, office buildings, depots, or were destroyed.

The Bolsheviks did not forget the western part of the old Russian empire. Lenin started in 1918 to try to return these states to his new Soviet empire by force. The peoples of the Baltic states, Lithuania, Latvia, and Estonia, as well as Finland and Poland resisted the pressure of the Red Army so well that Lenin and Trotsky had to finally capitulate to the inevitable, acknowledging their right to be independent.

There were many ethnic Russians in these Baltic countries who had lived there for many years developing diverse cultural and religious institutions. These Russians lived in peace from that time until the start of the Second World War when with the infamous German-Soviet pact of 1939, the Baltic states as well as the eastern part of Poland were virtually deeded to the Soviet Union. Stalin's method of annexing these three republics was not by armed aggression; cunning deception and military threats were effective instead. Moscow stated to them that they should sign treaties to provide for Soviet protection against possible aggressors. They were induced to believe that they should allow Soviet troops to be located within their borders, while still enjoying their national sovereignty. It was made clear, however, that if these demands were not met, their countries would be occupied forcibly by the Red Army and that they would lose their freedom. Summoned to the Kremlin, the three heads of state signed treaties within twelve days: Estonia, September 28; Lithuania, October 10; and Latvia, October 5, 1939. It took Stalin nine months to completely purge these states of their independence. The governments that had signed these documents and the parliaments that had ratified them were all imprisoned in concentration camps, to be followed later by one-third of their populations. Baltic state

Communists were then sent from Moscow to run in "free" elections in which they received the usual 92 to 99 percent of the vote. New parliaments were elected in the same manner in the summer of 1940 and passed legislation addressed to the USSR petitioning Stalin for admittance to the union. It is not surprising that the Kremlin answered in the affirmative.

In a similar event, the provinces of Bessarabia and North Bukovina were annexed from Romania, whose government gave in when faced with the specter of Hitler standing behind Stalin in accord with the nonaggression pact that had been signed previously. On June 27, 1940, the Red Army occupied both these territories. These and similar actions radically improved the territorial and strategic positions of the USSR in its western environs.

We have already mentioned the Treaty of Nonaggression Between Germany and the USSR which was signed by Ribbentrop and Molotov on August 23, 1939. This pact was made public and caused consternation in the rest of the world. What was unrevealed at the time was a secret additional protocol that was developed in the Kremlin and sent to Berlin beforehand. It provided for the division of Poland between the two countries, as well as permitting Germany a free hand in Western Europe. It further allowed the USSR to annex the Romanian provinces, the Baltic states, and Finland. After the signing ceremony, the signees had a victory celebration hosted by Stalin and Molotov. It took only two signatures and a few minutes to decide the fate of five independent states.

Stalin's plans were simple: to gain a large slice of the European pie with Hitler's help and later to confront the Germans with Western aid, dictating terms to nations exhausted by war. As an alternative plan, Stalin was even preparing plans for a preventive attack on Germany. Many documents in Soviet archives are evidence of such an intention. A planning document of the Soviet General Staff prepared in August 1940 was adopted in May 1941 with the title "Considerations of the Plan for Strategic Deployment of the Armed Forces of the Soviet Union." The plan stated not only the requirement for a preventive strike at Germany but specified the forces needed and various specific objectives. During this period the Red Army conducted numerous maneuvers and tactical field exercises to prepare itself for its part in carrying out the plan's provisions. Organizations designed for offensive operations were created, such as the Department of Airborne Troops, organized on June 12, 1941. Airborne formations had been employed in the Red Army since 1935.

It is not our purpose in this book to discuss the conduct of World War II from the Soviet viewpoint. Suffice to say that Hitler interrupted Stalin's aggressive plans by launching Operation Barbarossa, the invasion of the Soviet Union, on June 22, 1941. Political games of the Soviet Communist leadership plunged the peoples of our country into a hazardous and frightful war that cost us more than twenty-eight million lives. God only knows what the outcome of the war might have been had it not been for gifted military commanders who somehow managed to avoid the reprisals of the 1930s, particularly Semyon Timoshenko and Georgi Zhukov, who were able to lead the nation to ultimate victory despite Stalin's plans for grand offensive and aggressive actions.

After the war Stalin was able to consolidate his power and remain true to himself, although he surely was the greatest murderer of all time. After the victory, all Eastern European countries found themselves under the yoke of Bolshevism, moving from the domination of Fascism, a most unenviable switch. In place of the "paradise" promised, they were subjected to poverty, slave labor, and suppression of democratic rights.

A brief look at the history of Soviet oppressive actions in the postwar world is instructive:

1948: West Berlin blockade
1950-1953: Korean War
1953: Soviet troops suppress protesters in East Germany
1956: Soviet troops suppress Hungarian uprising
1961: Berlin Wall constructed
1962: Caribbean crisis
1964–1975: Vietnam War
1967: Soviet involvement in Arab-Israeli War

1968: Soviet invasion of Czechoslovakia
1973: Soviet involvement in Arab-Israeli War
1979-1989: Soviet war in Afghanistan

Apart from these involvements in the internal affairs of foreign countries, there were many instances of official participation of the KGB and the Red Army in "liberation" operations and subversive actions against constituted governments. Soviet "internationalists" in civilian clothes or the uniforms of local soldiers took part in combat in Egypt, Yemen, Syria, Angola, Mozambique, and Ethiopia, to name only a few such instances. Tens of thousands of Soviet soldiers laid mines, set ambushes, and raised their Kalashnikov rifles under the banner of "national liberation" movements against "world capitalism" in countries of the third world. To our shame, not all of these "volunteers" returned home healthy and unwounded. Many became "unknown soldiers" in anonymous graves in the jungles of Africa and Vietnam, the sands of Sahara, or the Golan Heights. Some 239,000 families get pensions because of the deaths of husbands or sons   soldiers who remain forever in remote foreign lands.

Soviet expansion also had the form of huge shipments of weapons to many client states. The share of the USSR in the total volume of weapons trade early in the 1980s amounted to forty percent; in some kinds of combat weaponry it rose to fifty percent. Some twenty-five percent of all types of combat equipment produced in the USSR was exported. Other countries known as arms sellers, like France, Britain, and China, lagged far behind. This reckless and criminal international "assistance" contributed greatly to the ruination of the Soviet economy. One might excuse this if the countries supplied with all this aid became prosperous. The opposite was true, as illustrated by the "divided" nations like Germany and Korea.

As is now well known, the triumphant parade of socialism failed dismally. The peoples of the world rejected the Communist nightmare at the first opportunity and overthrew the totalitarian governments supported by the Soviet Union.

Reading the foregoing must cause one to ask oneself why the

people of the USSR tolerated the Leninist-Stalinist regime as long as they did; how they treated the aggressive policies of their leaders with "wholesome approval." People living in free countries cannot understand this phenomenon from their own experiences. Powerful ideological pressures fooled millions of people; lies in the form of constant propaganda coupled with the distinct possibility of death or imprisonment for the slightest offense caused our people to toe the line and support what they thought was an honorable regime. As we look back on our lives spent in supporting this immoral system, we can only imagine the monstrous consequences of covering the globe with the Communist program of the Soviet empire. Mikhail Gorbachev tried to revitalize socialism in the country, but failed. The whole rotten system fell in shambles, with many new sovereign states resulting. It is our fervent hope that current world leaders will find a way to prevent any further arms race and reduce the number of nuclear weapons and delivery systems to the level where world peace can be assured.

The foreign wars participated in by the Soviet Union now belong to history, but we see their traces in various trouble spots today. Combat actions in Yugoslavia, Georgia, Azerbaijan, and Tajikistan, as well as terrorist acts that are taking place all over the world, have their genesis in the acts of the Soviet Union in the past. So our past continues to haunt the world.

Let us now proceed to more detailed examinations of the alien wars of the Soviet Union. Our analysis of these is based on documentary evidence derived from a number of previously inaccessible archives. These documents contain information on Soviet participation in wars known only too well by Americans, Koreans, Vietnamese, Africans, and Israelis who lost sons in these unnecessary incursions

The earth is given to us for creation and not for destruction. We should be able to awaken each morning with the happy thoughts that the skies are clear, the sun is shining, and we are the masters of our own destinies.

Chapter I

War in the Pyrenees as Directed in the Kremlin

The developments in Spain from 1936 through 1939 were seen in the Kremlin as a gift from God, just as they should have been. What other opportunity could have presented itself to allow Stalin and the rest of the leadership the opportunity to introduce Soviet arms into the very heart of Western Europe? Added to this was a noble purpose that could be trumpeted to the world, the saving of a democratic regime from the ravages of Fascism embodied in the Spanish revolutionary movement led by General Franco. In fact, however, our Communist government was not concerned with any of the niceties of international law and customs that prohibited interference in the domestic affairs of other nations. Our leaders adhered to other principles that justified any action of proletarian internationalism, particularly if it was to their benefit. They saw the game as worth playing.

In January 1936 the Spanish Popular Front was established with strong Communist and other left-wing influences. This was a kind of culmination of political activities in the Second Republic that came to power in 1931 as a result of King Alfonso's abdication in

April. The government from the start until 1933 had a decidedly left-wing hue, whereas its successor from 1933 to 1936 was somewhat right of center. The Popular Front lasted only from February through July 1933, when in Morocco a revolt within the army broke out, led by General Francisco Franco.

Actually neither tsarist Russia nor the Soviets after 1917 had anything like close ties with Spain. Even the dissolution of the monarchy and the formation of the generally left-wing republic did not cause much interest in the Kremlin and remained unknown to the Soviet public. At that time Stalin was so preoccupied with his internal problems—the collectivization of the farms and his purging of the "peoples' enemies"—he had no time for the situation in Spain.

But a visible turn in Soviet policy toward Spain happened in mid-September 1936 after the civil war had begun and blood had already been shed. The Political Bureau of the Central Committee ordered the chief of the Intelligence Department of the People's Commissariat of Defense, S. Uritsky, and the head of the Foreign Section of the NKVD, A. Slutsky, to work out a special assistance plan for the so-called Loyalist government of Spain. The plan, approved on September 29, 1936, envisaged the creation of special companies in other countries for the purchase of weapons, goods, and combat and combat support equipment, and sending it all to Spain. Various ministries of the Soviet government were directed to organize shipments of war materiel immediately from the USSR.

The plan also contained provisions for sending regular Red Army units to Spain, but this was vetoed by the military. Instead, initially only military specialists and advisers would be sent there to help Republican forces learn how to use the equipment being provided and to help organize and train the Spanish Army, as well as work on operational plans for its deployment.

Preparations for such a large-scale operation were conducted secretly, although they did not succeed entirely. An Italian foreign service officer remarked to the Soviet ambassador in Rome: "We are aware of the scale of Soviet assistance going to Spain. Ships with Soviet weapons aboard frequently pass our coasts. We have not undertaken any measures against them, not wishing to complicate further Italian-Soviet relations."[1]

The volume of shipments of Soviet-produced combat equipment, weapons, and materials to Spain was immense. Other goods were procured through dummy Soviet companies in other countries and transshipped to Spain. A report from Voroshilov's report to Stalin shows that from October 1936 until February 1937, thirty guns, photographic equipment, and gas masks were bought from France; seventeen aircraft from the United States; eight guns from Switzerland; and 145 machine guns and 10,000 rifles from Czechoslovakia. The total bill for all this equipment came to about 132 million dollars. They also managed to buy sixteen aircraft in Holland (twelve arrived in Spain) and twenty-five in Czechoslovakia (eight arrived).[2]

We should stress that mostly new types of Soviet combat equipment were shipped to Spain—aircraft, tanks, other armored vehicles, and guns. Two results were achieved at the same time. The Spanish Republican Army was equipped with the latest developments of Soviet designers, and this equipment was being tested under combat conditions. Spain was the ideal proving ground for rehearsing the larger scale combat operations to come in the future. Specialists returning home after combat in Spain were interrogated exhaustively on the effectiveness of the equipment being supplied and the methods of its employment. Modernization of aircraft and tanks, particularly, became possible because of these reports from the field.

The war in Spain was very important for Stalin's foreign policy. He kept aware of the military, political, and diplomatic situation in Spain and neighboring countries on a day-to-day basis. He was able to acquire vast information from the KGB, the People's Commissariat of Defense, and the Communist International, as well as from many other sources. Not a single document concerning the Spanish war avoided the dictator's attention. This allowed him to be knowledgeable on all developments and to react to them promptly. One cannot help but agree with the Italian historian D. Boffa, who stated that "the Spanish question was for Soviet diplomacy the soil which Moscow could exploit for imposing on

France and Britain strict obligations concerning opposition to Fascism and consequently getting from them solid mutual security guarantees."[3] So from this viewpoint, involvement in Spain satisfied long-term strategic plans of the USSR.

Judging from numerous papers that we have examined, Stalin began to see the Spanish government as some kind of branch of the Soviet government obedient to dictates from Moscow. For example, late in 1937 when the Spanish situation was discussed at a Politburo meeting, a comprehensive directive to the Spaniards was approved. It covered among other things that it was necessary to remove all saboteurs and traitors from the army, to develop measures to mobilize industry for military production, and to clear rear areas of Fascist spies and agents. Other matters were included in the directive, such as governmental programs and laws regarding agriculture, industry, trade and transportation, and propaganda in territories occupied by the enemy.[4] It is not just the listing of problems and points for attention that is important, but the language itself. The words chosen and the tone used were so bad that they resembled directives to a district Party committee or some ministry as opposed to friendly messages of advice sent to a sovereign state.

Although Kremlin policy in Spain was conducted by military advisers, they did not limit themselves to providing advice and issuing directives. Their functions were broad. This can be illustrated from a recollection by the chief military adviser, Marshal Meretskov:

> In the Spanish Army, the situation was so bad that our advisers were required to perform both organizational and operational combat tasks. . . . Advisers would suggest the concept of an operation to the Spanish commander. With his concurrence, they would work out the details of the plan. They then would write draft operational orders and train those responsible for executing them at the staff level. It was necessary to teach tactics to the highest commanders and show them how to teach their soldiers. Soviet advisers participated in organizing and forming international brigades

and a number of Spanish brigades. Later, they often led them in combat, especially in their first combat operations to show the officers how to command their units.[5]

As the Republican Army and its commanders accumulated combat experience, the role of advisers grew less important and their number could be reduced. Also the level of the advisers' professional competence diminished. During 1936 and the first six months of 1937, highly qualified specialists were sent to Spain, generals and other career officers possessed of rich experience in military and political matters as well as life itself. But we have to remember that this time period coincided with Stalin's purges and reprisals against the officer corps of the Red Army. Therefore, officers of much less capability started to be sent to Spain, many poorly educated in their professions. In some cases advisers to divisions and corps were only lieutenants and captains.

Upon arrival in Spain, Soviet military representatives were faced with numerous problems. The overwhelming majority of them could not speak or read Spanish and did not know local traditions and mores, the Spanish national character, the differences among various political entities, the rules of the Spanish military, and the peculiarities of the theater of war. This meant that on occasion their decisions and advice were not helpful in prosecuting the war. For example, as insisted by the advisers, political commissars were introduced into the various echelons of the army. They were not readily accepted and became the cause of sharpest conflict among various units having different political orientations. Certain non-Communist organizations viewed them as the manifestation of Moscow's striving to establish Soviet control over all the Spanish armed forces. So they tried to eliminate them at any cost. For this and many other reasons, operational decisions of the advisers were not always successful. An example was the failure to organize mass guerrilla forces in the enemy's rear.

In accomplishing his military-strategic goals, Stalin relied not only on his military advisers. An important role was played by the Committee for State Security, the KGB. They used the war in Spain for deep penetration into the military and the political structures of the republic. They created cells which the KGB planned to expand significantly in order to increase its secret operations in other European countries and the United States. KGB specialists were ostensibly sent to Spain to help the republic organize its intelligence and counterintelligence functions. Soon, however, they began to insinuate themselves into the political struggle itself, to recruit agents from the local people and soldiers of international brigades, and to conduct special operations against selected political parties and organizations. The most important KGB missions in Spain were like those in the USSR: provocations, shootings, persecution of people without trial or honest investigation, as well as torture. For example, in Barcelona, the home of the Unified Socialist Party of Catalonia, torture of dissidents occurred at the Colon Hotel and near Madrid in the Alcala de Enares jail. KGB activities permitted favorable conditions for liquidating the various rivals of the Spanish Communist Party and the virtual "Sovietization" of the nation. Later, as Soviet military involvement in the conflict increased with the introduction of entire armor, aviation, and artillery units staffed with Soviet "volunteers," the Kremlin was able to simply direct the war on its own terms and prepare everything to join Spain to the Soviet empire.

This is a good place in the narrative to make the point that in the Spanish Civil War the Soviet Union was not the only foreign country sending potent support to Spain. In fact, a rather gigantic rivalry was produced because both Germany and Italy were providing military aid to the rebel forces of General Franco at the same time that the Soviets were supporting the Republicans. For example, early in the war, Germany sent various military aircraft, including Junker bombers and fighters, to Franco. The Italians sent troops equipped with armor and their own aircraft. In addition, small contingents of anti-Communist volunteers joined the insurgents. The actions of the two opposing factions helped them in the subsequent hostilities in which they were involved.

Let us now return to the war itself and examine some of the military actions taken by both sides. The military coup against the Republican government was triggered by a radio broadcast whose words were "The skies above Spain are cloudless." This was the coded signal to the generals loyal to Franco that the coup plans were to be executed. "When, on July 17, 1936, Generals Franco and Mola started the rebellion, practically all the officers of the army were with them; only about 200 of 15,000 remained loyal."[6]

Jan Bursin recalls:

The coup decision had already been decided in January 1936. The only unsettled aspect was about tactics. On May 25, 1936, the General Staff sent to trusted officers in the various garrisons the initial operational plan which did not envisage employment of Moroccan troops or the Foreign Legion. Madrid was to be attacked from the north and northeast by the 5th (Saragossa) Division, 6th (Burgos) Division, and the 7th (Valladolid) Division.

This operational plan was superseded by a final plan that envisaged using Moroccan troops in an offensive from the south. A preliminary requisite for the success of the coup was a rebellion in the 2nd (Seville) Division. It became known that the rebels commanded by General Keipo-de-Liano managed to consolidate their positions in this area from the very first days of the coup.

The reasons for resorting to Moroccan regiments, in spite of serious national concerns, were purely military. Moroccan troops were the only truly seasoned units of the Spanish Army. They were privileged units with higher salaries, more comfortable living conditions, and better food. They were rather low culturally which made them a reliable political instrument in the hands of their officers. Their combat potential was higher than Spanish units in that they were armed with more modern weaponry and other combat equipment. Militarily they were better prepared because they had been trained rather well.

On July 17–18, 1936, General Franco signaled the start of the coup from Morocco. In Morocco and in the sectors of the 2nd (Seville), 5th (Valladolid), and 8th (Galacia) Divisions, the rebels were victorious at once. It was suppressed, however, in the sectors of the 3rd (Valencia) and 4th (Barcelona) Divisions. Judging by the orders issued, not a single attempt in support of the coup was undertaken in the sector of the 1st (Madrid) Division.

The coup, therefore, had already ensured two operational bases for itself, in the southwest and the north of the country. It was a development totally unexpected by the Republican government, which at this point was at a complete loss.[7]

Under these conditions the most important and difficult problem for the Republican government was reorganization of the regular army. The Popular Front was formed in Madrid under the leadership of Francisco Largo Caballero. This new government turned to the Soviet Union for help, despite the fact that they had no normal diplomatic relations with the USSR at that time. As a result of this plea, a diplomatic representative of the Soviet government arrived in Barcelona, followed a little later by Ambassador M. I. Rosenberg, Military Attaché Brigade Commander V. Y. Gorev, Naval Attaché Capt. N. G. Kasnetsov, and Air Force Attaché Col. B. F. Svechnikov, who went to work in Madrid. Somewhat later Corps Commissar Y. K. Bersin also arrived in Madrid and became the primary military adviser to the Republican government. He brought with him a group of infantry, armor, artillery, aviation, and other combined arms experts to advise the Spanish Army in their specialties.

Their mission was daunting: as soon as possible, to develop an estimate of the situation at the various combat fronts, to assist the Spanish leaders in establishing effective control of their troops, to strengthen the defenses of Madrid, and finally to create a real regular army from a mass of dispersed detachments and militia units. Commissar Bersin suggested to Largo Caballero that he appoint Comdr. K. A. Meretskov, an officer of extraordinary ability, as personal adviser to the chief of the General Staff. In a short time, working with Spanish colleagues, he started to form reserve units for the Spanish Army.[8] Under his guidance an overall defense plan was developed to include the organization of the army, creation and training of maneuver groups, training of commanders and other officers, providing for political orientation of the troops, organizing guerrilla operations in the enemy rear areas, establishing intelligence and counterintelligence activities at all echelons, distribution of weapons and ammunition, and other logistical matters.

In October 1936 a general military commissariat was established whose adviser was Division Commissar I. N. Nesterenko. Military commissariats were set up at major unit levels in military schools and in other military organizations. In practice, this system directly paralleled the commissar system of the Red Army in the USSR. In Albaseta, Nesterenko began to set up organization centers for the first new Spanish units as well as the various international brigades arriving on the scene. The first new unit, the 5th Communist Regiment, commanded by A. Lister, arrived on the front and became engaged in combat on October 29. Soon, five more infantry brigades were formed and were sent to the front. With the most active participation of the Soviet military advisers, the 11th, 12th, and 13th Spanish and some international brigades were quickly organized and incorporated with other units into the People's Army. Many of these new units participated actively in repelling fierce attacks by the rebels on the defenses of Madrid.

In later October 1936 the first ships carrying Soviet aircraft, armor, artillery, other weapons, and ammunition arrived at Spanish ports. Soviet soldiers and air crews accompanied the equipment on these first ships. The initial plans called for these personnel to instruct the soldiers of the Spanish forces on the use of their new Soviet equipment. The situation at the front was so severe, however, that many of these soldiers were needed for active fighting immediately. A tank unit commanded by Capt. Pol Arman was hastily organized and used in the defense of Madrid. This was, of course, a stopgap measure to gain some precious time to enable other units to get to a level of readiness needed for the stringent combat anticipated in the future. The same situation pertained to the first Soviet air crews to arrive. These experienced pilots performed many of the initial combat missions flown in support of the Loyalist forces. In addition to getting these initial tasks accomplished, these tankers and airmen served as role models for their Spanish counterparts.

Another large group of Soviet airmen and tankers came to Spain in November, accompanied by large numbers of I-15 fighter aircraft and T-26 tanks. They could not have arrived at a more critical time, because Franco's troops were pressing hard in their offensive against the defenses of the capital. A full armor brigade under the command of Soviet Brigade Commander D. G. Pavlov was formed, composed largely of Soviet personnel, and committed to combat with great success.

Paying tribute to the qualities of these Soviet soldiers, the American historian D. Kettel writes:

> Before the Russians arrived, there had been no army staff, only armed masses without organization or coordination of actions and plans. Soon after the Russians came, the whole defense system was drastically changed. Six months later the army managed to defeat a modern Italian army at Guadalajara and for almost three years to contain Franco's army, trained by Germans and Italians and reinforced by Mussolini's divisions.[9]

Because of the threat to Madrid, Largo Caballero moved his capital to Valencia on November 7, 1936. He left a defense staff under Gen. J. Miaja to coordinate the defenses of this most important city. In the meantime, on October 1, 1936, General Franco named himself the overall leader of Nationalist Spain, becoming a dictator something in the mold of Hitler and Mussolini. His political party was called the Falangists. Germany and Italy recognized the Franco government, but other Western nations such as Britain, France, and the United States remained officially neutral despite the fact that thousands of their citizens volunteered for service in Spain on the Republican side in non-Spanish units such as the Abraham Lincoln Brigade of the Americans.

Diaries and reports of Soviet commanders and advisers to the Spanish armed forces are interesting to read because they give a flavor of the day-to-day events of those intense days of the civil war. Certain of these we will quote in part; others will be summarized. A good example of a combat commander's experiences is that of Col. Nikolai Grusdev, who wrote:

> Our international tank regiment commanded by Col. S. I. Kondrat'yev was composed largely of Soviet soldiers but also had troops of the 5th Communist Regiment, many of whom were clothed in summer weight uniforms, which crossed snow-covered mountains and attacked consolidated positions of the enemy. Because of the heroic deeds of our infantrymen and armored crewmen, the enemy's defensive lines were penetrated. The city of Teruel was encircled and was finally captured from the Fascists on December 24, 1937.
>
> I had the honor of fighting with Soviet tankers who operated in the most dangerous sectors of the front. Companies of BT-5 tanks bravely counterattacked the enemy, defeating his infantry, tank, and artillery units. But a lack of combat equipment compelled the Republican high command to send the available tanks and aircraft from one sector of the battlefield to another. On some occasions, an individual tank company was engaged in as many as seven different attacks, using up its basic load of ammunition each time. Brave Soviet pilots were constantly in the air conducting bold attacks in support of the ground forces.[10]

Soviet troops took part in all major battles from the autumn of 1936 until spring 1938. Without armor support, any combat operation of Republican units, defensive or offensive, was unthinkable. The Soviet Union provided to the Spanish Republican government the best tanks and other equipment available at the time, the same equipment that regular Red Army units possessed. This equipment more than held its own against the German- and Italian-supplied troops of General Franco. Military experts of other countries came to this same conclusion, based on their analyses of the operations where similar equipment of one force faced that of another. The most dangerous threat against Republican troops in the war was not enemy tanks, but their artillery that had been lavishly supplied to Franco by Germany and Italy.

In many battles Soviet tanks provided the difference in combat power that produced victory. Such was the case in frontal lines to the northwest of Madrid in January 1937, especially during the bloodshed of the battle at Harama, where, as V. Renko said, "tanks played a most important role." Under the command of battalion commanders N. F. Petrov and S. F. Urban, tankers more than saved the situation, repelling and destroying groups of Moroccans and foreign legionaries who were trying to cut the Madrid-Valencia highway.

Earlier in the first combat near Madrid on October 29, 1936, in the region of Segesna, tank crews of the company commanded by Capt. I. Arman displayed extraordinary courage in inflicting heavy losses on the enemy and halted its offensive in that sector. For the next few weeks, when the fate of Madrid was in the balance, Soviet and Spanish tank units were constantly at the front. They constituted the only mobile strike force available to stabilize the situation, attacking the enemy and supporting the infantry. D. Ibarruri recalls:

> The tankers were constantly in combat and most of the time on their own with no support from the infantry. Republican tanks unexpectedly attacked the enemy, often creating panic, especially when attacking artillery units in the rear. From dawn to dusk these dedicated armor crewmen were busy clearing the city approaches from enemy incursions, returning to bivouac areas when it became dark. There they had little rest because this was the only time that the vehicles and other equipment could receive necessary maintenance to get them ready for the next day. They turned upside down the accepted norms for technical use of equipment and human endurance. They learned the hard way that people and vehicles can only function up to a certain limit. But each morning they returned to combat. Soviets and Spanish alike were heroes in those days.[11]

Combat experience acquired in the early battles was helpful subsequently, such as in operations near Guadalajara, Brunete, and other follow-on actions. One unit of seven tanks was sent to Guadalajara with the first available information on the Italian campaign in March 1937. They, together with an infantry battalion, met the vanguard of the Italian corps conducting the attack and bravely attacked it the entire first day of the battle. They were supported ably by the Soviet airmen who attacked the Italian armored vehicles held in place by the ground forces. Later, when reserves of the Central Front arrived on the scene, D. G. Pavlov's tank brigade took a prominent part in the victorious counteroffensive of Republican troops against the Italians. During the offensive near Brunete, Republican tank units suffered many losses in attacking strengthened Italian defensive positions, but were successful in assisting the attacking infantry brigades in capturing and holding them.

Examples of great courage abound. At Harama a tank commander, V. Novikov, was fighting his tank in an exposed area between Republican and rebel forces when his vehicle was hit by an enemy shell. He was wounded along with his driver and another crewman was killed. But Novikov refused to leave the tank, continuing to direct fire against the enemy until darkness, when the damaged vehicle was towed from danger. In the hospital medical technicians found twelve wounds on Novikov.

The same valor was displayed by tank company commander P. A. Tsaplin in a fight near Teruel in January 1937. Although wounded, he remained in a damaged tank for eight hours, fighting the enemy. After doing all that he could, he managed to make his way to his unit's position. In that same action, a tank commander, K. Y. Samohvalov, left the relative safety of the tank's interior to repair a damaged track and later lead his tank forward against the enemy. Later at Harama he was killed trying to save the crew of a damaged tank.

Soviet and Spanish tankers fought with the same enthusiasm and valor. Near Guadalajara in March 1937, a tank platoon commanded by Ernesto Ferrera ambushed some twenty Italian armored vehicles and a column of trucks carrying infantry, destroying the bulk of them. At the same place Soviet Lt. A. G. Abramovich led his platoon in an attack on a company of rebel infantry and captured four guns, several machine guns, and many rifles. Unfortunately on July 10, 1937, he was killed in an attack against the enemy near Brunete. Capt. G. W. Sklesnev, a tank company commander, was able to tow a tank damaged in a fight near Madrid to safety while under intense enemy fire. In February 1937 he and his company counterattacked Moroccan forces that had broken through Republican Army defensive positions near the Pindock Bridge over the Harama River. His prompt and effective action repulsed the enemy and restored the line. The next day he also was killed in still another counterattack. Others were equally valiant. S. Y. Laputin and F. A. Semyonov, although surrounded by the enemy, kept up covering fire to permit wounded members of their tank crews to escape to friendly positions, thus saving their lives.

Soviet naval personnel were also present in Spain as advisers to the Republican Navy. They concentrated their efforts on assisting Spanish sailors in getting deliveries of military supplies by sea. Spanish vessels, in accord with plans for each occurrence, met Soviet merchant ships in the open sea and escorted them to Spanish Mediterranean ports. These same advisers helped Spanish commanders in the operations of their ships and the training of their personnel for combat duties. Others worked in naval headquarters at the Cartajena Navy Base.

In some cases Soviet personnel commanded and manned submarines and motor torpedo boats in offensive and defensive actions against the rebel forces and their Fascist allies. This was necessary because of a dire shortage of trained Spanish sailors.

There was a problem in communicating between Russian and Spanish speakers that was solved in part with the help of interpreters. These men were graduates of language institutes in Moscow and Leningrad and were true volunteers who went to Spain at their own volition to help their fellow soldiers.

Still other Soviets were sent to Spain to instruct men in the Spanish defense industry in the latest techniques of manufacturing various types of combat equipment. They were involved in the actual running of industrial plants and repair and supply depots. The Soviet Union permitted free use of patents and plans and other engineering drawings to Spanish industry. This joint effort was invaluable in the supply and resupply of small arms, vehicles, artillery pieces, aircraft, armored cars and tanks, and all types of ammunition. Lt. Gen. (Eng.) A. Vetrov recalls:

> We had about 300 military engineers and technicians in Spain, among whom were highly qualified specialists in the maintenance of aircraft, tanks and other vehicles, artillery, small arms, engineer equipment, and communications equipment. In addition we brought other technicians who worked directly in Spanish industry, advising on the technicalities of actual manufacture and production. In all cases, their tasks were to give Spanish technical personnel the understanding of how to set up maintenance and rebuild shops and other facilities, not necessarily to perform such functions themselves. We were faced with the basic situation that industry in general in Spain was very poorly developed. This, added to the fact that the Spanish Army was mostly equipped with outmoded and worn-out equipment, made our task extremely difficult. We had to deal with tanks and aircraft of different types and nationalities and many different types and calibers of artillery and small arms. This made it necessary to try to obtain many disparate types of ammunition and spare parts, often without success. We, therefore, had to resort to manufacturing such items locally, a most difficult task.
>
> Naturally, combat equipment gets damaged or breaks down from use. One of our most important functions, therefore, was the evacuation of such equipment from the battlefield to repair facilities in the rear. Some of the most heroic individual exploits of the war happened when damaged tanks, for example, were towed away from the scene of action and brought to the rear. Despite the difficulties, Soviet technicians like Pyotr Gluhov, Nicolai Bebris, Pavel Salesski, Fyodor Rebrov, Isai Kabanov, Vasilii Rogov, and Stepan

Bespalov worked long hours in extremely disadvantageous circumstances to repair tanks and other equipment quickly so that this vitally needed equipment could be returned to fighting units on the front. They did this, of course, in conjunction with their Spanish comrades. Because of the shortage of spare parts, they often found it necessary to cannibalize broken down equipment to restore other less damaged things to an operative condition. Each combat vehicle was valued as its weight in gold. Many of these were repaired so quickly and returned to the combat front that the enemy was deceived into thinking that the actual number of tanks and aircraft was much greater than it was.

The life of these technicians was not confined to repair and maintenance facilities in the rear. They often had to go to fighting positions to retrieve damaged equipment. For example, during hostilities at Saragosa, a small Soviet evacuation detachment had the mission of evacuating a damaged tank from an enemy trench. Using cover and concealment they carefully moved toward the tank, riding an operable BT-5 tank into a large shell hole near their target. To divert enemy attention from this operation, Spanish infantrymen fired at the enemy on their right flank. Tank technician Konstantin Gur'yanov covertly approached the hurt tank to fasten a stout rope to it. At that moment an enemy soldier saw what he was doing and fired at him, fortunately missing his mark. Gur'yanov then attacked the enemy soldier with a knife, killing him. After this struggle, he managed to get his rope attached and signaled the rescue tank to pull the damaged vehicle to friendly territory. All members of the recovery squad were able to return safely. Such initiative was demanded of Soviet engineers and technicians on a constant basis.

Much was done by Soviet engineers and technicians to update weapons and other combat equipment. They were able to fabricate field modifications such as safety devices for aircraft and expedients to ensure synchronized fire from aircraft and armored vehicles. They modified ammunition to permit it to be fired from weapons of slightly different calibers. Their innovations went a very long way toward improving battlefield reliability.[12]

Since tanks were so important to the overall war effort, a higher-echelon tank repair facility was established at Alcala de Enares, about thirty kilometers from Madrid. This became the principal tank maintenance base in Republican Spain. Overall repairs of T-26 and BT-5 tanks was done here, especially rebuild on engines and associated systems. Because of the tight blockade imposed on Republican ports and borders, technicians at this base had to produce their own spare parts and system components. Another important function they were assigned was the writing and production of user and technical manuals for the equipment in the field so that using units would be able to better maintain their assigned equipment.

There were other manufacturing plants in Republican Spain, such as Ispano-Suiza de Automobiles, Elisalda, and Ford Motor Iberico. Various items were produced at these plants, such as I-15 and I-16 aircraft. So effective were these efforts that the plants became targets for the bombers of the enemy, resulting in Soviet personnel being injured or killed. In mid-1937 in the workshops of the Union Naval de Lavante, a tank engineer was able to modify the ZIS armored vehicle to add machine guns to it. It became a very important vehicle in the Spanish Army with more than thirty percent of the overall inventory of vehicles in tank and cavalry units being equipped with this modified ZIS. Production of armor plate for tanks was started at the metallurgical plant in Sagunto under the guidance of military engineer Andrian Vorob'yov. This became a main producer of armor plate and other parts for other industrial plants and the maintenance units of the Spanish Army.

Plants producing ammunition had to be remarkably innovative. For both small arms and tank and artillery ammunition it became necessary to recycle the spent shell cases after firing. Special detachments on the battlefields were assigned to salvage such metal cases and return them to the rear, where they could be reused and sent back to the front for action against the enemy. This idea came from recollections of some of the technicians of a similar situation that happened during the Russian Civil War, when Bolshevik forces were faced with the same acute shortages of all kinds of ammunition and spent cases were recycled to good effect.

Equipment and supplies were of little value if the soldiers were not well trained in using them. In various locations throughout Republican Spain, training centers were set up with Soviet soldiers and officers as instructors. Many of the Spanish soldiers joining Loyalist forces arrived with no practical knowledge of military matters. This was true also for soldiers of the international brigades. The new soldiers had much to learn, both tactical lessons and instruction on how to operate and maintain their new equipment. This was true even for men who came from militia units and had already understood the school of the soldier to some extent. They would not have knowledge of the strange new Soviet equipment they were to use in combat. So a great part of the Soviet soldiers' duties was to be trainers and teachers. Since most of this had to be done through interpreters, the task was even more daunting. In this and all their myriad other duties, Soviet soldiers and civilian technicians performed very ably and were a credit to the USSR and their leaders.

Most of the Soviet pilots and other technicians were returned to the USSR during the months of September and October 1938, followed by the remnants of the international brigades that had suffered badly in the war. The government staged a farewell parade for them in Madrid on November 15, 1938. The war itself ended on April 1, 1939, with the surrender of Republican forces to the insurgents after a strong general offensive by Franco.

The Spanish Civil War demonstrated forcefully that one cannot immediately create an army capable of effective operations against a disciplined and well-equipped foe. It does show, however, that a new army can be marginally effective when in a defensive situation. The defense of Madrid is proof of this. This lesson should have been studied by all belligerents in the Second World War: that new developments in military equipment seen last in

World War I, principally machine guns, tended to favor the defense. We feel that despite using the most modern tanks and aircraft available, the offensive is more difficult than the defensive. This was seen clearly in the Spanish Civil War. We feel that today's antitank and air-defense means are more developed than they were ever before.

During the Spanish Civil War, more than two thousand Soviet citizens fought and worked in Spain. This number includes 772 pilots, 351 tankers, 222 combined arms advisers and instructors, 77 naval personnel, 100 artillerymen, 52 logistics technicians, 130 workers and engineers at aviation and other industrial plants, 156 communication specialists, and 204 interpreters. At any given time, however, there were never more than 600 to 800 personnel in Spain.

Great numbers of military goods and equipment were shipped from the Soviet Union to Spain: 806 combat aircraft, mainly fighters; 120 armored vehicles; 1555 artillery pieces; about 500,000 rifles; 340 grenade launchers; 15,113 machine guns; more than 110,000 aerial bombs; about 3.4 million tank and artillery shells; 500,000 grenades; and 862 million rounds of small arms ammunition. As described earlier, a good deal of logistics help as well as military equipment came from other countries.

The war in Spain was, despite the propaganda of the Stalinists, a foreign war to the people of the Soviet Union. In this unnecessary war, many hundreds of Soviet young men suffered and died for no good purpose. Stalin and his team pursued an unrealistic goal: to turn Spain into a Communist country beholden to the Soviet Union as a first step to creating Communist governments in other countries of the Western world. As with the Germans and Italians, it gave Stalin a fine place to test Soviet equipment and procedures in a modern war. Soviet participation in this war was the first serious attempt to change the social system of another state by force after the Revolution of 1917. It failed dismally.

The next attempt with use of regular troops in implementing the idea of global conquest by Communism was the provoked war against Finland.

Chapter II

Soviet Shadow over Suomi

As countries are classified by age, Finland is rather on the youthful side, dating only from the Treaty of Tartu with the Soviet Union on October 14, 1920. Prior to that date, it had been a vassal state of Sweden (1155–1809), and then a grand duchy of the tsarist governments from 1809 to the time of the Russian Revolution in 1917. During these centuries, the Finns desired to have their freedom. They had their own ancient culture and language and felt they had every right to govern themselves. When the revolution occurred, they saw a golden opportunity to shed the yoke of foreign domination. They proclaimed a republic in 1919, and organized resistance to Bolshevik elements that were trying to annex Finland to the new Soviet Union. They were led by a former tsarist general, Carl Gustaf Mannerheim, with help from Germany. That they succeeded in repelling the Bolsheviks at this time should have been a lesson to those who showed aggressive tendencies later.

But in 1939, following the combined Soviet-German war against Poland and Soviet actions against the Baltic countries, Finland again found itself having to defend against Soviet domination. Despite two nonaggression treaties between the two countries, the Soviet Union invaded little Finland on November 30, 1939, by sea, land, and air.

In official circles of the Soviet Union and in propaganda published in many media to the entire world, the government attempted to justify this aggression by claiming that the war was instigated by "reactionary circles in Finland."[1] In other words, Finland should be blamed for everything that occurred. It was this tiny nation that decided to assault its huge neighbor and thus provoke a counterattack on itself. Even for a person without knowledge of the overall situation between the countries, but with a modicum of common sense, it was obvious that things could not have developed like this; that the very idea was laughable. Our research into the history of the war proves conclusively that it was started without provocation by Stalin using the utmost in treachery and deceit against a country willing to grant logical concessions to its mighty neighbor.

The war cost both sides combined hundreds of thousands of casualties, but gained little in fact for the Soviet Union. Stalin and his accomplices apparently had trouble tolerating a sovereign and successfully developing a state so closely allied to the West and at a strategically disadvantageous location to the Soviet Union. It looked like a good bet for them to accomplish the Sovietization of Finland, or even better, to return it to the Soviet empire. This was the goal in 1917. It seems to have persisted until 1939.

In planning a quick war against Finland, the Soviet leadership had already designed the postwar organization to be installed there. The creation of a puppet pro-Soviet government headed by the secretary of the Executive Committee of the Communist International, Otto Kuusinen, was seen as the best solution. Moscow thought that this government to be based in Helsinki was to be the head of the ". . . leadership of the people's power in the liberated territories (from legal Finnish authorities)."[2] The Kuusinen "government" was organized in Moscow and was actually recognized by the Soviet government. It proclaimed itself as the People's Government of the Democratic Republic of Finland, promising to rely on wide support by the liberated Finnish people. Until the war ended in 1940, Stalin refused to communicate whatsoever with the legitimate government of Finland. Only after Finland turned to Sweden as an intermediary on January 24, 1940, did the Soviet leadership become at all ready to begin peace talks. But success toward peace had to wait until the end of February, when the situation changed.

The situation at that time was that the Soviets had finally broken through the Finnish main defense line (Mannerheim). England and France decided to provide support to Finland, having developed a plan of joint operations near Petsamo. The Soviet government became afraid of the possibility of armed conflict with these Western nations and decided to limit its acquisitions to territory adjacent to the Soviet border. Finally, on March 12, 1940, Finland capitulated and by treaty ceded to the Soviet Union the entire Karelian Isthmus and the industrial city of Viborg. But Stalin again showed his treacherous and cruel nature. Despite the fact that Viborg was included in the treaty, he ordered the Red Army to conduct a brutal attack against the city as the last operation of the war, an utterly senseless and wicked act. Viborg was to become part of the Soviet Union without firing a single shot, but Stalin was so obsessed with a spirit of revenge that he needlessly sacrificed many lives of both Finnish and Soviet young men. This was only typical of Stalin's crimes, provoking a tragedy when there should have been peace.

Let us now examine the reasons for the conflict and more details of the war itself. We cannot depend on the official history of the political aspects leading to the war nor the military operations themselves. We instead will use the archives to learn as much of the truth as is now available to provide the reader with dependable information.

The whole world knows that in the 1920s and 1930s the Soviet-Finnish frontier was a place for all manner of incidents. Usually these were settled through diplomacy and negotiations and direct armed conflicts were averted. It was an uneasy peace that prevailed between the two countries. The two nations, as we have covered above, were parties to two separate treaties of nonaggression during this period. Years went by with no appreciable improvement in Soviet-Finnish relations.

As the latest example of German aggression, the Munich accords happened in September 1938, after which Germany annexed Czechoslovakia and openly headed for satisfaction of its expansionistic tendencies by military action. Many countries were thus at the brink of war. In March 1939, the Soviet government through diplomatic channels offered another pact to Helsinki to guarantee the inviolability of Finland, supporting it against any possible aggression and backing its application for review of the status of the Aland Islands. Finland, in turn, was asked to defend itself against any aggression and provide the Soviet Union assistance in strengthening the security of Leningrad and for that purpose to grant Sursari Island (Gogland) and several other small islands in the Gulf of Finland on a thirty-year lease to the USSR. Finland reacted unfavorably to these proposals, feeling that its own neutrality and sovereignty would be compromised.

Both countries decided to move on parallel roads. While not abandoning political talks, they individually began to build up their military power in the area, the Soviets in an offensive manner and the Finns, defensive. Finland intensified its military contacts with Great Britain, France, Sweden, and even Germany. Helsinki was often visited by military delegations from these and other countries. For its part, Finland's main preparation for possible hostilities was the improvement of the Mannerheim Line, a system of fortifications somewhat similar to the defenses used by the combatants in World War I, capable of thwarting an attack by an aggressor, but hardly conducive to offensive warfare.

But hopes for a political solution to the problems of the two countries were still alive. Negotiations were resumed between them on October 12, 1939, when J. K. Paasikivi, the experienced diplomat who had helped negotiate the 1920 accords between the two parties, arrived in Moscow at the invitation of the Soviet government. During the talks, Stalin proposed a Soviet-Finnish pact similar to those signed earlier by Latvia, Lithuania, and Estonia. One of the provisions forced on these three countries was the establishment of Soviet military bases therein. Finland feared that such bases would likely be placed in its territory if it acceded to the pact requested. It rejected this proposal on the basis that its own desire for neutrality would not be respected.

The Soviets at once put another proposal on the table: to shift the frontier in the Karelian Isthmus several dozen kilometers in depth and to give over to the USSR several islands in the Gulf of Finland and parts of the Rybachiy and Sredniy Peninsulas, as well as the port of Hanko, which was to be used as a Soviet naval base. The Finns agreed to some of the proposals but felt that others, like demilitarizing their frontier fortifications and turning over Hanko, were too much to give up. Passikivi stated that these kinds of demands would have to be approved by the Finnish parliament by a two-thirds vote of legislators. Stalin reacted very belligerently, saying: "You will receive more than two-thirds and moreover you should take into account our votes."[3] These words were considered to be an unconcealed threat to use force in case of refusal by the parliament. On November 13, 1939, the Finnish delegation left Moscow with the breakdown of the negotiations. The events following their departure were full of potential danger because it was assumed that the military solution would now dominate Soviet thinking.

On November 26, 1939, a disputed incident took place in the village of Maimila, a supposed bombardment of Soviet positions by Finnish artillery. Accepting that the attack actually did occur in the manner stated, the note protesting it was delivered to the Finnish envoy in Moscow so quickly, that one must view the whole affair with suspicion. The note stated that the Soviets would not escalate this "outrageous act of aggression of the Finnish Army," and demanded that Finland withdraw its troops from the Karelian Isthmus up to twenty-five kilometers in depth.

The return note from the Finnish government denied the provocation on the part of its troops and proposed that a joint inquiry into the incident be made in conformity with the convention between the two countries of September 24, 1928. They further proposed that the two sides begin negotiations for a bilateral withdrawal of Soviet and Finnish troops to given lines on both sides of the frontier. One might think that this was a reasonable proposal, one that could have been accepted by the Soviets. Their response, however, was one of angry rejection, describing the Finnish note as "a document reflecting the cutthroat hostility shown by the Finnish government toward the Soviet Union, intensifying the crisis between both countries."[4] On the evening of November 29, the political and economic representatives of the Soviet Union were recalled to Moscow from Helsinki.

When the Red Army attacked Finland at eight A.M., November 30, 1939, the Soviet government did not officially declare war against its neighbor. The commander of troops, Gen. K. A. Meretskov, received the following order from the Kremlin: ". . . to be prepared for any kind of eventuality and to immediately rebuff any aggressive actions on the part of the Finnish militarists."[5] Shortly after this, Meretskov ordered his troops to cross the border and destroy the Finnish troops in that area. His order contained some strange positions that far exceeded the notion of ensuring the security of the city on the River Neva, Leningrad. His order contained the words ". . . we are the friends and liberators of the Finnish nation and are removing from the people the yoke of landlords and capitalists."[6] The same day as the attack, the president of Finland, Kjosti Kallio, issued a statement declaring that a state of war existed between the two countries.

During the next few days, our public media seemed to forget completely the concept of securing Leningrad, emphasizing only a "liberating" mission of the Red Army in Finland. Stating that the Finnish working people were waiting for "liberation from exploitation" with the help of Soviet bayonets meant nothing but illusive and dogmatic views which in those days were unfortunately very popular in the international Communist movement as it danced to the tune of Soviet propaganda.

If Finland, as the Soviet side alleged, had really provoked the war and thus had been the aggressor with the USSR as its victim, one could logically believe that we would have appealed to the League of Nations, but not Finland. This before resorting to force. But the reverse was true. It was Finland that made the logical appeal. Moreover, on November 4, in response to inquiries from the League of Nations, Soviet Foreign Minister Molotov rejected its "interference" and declared that the Soviet Union was not at war with Finland and was doing nothing to menace that nation. In another letter to the League on November 14, Molotov refused to participate in the sessions of the Council or Assembly of the League of Nations.

Stalin's plans for the offensive against Finland were overly ambitious, as later events proved abundantly. An imperial mentality dominated Stalin's thinking. His position is obvious in his "Plan of Operations Aimed at Destroying the Land and Naval Forces of Finland."[7] It was prepared under his personal direction and provided on October 29, 1939, to the People's Commissar of Defense, Kliment Voroshilov, by the Military Council of the Leningrad Military District. We will quote a few pertinent portions of the lengthy text of the document:

> On receiving the orders for offensive action, our troops will immediately invade the territory of Finland in all directions with the aim of splitting the enemy into groups and to decisively destroy them in conjunction with aviation assets. . . .
>
> . . . The steps listed above will ensure the conduct of operations in the direction of Vidlitsa for fifteen days and at the Karelian Isthmus for eight to ten days with the average speed of the advance ten to twelve kilometers each day. . . .

The actual conduct of the Soviet-Finnish War went far differently from what Stalin had planned. The Red Army offensive faltered on its very first day. This was true of both land and amphibious attacks against the Finns during early December. In particular, the Soviet plan called for a major thrust against Finnish fortifications at the Mannerheim Line in the Karelian Isthmus. Later in the month, mobile Finnish troops using skis increased resistance against their invaders, resorting to counterattacks that encircled whole Red Army divisions. Being highly mechanized and thus dependent on the road network, the Soviet formations were unable to operate in the forests or in the snow, thus affording their enemy excellent opportunities. Tanks and heavy combat equipment became bogged down in the deep snow and ice along with supply vehicles that had great trouble in reaching the troops they were supposed to be supporting. In many cases and in many units, command and control became nonexistent. Many soldiers suffered frostbite and became incapacitated due to respiratory infections.

One important reason for the failure of Stalin's sought-after blitzkrieg had to do with his commanders. Many of the best and the brightest of commanders and staff officers in the Soviet armed forces were eliminated during Stalin's purges of the military several years earlier. Some fifty thousand of our most qualified officers perished during that bloody time. Their places were filled with officers far less qualified who in many cases did not have the confidence of their troops. This obvious fact did not dawn on Stalin. When faced with the army's lack of success, he blamed these inexperienced commanders, accusing them of cowardice and treason, with, of course, fatal consequences.

People's Commissar of Defense Kliment Voroshilov wrote to Stalin and Molotov in late December 1939 in an attempt to shift the responsibility for the lack of success of the offensive to his subordinates for the failures and generally poor combat readiness of the troops: "I consider it necessary to conduct drastic purges in corps, divisions, and regiments to replace cowards and lazy people [referred to as "bastards"] with honest and energetic officers."[8] Waves of repressions followed, instilling fear in all ranks. Speedy trials were common and frequent, resulting in executions by firing squads in front of troop formations. By order of Stalin, KGB guard detachments were placed in the rear of the major troop units to discourage disengagement from the enemy.

Because of the initial lack of success in December, STAVKA decided to halt the offensive and begin a comprehensive preparation to pierce the Mannerheim Line. They found it necessary to define better the nature of the defense and the Finns' system of fire and their tactics. Plans were made and executed to replenish the losses, to reinforce with additional artillery, especially siege guns, to better organize the terrain, to restock ammunition, and otherwise make troops and the various headquarters capable of continuing the fight.

To improve basic command and control, an order was issued on January 7, 1940, creating in Karelia the "Northwestern Front" under the command of Army Commander First Rank S. K. Timoshenko. Its mission was to break through the Mannerheim Line, occupying positions along the line, Keksgolm-Antrea-Viborg. The main blow was to be delivered at Viborg, another at Keksgolm, and across the Bay of Viborg. The Front staff was certain that the attack at Viborg would make it possible for the troop formations to cut off the Finnish troops in the isthmus and thus be able to destroy them. To envelop the fortified line from the southwest, a special force from the STAVKA reserve was organized under the command of Corps Commander D. G. Pavlov. It consisted of three motor rifle divisions, a separate tank brigade, and a reinforced cavalry corps. Its mission was to cross the Gulf of Finland on the ice and penetrate deep into the rear of the Vyborg defenses.

STAVKA approved of the general idea of the Front's plan for the offensive and assigned the following formations to complete the task: Thirteenth Army (nine divisions, six artillery regiments from STAVKA reserve, two heavy artillery battalions, one tank brigade, two separate tank battalions, one cavalry regiment, and five aviation regiments) and Seventh Army (twelve divisions, six artillery regiments from STAVKA reserve, four corps artillery regiments, two heavy artillery battalions, five tank and one rifle-machine gun divisions, and two separate tank battalions). These troops carefully prepared for their offensive for about one month, using specially constructed models of the Finnish fortifications as well as some of the frontier emplacements captured early in the war.

Essential materiel and goods were resupplied and special devices were made for the assaulting troops. Leningrad industrial plants provided many things unavailable previously such as mine detectors, armored shields and sleighs, and means for the evacuation of wounded soldiers in icy weather conditions and terrain. Ammunition stores were resupplied and dumps were established with easy access to the front lines. During the first few weeks of the war, some of the soldiers were not equipped with winter clothing and therefore suffered greatly. This deficiency was remedied and special rations of richer food provided. To escape the bitter cold, warm dugouts and special structures were erected where soldiers could congregate and be warmed.

Engineer work to improve the physical condition of the terrain received a high priority. The railway capabilities of the Leningrad area were enhanced. New roads, bridges, and special routes were built. Jump-off trenches to the enemy fortifications were dug as well as individual troop positions, command and observation posts, artillery bunkers, and protected areas for tanks.

By late January, most of the preparations for the offensive had been completed. Veteran troops were reinforced and replacements assimilated. Newly arrived troop units were oriented on the situation and received additional training. Commanders at all echelons visited the front lines, where they were able to meet and talk with the soldiers and inspect them to ensure their readiness. Patrols were sent out and small-scale attacks against the enemy were integrated into the overall training program. They were careful to keep their real strength secret from the enemy commanders as well as any of the plans that had been developed for the offensive.

On February 9 orders were issued for the start of the grand offensive on February 11. The offensive began at five A.M. with a massive artillery barrage. Because of extremely bad weather conditions, the attack had to be made without air support. Artillery fire destroyed some Finnish strong points, but as is so frequently the case, many of the Finnish troop units survived with defensive capabilities intact and were able to direct intense and accurate fire against the assaulting troops after cessation of the artillery barrage. This made the fight most intense. On February 12, the Finns counterattacked in several places without much success.

By February 14 Soviet troops had broken through the Finnish defenses at Summa, some four kilometers in width and six kilometers deep. The 123rd Infantry Division was able to occupy the region between some lakes, destroying eight reinforced concrete and twelve wood-stone bunkers. The 90th Division, commanded by Colonel Zaitsov, occupied Markki. Exploiting the breakthrough of I Corps, by February 15 two motor-rifle divisions of XIX Corps destroyed extremely powerful points of resistance comprised of more than sixty different fortified positions.

Sufficient success had been achieved by both armies by mid-February to begin the exploitation phase of the offensive. Both armies had special mobile groups organized for this purpose. Seventh Army had three such groups. The first one, under the command of Col. V.I. Baranov, was to exploit the success of the 123rd Division and to occupy Kyamyarga and Lyahde. The second group, under Brigade Commander S. V. Borzilov, was to operate through the 90th Division and capture Humola. Brigade Commander B. G. Vershpnin's third group was to add to the success of the 24th Division and occupy Leipyasuo. The mobile group of the Thirteenth Army was led by Col. D. D. Lelyushenko and was to exploit the success of XXIII Corps and capture Heinioki. These mobile groups were composed of armored brigades reinforced with infantry battalions and engineers. Until contact with the enemy was achieved, the infantrymen remained on or in vehicles, dismounting to reduce enemy positions with close-in fire and grenades.

By the evening of February 16 the breakthrough in the Seventh Army's sector was about twelve kilometers wide and eleven kilometers deep. In the Thirteenth Army zone, units of XXIII Corps Rifle Corps commanded by Brigade Commander S. D. Akimov approached the reinforced region of Muola-Il'vas. Particularly successful were the infantry division of Col. S. I. Chernyak and the mobile group of Col. D. D. Lelyushenko. Up to this time the III Corps of the Thirteenth Army had been unable to advance, so on February 16, sixteen reserve divisions were committed to augment the main thrust. This massive blow caused the Finnish defenders to withdraw, leaving their fortified positions from Muolan'yarvi to Karhula to the Gulf of Finland.

On February 21 the Front commander ordered the forward divisions to be withdrawn from the intense combat to which they had been subjected and go to the rear for rest and replenishment. These front-line troops were regrouped and reserves moved closer to the lines. All operations had to cease because of a three-day heavy snowstorm that hit the Karelian Isthmus. All roads disappeared under the snow, making any kind of operations there much more difficult. On February the order was given to resume the offensive in two days time and break through the second line of Finnish defenses and capture Viborg.

The Finnish defenders in the area of the Saimen Channel, however, opened locks and flooded the area to a depth of six meters in places, and icy water began to run down the system of lakes and rivers, flooding all the land area in its way. Near the station of Tali, the water level rose by 2.5 meters and everything there turned into an impassable icy swamp. Despite these frightful conditions, Soviet soldiers tried to attack the Finnish defenses while up to their waists in water. They managed to cross the flooded areas, but made little headway in their attack.

This was a kind of last-ditch defense of the Finns. Viborg did not fall, but elsewhere the entire defensive front was collapsing. On the right flank, the Finns had to retreat to Viipuri on March 1. The end was in sight for the valiant soldiers on both sides.

Overtures for an armistice were being made by the Finnish ambassador in Sweden to the Soviet envoy there. On February 23rd the Soviet government through A. M. Kollontai provided the following conditions to the Finns: transfer of the Karelian Isthmus to the USSR as well as the northeastern shore of Lake Ladoga and the lease of the Hanko peninsula with nearby small islands for the establishment of a naval base. In short, the conditions were roughly the same as those demanded back in November. As part of this, the Soviets agreed to evacuate the region of Petsamo and to defend the Gulf of Finland jointly with Finland and Estonia.

On March 12, 1940, peace accords between the USSR and Finland and a protocol to them were signed. The hostilities between the two nations were to cease at noon March 13 Leningrad time. Generally, the terms stated above were finally agreed to by both parties.[9]

As an important aftermath to the war, its lessons were the subject of a high-level discussion at the Kremlin between April 14 and 17, 1940. Present were officials from the People's Commissariat of Defense and the General Staff and representatives of the militaries and military academies. It was a unanimous conclusion that the Red Army had reliable armaments and combat equipment. But the army's soldiers were poorly trained in their use and had grave difficulties operating under the stringent winter conditions to which they were exposed. Artillery was effective, particularly the heaviest kinds used, but there were deficiencies in the fields of small arms, mortars, and other crew-served weapons. There was a definite weakness in the volume of small-arms fire because of a lack of automatic weapons and their unreliability in the extreme cold. Command and control suffered because of poor organization and unreliable officers as well as shortages of radios and other communications means.

The organization of the troop units did not meet the demands of the Finnish theater of war. Rifle divisions proved to be too bulky, with huge rear areas that became difficult to manage. The so-called "light" motorized divisions turned out to be "heavy" under the conditions present in the combat zones. They tended to block the roads and become immobilized in the deep snow. Infantry troops could not match the mobility of the Finns, who were extremely adept at moving and fighting on skis. Our infantrymen were generally incapable of using skis for cross-country movement. As the war progressed, we started to form special units of ski troops, but this measure came too late to have any decisive effect. Again later in the action, special road construction units were formed and they were greatly helpful in opening blocked roads and in building new ones. A serious deficiency at the start that was improved as the war progressed was medical care and medical evacuation. Under cold-weather conditions, it was imperative that wounded or injured soldiers be evacuated with dispatch. And conditions in rear areas were gradually improved.

Supplies of all commodities of troop units in internal military districts were at satisfactory levels in peacetime situations. This was not true under wartime conditions in Finland, a fact that quickly became obvious. This had a decidedly negative effect on the fighting capabilities and morale of the troops and the overall conduct of the war at all echelons. One deficiency that should have been anticipated before beginning this grand adventure was the fact that some troop units went into this extremely cold climate without proper winter clothing. Some Ukranian formations, for example, arrived at the front in warm-weather clothing. This problem was exacerbated because not enough heaters for motor transport and tents had been provided. Also unanticipated was the continual exposure of oils, fuel, and other lubricants to the extreme cold. Trucks, tanks, and other vehicles were immobilized frequently for this reason and because of shortages of spare parts for them. Trying to perform maintenance on the vehicles and other equipment while bundled up against the cold proved to be extremely slow and difficult.

Roads were unsatisfactory. Until February the Front did not have enough road-repair and special engineer units. Added to this was a shortage of traffic regulatory means. As stated above, although we had a great number of trucks, many were immobilized because of a shortage of block heaters and spare parts.

The Soviet Union went to war in Finland seemingly not aware of the peculiarities of the Karelian Isthmus in geographical terms or of the very strong defensive line that the Finns had developed there. They also underestimated the fighting qualities of Finnish soldiers and knew little of the armaments available to their enemy and their state of training and the tactics they were apt to use. The Finns were used to their country and did all their training and war games there, whereas Soviet soldiers were not experienced in operations in forests and open terrain. The cold was an ever-present factor. Russian soldiers could stand severe cold well, but troops from the southern republics of the Soviet Union were also a part of the army that fought in Finland and they were ill prepared for the horrible conditions they found.

Commanders and staff officers had only general and vague impressions and understanding of the fortifications they were to face in Karelia and did not know how to attack them effectively. They did not understand how to reduce and eliminate ferro-concrete or granite bunkers erected by the Finns. They had to learn the hard way, by getting the experience they needed on the job in mortal combat. Many commanders, because of the earlier purges, had been appointed to their posts just before the war began, so they did not know their own troops well and because of their youth and inexperience made bad decisions, failing to attain objectives on time and causing needless casualties.

Training of soldiers in units was unsatisfactory, as was unit training. They had received no training for fighting against men in

trenches, in forests, or when encircled. They did not understand
the importance of camouflage and because of their dark uniforms
against the snow could not operate covertly, as compared with the
white smocks the Finns used. They were careless in intelligence
measures, particularly not observing good radio discipline.

Another conference of STAVKA was held on April 17, 1940.
Commanders present stressed that the final victory in the war
against Finland had cost us entirely too many casualties, many of
which could have been avoided. They insisted that the organization for combat be revamped and that training and motivation
of the troops be radically improved. Command and control was
seen as a problem, and one of the solutions was to decentralize
decision making. They felt that there was too much control ex-
ercised from above by the highest superiors. They demanded that
various regulations and field manuals be rewritten, taking into
consideration the lessons from this war and also what was known
from what had already happened in World War II. They felt that
the people living in the country should receive a certain amount
of orientation on the border conditions and their part in defending the Motherland if the country should find itself at war.
Stalin was present at the conference. He stated that it was necessary for all commanders to study modern methods of waging war.
He pointed out that the traditions and recollections of the civil
war in 1918–1920 prevented officers from adjusting their thinking to the present day, when things were far different. A commander thinking that he could fight and win with only the help
of civil war experience would soon be dead along with the rest of
his command. He must adapt to the conditions of modern warfare.[10]

STAVKA immediately took the required steps to improve the
overall situation. Outdated types of combat and combat support
equipment would have to be replaced. In particular, aviation and
armored vehicles had to be improved, as well as radios and other
means of communicating. Improved methods of training, both
individual and unit, were to be instituted, and deficiencies in organization and command and control corrected. Unified tables

of organization and equipment were designed for units at every level, responsive to both peacetime and wartime conditions. Measures were taken to supply the troops with new manuals.[11]

It was not just STAVKA and other Soviet ministries that were interested in the Soviet-Finnish war. Military thinkers in Germany, Italy, and their current adversaries like Britain and France also closely studied the state of readiness and the combat actions taken by the Red Army. The messages and reports of their military attachés were practically unanimous in their favorable opinion of the dogged persistence of Soviet soldiers in combat situations and of the high efficiency of the massed employment of artillery, tanks, and aircraft. They were critical, however, of the professionalism of Soviet commanders at all echelons, their lack of ability to provide cooperation on the battlefield, and their lack of care concerning living conditions and the health and welfare of their soldiers. They were especially concerned about the lack of discipline prevalent in the Red Army. These reports from ambassadors and attachés made many of the Western nations believe that the military of the Soviet Union was generally weak. London and Paris did not consider the USSR as a serious partner or ally against the Rome-Berlin Axis. In Berlin, the prevailing opinion was that the USSR was a giant with earthen legs that would be easy to defeat in a future war.

In this winter war, the Soviet side suffered a disproportionately large number of casualties as compared with its foe. This, of course, was not the propaganda story of the Soviet leadership that stated that Finland had lost one and one-half times the number of men as the Soviets. The facts from the archives tell a different tale.

Soviet losses were as follows: 72,408 were killed, 186,129 wounded, 17,520 missing in action, 13,213 severely frozen, 240 hospitalized for battle fatigue, and 5,489 prisoners of war.[12]

Finnish casualties were far fewer: 19,576 killed, 48,357 wounded, 4,101 missing in action, and 825 prisoners of war. We have no other information on battle fatigue or cold casualties.[13]

The treatment accorded Soviet prisoners of war was tragic. After repatriation from Finnish prison camps, they marched along the streets of Leningrad, where people threw flowers at them. Then they were separated from the "winners" and all of them were executed.

We have no doubt that Stalin planned through this aggressive war to turn Finland into another Soviet republic like the Baltic nations. But the stubborn resistance of the Finnish Army and the people of that nation combined with criticism by the rest of the nations of the world caused the dictator to have second thoughts. He did not need to face a nation of determined guerrilla fighters on his northern border when his ambitions pointed elsewhere.

After Stalin, his successors and their history books proclaimed the Finnish War as "the Finland-USSR military conflict." This official view was done to avoid worsening postwar relations between the two countries. But the party line stayed the same: that Finland was responsible for starting the war; hence, the use of Finland as the first word in the quotation cited above. As with many events of the Soviet reign, historians operated under strict guidelines to reflect "history" in ways to glorify the leadership, and not to describe the real facts. In the Soviet Union the study and research into the war as well as any written word about the actual events were strictly forbidden. Things changed only after the collapse of the USSR in 1991. The war remained unknown for the succeeding generations of Soviet youth, but in the minds and souls of the older citizens, it left not a heroic feeling, but mixed feelings of sorrow, bitterness, and doubt and a real feeling of guilt. The aggressive colonial war unleashed by the Soviet Union against Finland and the almost simultaneous occupation of Poland and the Balkan states were parts of Stalin's far-reaching strategy that centered, as later events demonstrate, around the plan of dividing Europe between the USSR and Germany, and, if and when circumstances permitted, the swallowing of Germany itself.

The Soviet regime after 1917 developed a party line of propaganda that "true to the Leninist ideal," the Soviet Union had never been the aggressor in any armed conflict. But it is an indisputable fact that in the early morning of November 30, 1939,

the "peaceful Soviet great power of 250 million people" assaulted
Finland in an undeclared war against a nation of three million.
By its nature it was a full-scale war involving a major part of
the Soviet armed forces and mass employment of troops and
combat equipment. The outcome was a historic tragedy in which
we lost hundreds of thousands of our young men: irretrievable
sacrifices.

Chapter III
Vicious Partnership

The written histories of World War II are full of contradictions. The majority of Soviet historians described it solely on a single notion: that Hitler's Germany and the other Axis powers were the aggressors and Stalin's Soviet Union was the victim of the aggression. Western researchers in studying the facts differ in many ways in trying to assess the blame for the war.

More and more researchers are tending to believe that the primary cause of the conflict was the Leninist-Stalinist policy of world revolution under the red banners of Communism. They see the direct responsibility for unleashing the forces of death as resting with two dictators, Stalin and Hitler. Our personal research into the archives of the Soviet state and especially from the classified papers of the Central Committee of the Communist Party confirm this conclusion. We now have all the proof necessary for stating that Stalin was doing everything possible to give up any friendly alliances with Western nations in the 1930s in order to get closer to Fascist Germany. This country, under its growing Nazi regime, was quickly turning its economy to military production and rearmament, not concealing its aggressive plans and goals.

Had the USSR oriented its foreign policy toward the United States, France, and Britain, Hitler would not have had the chance to direct his armies in an easterly direction. But that would have meant that Stalin would not have had a free hand either and his plans for the division of Europe would have had to be scrapped, or, at the least, modified. The Communist dictator had other plans for the future connected with dominating Europe with the help of Hitler's war machine and then later eliminating Germany as a rival for total hegemony over the continent.

In his report at the Eighteenth Party Congress in 1939, Stalin made it clear to Hitler that their interests in a future European war were identical. He was insistent in making Hitler think that the US, Britain, and France desired to foment a war between Germany and the USSR. The idea was that the two great dictatorships would exhaust themselves in a prolonged and disastrous war that would leave them open to political domination by the democracies.[1]

As he made these ideas public, Stalin intentionally ignored all the warnings given him by the democratic states about Hitler's intentions for eventual conflict with the USSR. He wanted to ensure a good psychological basis for the forthcoming alliance with Germany that he was planning. We believe that he wanted Germany to start a war with the democracies that later he could join on his own terms to exchange Hitler's new order for Communism. Stalin was persistent in implementing his strategic plan. The resolute start of this was the infamous Molotov-Ribbentrop nonaggression pact. Its consequences were horrible for the world. It practically provided for Europe to be divided into spheres of influence between Germany and the Soviet Union. Hitler was guaranteed a free hand in Western Europe with the USSR supplying him with various kinds of militarily significant raw materials. In its practical aspects, however, the Wehrmacht was given the chance to overrun France and other countries and simultaneously to prepare itself for offensive operations against the Soviet Union.

The USSR and the Western democracies were effectively isolated from one another by this pact.

This agreement between Stalin and Hitler was concealed from the general public for many years. Soviet historians were unanimous in writing that the initiative and pressure for the pact came from the Germans. This assertion was made in the six-volume official *History of the Great Patriotic War, 1941-1945*, for example. But with Gorbachev's policy of *glasnost,* many previous secrets of the agreement were available to the general public. The line presented in the official history was that overtures were made by the Germans in Berlin to our envoy, but that the Soviet government rejected the proposals. But there is no confirmation of this anywhere we have looked. But we have found documents that disclose quite another picture, that the initiatives actually came from the Soviet side. What really happened?

On May 20, 1939, reacting to a proposal from the German ambassador to Moscow, Schulenburg, regarding trade talks between the two countries, Molotov replied that prior to any economic deals, the "political basis" for them should be created. Then, about eleven weeks later, Hitler sent a personal telegram to Stalin in which he asked him to receive the German foreign minister to implement the Soviet proposal and to conclude the nonaggression treaty between the USSR and Germany. Stalin replied in agreement.

It is interesting how these facts are covered in official Soviet sources. The previously mentioned official history reads: "The USSR might either have rejected the German proposals or agreed to them. In the first case, war with Germany might have been inevitable within two weeks. In the latter case, the USSR might have been able to win some time."[2] If we believe this, we also have to believe that somehow Hitler forced Stalin to approve the document presented within only a few hours. In fact, the eleven weeks were full of intense diplomatic talks and political trades between Soviet and German officials concerning the division of their respective spheres of influence.

On June 15, the Soviet envoy to Berlin, Astahov, visited the Bulgarian ambassador, Draganov. Bulgaria had close ties with Germany, and Stalin was quite confident that the contents of Astahov's conversation would immediately be reported to Ribbentrop, the German foreign minister. Astahov told Draganov that in considering the current international situation, the Soviet Union had two options: sign a pact with Britain and France, or mark time by signing an agreement with Germany. He put the Kremlin's desire quite clearly: "If Germany were to announce that she would not attack the Soviet Union and signed a nonaggression pact, the USSR might well restrain from signing an agreement with the British."[3]

On July 4 Astahov was invited to the German Foreign Affairs Ministry, where he had a conversation with Doctor Schnurre, an official very close to Ribbentrop. Schnurre informed him that the Soviet-German talks could consist of three stages: first, signing a trade agreement; second, normalizing political relations; and third, either returning to the treaty of April 24, 1926, that provided for friendship and neutrality between the two countries, or signing a new nonaggression treaty. At the end of this meeting he told Astahov that the ideologies of Bolshevism, Fascism, and National Socialism were identical. He said:

> There is one thing common in the ideologies of Germany, Italy, and the Soviet Union; it is opposing the capitalist democracies. Neither we nor the Italians have anything in common with the democracies of the West. That is why it would seem quite a paradox to us if the USSR as a socialist state found itself allied with the western democracies.[4]

In other words, neither Bolshevism or Fascism have any foundations for ideological differences. The only disputes are of a territorial-strategic nature: who will obtain the bigger slice of the European pie.

Stalin was not bluffing in his political game with Hitler. England and France had already proposed a defensive treaty with the USSR to collectively oppose the increasing threat emanating from Germany. The proposition was similar to the grand alliance that came into being just after the turn of the century: the agreements between the three great powers, Russia, France, and Britain, to oppose the bellicose tendencies of Germany and her allies. In these negotiations with the Western powers, Stalin was playing his usual double game.

On July 2, in the heat of Soviet-German talks in both Berlin and Moscow, the Kremlin gave a draft of a treaty with the USSR to Britain and France that would put the three powers against Germany. The chief feature in the treaty was the necessity to grant to the Soviet Union the right to invade Poland, the Baltic states, and Finland. On August 11, French and British military missions traveled to Moscow to discuss this draft. The Soviet delegation was headed by Generals Voroshilov and Shaposhnikov. As might be expected, the meeting lacked results because the French and British could not agree to Soviet occupation of presently sovereign states. But these talks had the desired effect on the Germans, alarming them greatly, just as Stalin had planned.

On August 14 Schulenburg informed Molotov that Ribbentrop wanted to come to Moscow to meet personally with Stalin and give him Hitler's personal viewpoints on the principal problems for both sides involved in the negotiations. Molotov diplomatically refused, stating that much more preparatory work was required for this visit. Stalin wanted to heat up the Germans even more. Soviet intelligence agencies through various channels put out false information concerning the progress of the talks with England and France. On August 16 Schulenburg again met with Molotov and informed him that Germany was now prepared to enter into a political pact with the USSR. Molotov replied that Moscow was ready to sign such a treaty, but it should be accompanied by a secret additional protocol in which the spheres of influence of the parties in Western Europe would be delineated. On August 19 a trade treaty between Germany and the Soviet Union was signed. On August 22, Ribbentrop arrived in Moscow to sign the political treaty and its infamous protocol.

In order to obtain the political treaty so desired by Stalin, the

USSR had to give in and sign an utterly unprofitable trade treaty. According to it provisions, Germany was able to obtain not only foodstuffs such as sugar, wheat, butter, and meat, but also strategic raw materials to the benefit of the German war effort and naturally to the detriment of Soviet defense. What he really wanted, of course, was the advantages gained in the secret protocol. This was drawn up in the Kremlin and sent in advance to Berlin.

For the first time, Westerners are able to read the Soviet-German documents of 1939–1941 from the archives of the Central Committee of the Communist Party of the Soviet Union. The original versions of these Soviet documents marked "Top Secret" had been considered lost for a long time because they were kept in a "Special Dossier" at the offices of the Central Committee in Moscow.[5]

Diplomatic documents of the German Ministry for Foreign Affairs concerning Soviet-German relations from 1939 to 1941 were first published in German and English by the United States State Department. These documents were also published in Russian but were translations from other languages and differ in many respects from the originals in the archives. The first official publication of the nonsecret portions of the papers took place after the Second World War. Also published under the classification of "For Restricted Use Only" are papers entitled "Signing the German-Soviet Treaty of Friendship and Borders Between the Soviet Union and Germany (two dates, September 28, 1939 and October 28, 1939)," and a letter from Molotov to Ribbentrop dated September 28, 1939. All these were contained in a book entitled *The USSR Foreign Policy*. Ribbentrop's reply to Molotov was not published in this book, but was contained in the November 29, 1939 issue of *Izvestia*. Maps of Poland with Stalin's and Ribbentrop's signatures were published also on November 29, 1939, in *Pravda*.

In 1989 at the Second Congress of the People's Deputies of the USSR, the Commission on the Political and Legal Assessment of the Soviet-German Treaty on Nonaggression was convened under the chairmanship of A. N. Yakolev. The commission introduced the "Secret Supplementary Protocol on the Borders of the

Spheres of Interest of Germany and the USSR of August 28, 1939."[6] The resolution of the congress stated that ". . . the original version of the protocol had not been found in either Soviet or foreign archives. But . . . expert analysis of the copies, maps, and other documents and the coincidence between the events as they took place and the contents of the protocol testify to the fact of its signing and its existence."[7] The primary documents signed in the period August 15–September 3, 1939, including all the copies of the treaty of August 23, were first published officially in the USSR in September 1989 in *International Life* and were based on copies from the archives of the Federal Republic of Germany. Official Soviet texts of the documents are reproduced herein from the originals in the archives.

The papers containing the Soviet-German secret agreements of 1939–1941 were received in the archives of the Communist Party Central Committee on October 30, 1952, from the secretariat of V. M. Molotov.

On July 2, 1956, the Presidium of the Central Committee adopted a resolution on the systematic publication of official documents. With the permission of the Party, officials of the Foreign Affairs Ministry began to read documents from the archives relating to the years 1923 to 1933. On February 21, 1974, the CPSU Secretariat were persuaded by the General Department of the Central Committee to deny access of these Foreign Affairs personnel to the archives. Instead, the Ministry could request the loan of certain documents, and after checking by the Committee, they were available for loan. Copies of secret Soviet-German agreements (1939–1941) were sent there twice, July 8, 1975, addressed to Deputy Minister L. N. Zamskov but for the attention of A. A. Gromyko. The copies were returned and destroyed on March 4, 1977. On November 21, 1979, they were requested again and were returned and destroyed on February 1, 1980.

These documents were sent to nobody else. They were never referred to. Only those responsible for studying and storing them in the CPSU archives had access to them. The original versions were kept under conditions of extreme secrecy. But the major documents were published in English in the book, *Nazi-Soviet Relations in 1939–1940: Documents from the Archive of the German Ministry for Foreign Affairs*. This publication was done under the auspices of the State Department of the United States in 1948.

The following list is from the Chief of the IX Section of the General Department of the CPSU Central Committee, D. Moshkov, December 10, 1987, Number 20-06-197, classified Top Secret.

1. Original texts of Soviet-German secret agreements signed in 1939–1941.

a. Secret supplementary protocol concerning the borders of the spheres of interest of Germany and the USSR, signed by Molotov and Ribbentrop on August 23, 1939.

b. Clarification of the secret supplementary protocol of August 23rd, signed by Molotov and Schulenburg on August 28, 1939.

c. Confidential protocol on the probability of deporting the population of the countries comprising the spheres of interest of the governments of the USSR and Germany, signed by Molotov and Ribbentrop on September 28, 1939.

d. Secret supplementary protocol on preventing Polish propaganda in the territories of either party to the treaty,

e. Secret supplementary protocol on changes in the agreement of August 23rd on spheres of interest, signed by Molotov and Ribbentrop on September 28, 1939.

f. Protocol stating that Germany relinquishes any claims to the parts of the territories of Lithuania marked in the secret supplementary protocol of September 28, 1939, signed by Molotov and Schulenburg on January 10, 1941.

g. Announcement by the Soviet and German governments of September 28, 1939, on mutual consultation (in Russian and German).

h. Letters exchanged by Molotov and Ribbentrop on September 28, 1939, on economic relations between the USSR and Germany (in Russian and German with draft copies).

i. Two maps of Poland with signatures of Stalin and Ribbentrop.

2. Original Texts of Soviet-German Secret Agreements signed in 1939–1941.

a. Secret supplementary protocol concerning the borders of spheres of interest of Germany and the USSR signed by Molotov and Ribbentrop on August 23, 1939, with copy to Stalin.

b. Clarification to the secret supplementary protocol of August 23, 1939, signed by Molotov and Schulenburg on August 28, 1939.

c. Confidential protocol on the probability of deporting the populations of the zones of interest of the USSR and Germany signed by Molotov and Ribbentrop on September 28, 1939.

d. Secret supplementary protocol on changes in the Soviet-German agreement of August 23rd on the subject of the spheres of interest of Germany and the USSR signed by Molotov and Ribbentrop on September 28, 1939.

e. Secret supplementary protocol on preventing Polish propaganda in the territories of either party signed by Molotov and Ribbentrop on September 28, 1939.

f. Protocol stating that Germany relinquished any claims on the territory of Lithuania as marked in the secret supplementary protocol of September 28, 1939, signed by Molotov and Schulenburg on January 10, 1941.

g. Declaration by Soviet and German governments of September 28, 1939, on mutual consultations.

h. Letters exchanged by Molotov and Ribbentrop on September 28, 1939, concerning economic relations between the two countries.

i. Two maps of Poland with the signatures of Stalin and Ribbentrop.

We have obtained the secret supplementary protocol signed by Molotov and Ribbentrop in Moscow, August 23, 1939, on the borders of the spheres of interest of Germany and the USSR:

MINISTRY OF FOREIGN AFFAIRS OF THE USSR

In signing the nonaggression treaty between Germany and the Union of Soviet Socialist Republics, the signatories discussed confidentially the question of dividing the spheres of mutual interest of the countries in Eastern Europe. The discussion resulted in the following:

1. In case the territorial-political regions are restructured, making part of the Baltic States' (Finland, Estonia, Latvia, and Lithuania) border be the northern border of Lithuania, this simultaneously marks the border dividing the interests of Germany and the USSR. The interests of Lithuania concerning the Vilna district are recognized by both parties.

2. In case the territorial-political regions are restructured, making part of the State of Poland be the border between the spheres of interest of Germany and the USSR, the border for this purpose will be approximately along the Rivers Nareva, Visla, and Sana. The question of preserving an independent Polish state and the actual location of its borders can be answered definitely only in the course of further political developments. In any case, the two governments will solve this problem with friendly mutual consent.

3. As far as Southeast Europe is concerned, the Soviet Union stresses its interest in Bessarabia. Germany declares its complete disinterest in those regions.

4. This protocol will be kept strictly secret.

The next document from the same source was signed in Moscow on August 28, 1939 by Molotov and Schulenburg. It is entitled:

CLARIFICATION OF THE SECRET SUPPLEMENTARY
PROTOCOL OF AUGUST 23, 1939

To make the first paragraph of Item 2 of the "Secret Supplementary Protocol of August 23, 1939" more precise, it should read as follows:

2. In case the territorial-political regions are restructured, making part of the State of Poland be the border of the

spheres of interest of Germany and the USSR, the border for this purpose will be approximately along the Rivers Pissa, Nareva, Visla, and Sana.

Next is the secret supplementary protocol signed in Moscow on August 28, 1939 by Molotov and Ribbentrop on changes to the Soviet-German treaty of August 23rd concerning spheres of influence of Germany and the USSR:

SECRET SUPPLEMENTARY PROTOCOL

The signatories of this document state that the German and Soviet governments agree that:

The secret supplementary protocol signed on August 23, 1939 is changed in Item 1, stating that the territory of Lithuania is included in the sphere of interest of the USSR, and on the side of the other party, the Lublin district and part of the Warsaw district are included in the sphere of interest of Germany. (See map to the treaty of friendship and the border between the USSR and Germany signed today.) As soon as the government of the USSR undertakes special measures to protect its interests in Lithuania, with the aim of a simple and natural delineation of the border, the present German-Lithuanian border is changed, so that Lithuanian territory to the southwest of the line will be part of Germany.

Further, it is agreed that actual economic conditions between Germany and Lithuania should not be influenced by any measures taken by the Soviet Union as mentioned above.

Still another secret supplementary protocol was signed by Molotov and Ribbentrop on August 28, 1939 on preventing Polish propaganda in the territories of either party:

SECRET SUPPLEMENTARY PROTOCOL

In signing the Soviet-German treaty of friendship and their borders, the signatories hereby state that they agreed that:

Neither side will allow on its territory any Polish propaganda to enter the territory of the other nation. They will prevent the emanation of such propaganda in their countries and will inform each other on any necessary steps taken.

On January 10, 1941, only a few months before the invasion of the USSR, the following protocol on Germany relinquishing any claims to that part of Lithuanian territory agreed to in the secret supplementary protocol of September 28, 1939 was signed in Moscow by Molotov and Schulenburg (Strictly Confidential).

SECRET PROTOCOL

By the authority of the Government of the USSR, the Chairman of the Council of People's Commissars of the USSR, V. M. Molotov, on one side, and by the authority of the Government of Germany, Ambassador Count von der Schulenburg, on the other side, it is agreed that:

1. The Government of Germany relinquishes its claims on that part of Lithuanian territory mentioned in the Secret Supplementary Protocol of September 28, 1939, and depicted on the map accompanying this protocol.

2. The Governmant of the USSR agrees to provide to Germany compensation for the territory mentioned in paragraph 1 above and will pay to Germany $7,500,000 in gold which equals 31 million 500 thousand German marks.

This sum of 31.5 million German marks will be paid as follows: one-eighth part (3,937,500 marks) in the form of shipments of nonferrous metals within three months from the signing of this protocol, and the remaining seven-eighths (27,562,500 marks) by reducing existing German debts up to February 11, 1941, on the basis of the exchange of letters between the People's Commissar of Foreign Trade, A. I. Mikoyan, and the chairman of the German Economic Delegation, Herr Schnurre, concerning the signing of the agreement of January 10, 1941, on Mutual Shipments for the Second Agreed Period in Accordance with the Economic Agreement of February 11 between the USSR and Germany.

3. This protocol has two originals in Russian and two originals in German. It goes into force immediately upon signing.

The Molotov-Ribbentrop pact set up a vicious partnership between Stalin and Hitler. It gave the two dictators a free hand in determining the destinies of other peoples, allowing them to occupy other countries' territories and to establish ways of living by the standards of their own nations, Bolshevism and Fascism, differing only a little. The law of the jungle was validated by the official documents. The USSR was able to annex the Baltic States and parts of Romania, Finland, and Poland. Stalin's KGB agents shot 15,000 Polish Army prisoners of war, 5,000 of them at Katyn in 1940. The Soviet mass media in those days not only persuaded our people that the occupation of foreign territories by the Soviet Union was necessary and just, but excused the combat actions of Hitler's Germany against democratic nations, depicting them as defending the German people against aggression. Thus is the nature of propaganda. At the same time, the USSR was supplying Germany with many things necessary for aggression against her neighbors.

The real plans of the two dictators, Hitler and Stalin, were not yet fully realized. Each of them had secret-planning offices where directives for mutual destruction and occupation were being worked out. Hypocritically smiling at each other and keeping up false pretenses, each had diabolical ideas relative to the other. Hitler was preparing for "Operation Barbarossa," the invasion of the Soviet Union, and Stalin was preparing a preventive strike at Germany.

But Hitler was the first to act. On June 22, 1941, Nazi airplanes and tanks, filled with Soviet fuel, invaded the Soviet Union. Hitler's soldiers, well equipped with German vehicles and also with Soviet bread, meat, and butter, followed the tanks and aircraft into the interior of our country. This was the Great Patriotic War of the Soviet people against Nazi Germany. The Soviet people were fighting against foreigners in their motherland. This war is described as just and liberating. That is correct, but not all of the story.

Unwillingly we ask ourselves a question and search for an answer. Chronologically the beginning of our war with Germany is June 22, 1941, when *Wehrmacht* troops began to flood the borders of the Soviet Union. The end of the war is May 9, 1945, when Germany surrendered to the allies and the documents of surrender were signed by the Nazis. But our Soviet troops had largely expelled the Germans from our territory by the middle of 1944. So for the last six months of 1944 and up to May 1945 they were fighting on foreign soil in Eastern Europe and the Balkans with the stated purpose of liberating the peoples there from their Fascist yokes. Had this great and good deed stopped there, we would have no argument with our leadership.

As it turned out, this "liberation" moved these countries from one undesirable regime under Hitler to so-called "people's democracies" that answered to the leaders in the Kremlin. These Eastern European countries were turned into socialist clones that followed the leadership from Moscow closely. We have trouble seeing how the word "patriotic" can logically be applied to the war once it left the territory of the Soviet Union; "liberating," perhaps, if the countries involved had been really set free, but not even that with what actually happened. What occurred was while we were beating the enemy (Germany) to death, we were simultaneously implementing Stalin's dream. His strategic plan was realized in full scale as he became the "inspirer" and "organizer" of all the victories of the Soviet people and its armed forces. He awarded himself the highest possible military rank of "generalissimo" (as the Fascist Franco had done in Spain earlier) and been rewarded in all thinkable and, yes, unthinkable ways.

So the pro-Soviet socialist states—the German Democratic Republic, Hungary, Bulgaria, Czechoslovakia, and Poland—were united under the mantle of the Warsaw Pact and its "Political Consultative Committee." Albania and Yugoslavia, while not members of the Warsaw Pact, still became Communist states with friendly relations with the USSR. Internally, as new parts of the Soviet Union we saw the Western Ukraine, Bessarabia (which became the Moldavian Soviet Socialist Republic), Latvia, Lithuania, Estonia, East Sakhalin, and the Kuril Islands (the last two seized from Japan). In the Far East, China, North Korea, and North Vietnam became Stalin's firm allies. In the latter two, Kim Il Sung and Ho Chi Minh were dictators with immense power who strictly toed the Kremlin's line and who in turn were heavily supported with Soviet arms, goods, and services. Stalin gave them both a great deal of thought and attention, constantly mulling over plans for unifying these two countries under the red banner and thus creating new opportunities for spreading Soviet Communism farther into Asia. Stalin was in an excellent position to fulfill the rest of his dreams. Where would he turn next?

Korea appeared to be the first in line.

Chapter IV

Stalin's Last Military Adventure

In attempting to achieve his strategic mission of worldwide revolution, Communist penetration into Asia played a prominent role in Stalin's foreign policy. As history tells us, the USSR finally joined the Allies against Japan in the last days of the war in the Pacific. Stalin saw this attack against the Japanese in August 1945 as a chance to cause the capitulation of the Kwangtung Army, seize Japanese territory like Sakhalin and the Kuril Islands, and position himself to make other inroads in this vast and important part of the world.

Korea is a major state in East Asia located mainly on a peninsula extending from Mongolia and having a population of over 60 million people. In 1904 and 1905, Japan established a protectorate over the peninsula and in 1910 formally annexed it. Korea remained a virtual part of the Japanese empire until it was liberated by the Allies in 1945.

On August 15, 1945, a United States military mission presented to Stalin in Moscow a far-reaching proposal from General MacArthur. In it he suggested that the USSR accept Japan's capitulation on that part of the Korean peninsula north of the 38th parallel and that the United States do the same south of that line, thus dividing the country roughly in half. Stalin telegraphed his positive response to this proposal on August 16. An unfortunate agreement thereby was concluded, perhaps too quickly, one that was to prove highly advantageous to the Communist side. For Stalin this was yet another step along his path toward annexation.

The American administration under Harry Truman was well aware of the artificial nature of a divided Korea and looked on it as a short-term expedient. The United States constantly strove for unification of the two pieces in many ways. In response to an American initiative, a Soviet–United States conference was held from January 16–February 5, 1946, but it failed to achieve its goal. The primary reason for its failure can be ascribed to the different ways the two parties saw the future of Korea. The United States wanted to have the country united as a democratic nation. Stalin objected to this concept, insisting on preserving the division, stating the Koreans should have the chance to settle the problem themselves in the future. In fact, the USSR desired to bring North Korea under its own political wing.

The United States advanced the question as an agenda item to the newly formed United Nations Organization (UNO). Despite resistance from the USSR and its allies, a temporary UNO commission was established to observe elections in Korea on November 14, 1947. When the time came for the elections, the Soviet authorities refused to permit the members of the commission to enter the occupation zone north of the 38th parallel, so the only part of the elections to be monitored was in the southern United States zone.

On May 10, 1948, free elections were held in the southern zone, resulting in the birth of the Republic of Korea. On September 9, 1948, the new Korean People's Democratic Republic was proclaimed in the northern sector of Korea. The UNO commission characterized it as an "occupation and antidemocratic regime."[1]

The division of Korea at the 38th parallel came as a result of a shortsighted decision of the United States at the end of the war and the acquisitive policy of the Soviet Union as it began to establish its "iron curtain" in both Asia and Europe. With Korea,

Stalin began his practice of dividing states with a final objective of unifying them under his own auspices. This began in Korea and was repeated in Germany and Vietnam. The Stalinist leadership in North Korea commenced the huge task of converting the country into a puppet regime subservient to Moscow. The Soviet dictator realized that to accomplish his mission, careful preparation and caution were needed.

In those days, the end of the 1940s and the beginning of the 1950s, the frost of the cold war was getting even icier. Allies who had fought Hitler in harmony were now looking through gunsights at each other. Stalin recognized the indisputable fact that the United States was stronger than the USSR, virtually invulnerable. So he could not act by his tested principle: "I do what I want to do."

Beginning his working day in the Kremlin, Stalin attentively read through lavish reports concerning international affairs from the State Security Minister (KGB) Beria, other ministries, ambassadors, and international agencies from various places in the world. Special attention was devoted to Asia, where Mao Tse-tung, supported by Moscow, was achieving victory after victory over his Nationalist Chinese leader Chiang Kai-shek. Stalin was also quite content with the activities of his puppets in Mongolia and North Korea.

In Korea, Kim Il Sung, closely monitored by Soviet advisers, became significantly better educated politically as he gained experience in Communistic thought and practices. From his capital in Pyongyang he wrote a personal letter to Stalin, reporting "progress in Socialist construction" in the country and asking to be received by him in Moscow. Upon receiving the letter, Stalin ordered that Kim be invited to the Soviet capital because the two men should become more closely acquainted, but the date would be set later.

In the meantime, on January 19, 1950, Ambassador T. F. Shtykov reported the following from Pyongyang:

> There was a reception in the Chinese Embassy in honor of the ambassador's departure. During this affair, Kim Il

Sung and I had a conversation in which he stated that now
that the liberation of China was about finished, the time had
come for the liberation of South Korea and the unification
of the country. Mao does not believe that we should attack
the south, but should counterattack if the south initiates an
attack. But South Korea is not apt to attack. So Kim wants to
visit Comrade Stalin to ask for permission to make an attack
on South Korea to liberate it. Mao has promised support and
Kim Il Sung will also meet with him. Kim insists on personally reporting to Comrade Stalin on his plans for the attack
on South Korea.

Stalin's answer was prompt. He sent a telegram to Shtykov saying: "Everything should be organized so as to avoid great risks. I
am ready to receive Comrade Kim Il Sung."[2] In Pyongyang the
telegram was interpreted as Stalin's approval of planning for the
operation, provided success could be guaranteed.

Also in January, following a telephone conversation between
Stalin and Mao, a detailed discussion of the Korean problem took
place in Moscow when the Chinese leaders Mao Tse-tung and
Chou En-lai made a month-long visit. On January 22 they had a
lengthy meeting with Stalin.

During these talks, all parties agreed that Soviet military contingents and Chinese "volunteers" would take part in the war by
North Korea against its southern neighbor. They agreed to send
to North Korea food and other supplies, weapons, fuel, ammunition, medical supplies, and anything else necessary for the waging of large-scale war. The Soviets were willing to provide not only
military contingents, but also many military specialists, instructors,
advisers, and interpreters. All the obligations under these agreements were recorded in the proceedings of these high-level talks.[3]

On February 4, 1950, Shtykov notified Stalin through Vishinsky that Kim had requested credits from the Soviet Union for the
purchase of weaponry. In addition, he asked for permission to increase the number of infantry divisions from seven to ten, with
three new divisions to be organized.[4]

After consulting with Beijing, on February 9, 1950, Stalin gave his approval for the preparation of plans for a large-scale operation on the Korean peninsula and thus approving Kim's wish to unify the country by force. This date is the practical official start of North Korean military preparations for the war. Shipments of tanks, small arms, ammunition, medical supplies, and other vital supplies such as gasoline and oil from the USSR were intensified. Under strict secrecy, the North Korean Army headquarters aided by Stalin's advisers worked on the details of the plan for ambitious offensive action against the southern territory. Rapid formation of new Korean units was under way. The world did not know yet that it would soon see one of the biggest bloodbaths of the twentieth century.

On May 30, 1950, Shtykov reported the following to Moscow:

> Kim Il Sung informed me that the chief of the general staff has finished formulation of the principal operational plan in conjunction with (Soviet) adviser Vasil'yev for the upcoming offensive. Kim Il Sung has approved the plan. Organizational work will be completed by June 1st. Out of twenty divisions, seven are ready for the offensive. In July the rains will begin. Generals Vasil'yev and Postshev informed me that more time will be needed for assembling the troop units. The general staff suggests that the operation be started late in June. My opinion is that we can agree to this date. The Koreans are asking for fuel and medical supplies. I request expedited directives.[5]

Stalin himself wrote the answering telegram to Shtykov: "Your suggestions have been approved. Fuel and medical supplies will be shipped on an expedited basis."[6]

The period from June 1, 1950, until the 25th was used by the North Koreans and their Soviet advisers to perfect their plans, conduct rehearsals, perform needed maintenance on the equipment, and otherwise get themselves prepared for the great adventure that lay ahead.

On June 25, 1950, North Korean troops crossed the 38th parallel, seven divisions strong along with a tank brigade. They were able to make rapid headway, advancing about two kilometers into South Korea. This is not surprising considering the lack of strength of their adversary. The South Koreans were not prepared for any kind of extensive combat, offensive or defensive. They lacked many of the implements of war that the North Koreans possessed abundantly, such as tanks, heavy artillery, and crew-served weapons. The excuse given to the world for the attack was that their southern brothers had attacked first; this seems reminiscent of the Soviet attack on Finland in 1939. This charge is, of course, ludicrous. How could South Korea have been ready to attack North Korea and find the North Koreans in their capital, Seoul, in a short three days?

Having started the war with such great success, Kim Il Sung felt as though he had wings. His Soviet advisers insisted that the initial success be exploited in a systematic way with all forces being mobilized to achieve a quick and complete victory.

Despite the indisputable fact that there was considerable Soviet involvement in all phases of the war and the preparations thereof, Stalin did his best to deceive the rest of the world by concealing the facts. For him, it was important to support the story that North Korean actions were only defensive in nature and that any Soviet involvement was merely "technical." He was able to sell this fable to the Soviet people, who believed it as the truth for decades.

Soviet newspapers and other media reported that an aggressive South Korea, supported by the United States, was ready to attack and occupy North Korea, but miscalculated the strength of the People's Army and were severely punished. In the *Soviet Military Encyclopedia* it was written: "The Korean war of 1950–1953 was unleashed by the South Korean military and United States ruling circles with the aim of eliminating the Korean People's Democratic Republic and turning North Korea into a bridgehead for an attack at China and the USSR. This offensive plan was devised by the American military mission and the South Korean military command in May 1949."[7]

This may have fooled the Soviet people and other Communist-oriented nations, but was not very effective throughout the world. The United States brought the matter to the Security Council of the United Nations on an emergency basis. The Security Council condemned the invasion and asked the North Koreans to cease their offensive at once and to leave the territory south of the 38th parallel and return to North Korea. The Council also requested member countries to aid the South Koreans in their struggle. For reasons that are hard to understand, the Soviets boycotted this session of the Security Council, when they were in a position to veto the action taken. The United States took rapid action starting on June 30 to implement the Security Council request by sending occupation troops from Japan to Korea to help the South Koreans in repelling the juggernaut from the north.

Although the Americans and other UN member states sent troops to South Korea and fought hard, they were badly outmatched by the North Koreans. In particular, the American divisions in Japan were poorly equipped and badly trained, as the United States government had downsized the victorious American Army of World War II and was not providing sufficient funding for the troops that remained. Units were short of personnel and equipment, and such equipment as was present was outmoded, certainly not a match for Soviet supplied items as the T-34 tank. Achieving operational success starting with the surprise initial attacks, the North Korean army was able to capture Seoul and many other important population centers. The outcome of the war seemed predetermined as Stalin congratulated Kim on his great victory.

The United Nations forces, although bloodied badly by the persistence of the North Korean assault, finally established a manageable defensive line in a perimeter around the southern port of Pusan, around the first week of August. This defensive line was able to hold for a variety of reasons, such as the long lines of communications and logistic support from the north to that area when the North Korean troops and supply convoys were subject to interdiction from the air and from guerrilla forces operating in their rear. Added to this was the fact that the United Nations forces were reinforced with new units consisting of two army infantry regiments and a brigade of marines, as well as individual replacements for soldiers killed or wounded and for bringing platoons and companies up to authorized strength. Fighting around this perimeter raged until September 16, when a highly dramatic event occurred, a mighty counterattack.

On this date, an entire army corps was moved by sea to assault the port of Inchon on the western coast of Korea, near Seoul, the capital. This invasion by X Corps of the United States Army came as a complete surprise to both the leadership of North Korea and their Soviet advisers. Coincident with the invasion, US Eighth Army troops consisting of both South Korean and American units launched a massive offensive against the North Korean troops opposing them in the Pusan Perimeter. Both UN operations succeeded in breaking the North Korean Army, which began to dissolve. Kim Il Sung's forces were seriously defeated, with over 100,000 men being captured. They lost the majority of their artillery and tanks to capture on the ground and from the air, where the Americans enjoyed superiority as they destroyed most moving items in North Korean–held territory. It became clear that without rapid additional steps by the USSR and China, North Korea would cease to exist as a country.

On October 1, North Korea's foreign affairs minister handed an urgent letter to Shtykov for delivery to Stalin personally. In this document, seemingly written with the help of Soviet advisers, Kim Il Sung addressed the problem as follows:

> The enemy, after having suffered one defeat after another, was restricted in a small sector in the southern part of South Korea; we therefore had significant chances for victory in the latest decisive battles. . . . But the USA, having mobilized almost all land, naval, and aviation forces in the Pacific, on September 16 conducted a sea landing at Inchon. Having captured Inchon, the enemy is waging warfare in the streets of Seoul. . . . Enemy avaition, encountering no resistance, dominates the air. . . . Some of our troops are encircled by the enemy. . . .
>
> Dear Comrade Stalin, if the enemy continues offensive actions at North Korea, we will not be able to stop the enemy by ourselves. That is why, dear Iosif Vissarinovich, we ask for special military assistance.

If for some reason this is impossible, then help us to organize international volunteer forces in China to provide military support in our struggle.[8]

Political prestige of all parties sat in the scales of ambition of three leaders, Kim Il Sung of North Korea, Mao Tse-tung of China, and the Soviet dictator, I. V. Stalin. The leaders of China and the USSR had encouraged and aided Kim and his other leaders to begin the mad adventure of overwhelming his South Korean cousins. So Stalin wrote a letter to Mao in energetic terms. These are words that even today give a feeling of cold death. In essence, the possibility of a third world war was contained in the sentences written by the Soviet dictator:

The USA cannot allow itself to be involved in a large-scale war. Consequently, China will be involved in conjunction with the USSR as we are tied together by our mutual assistance treaty. Shall we be afraid of this? To my mind we shall not, because together we will be stronger than the USA and England. Other capitalist states, except for Germany, which cannot provide any help to the USA, constitute no serious military force. If a war is inevitable, let it come now and not several years later when Japanese militarism is restored as an ally of the USA. . . .[9]

We feel somehow out of place when we realize that the third world war almost became real when the two blocs confronted each other in Korea (the situation was repeated in the Cuban crisis when we came close to nuclear war). We think that the Korean War might have been initiated by those who were thinking constantly of world domination, as the leaders of the Communist International did.

Mao responded: "I am very glad that your letter describes the joint fight of China and the USSR against the USA. . . . Undoubtedly if we have to fight, it will be better to fight now. . . . It will be good to employ not as few as five or six divisions, but nine, at least."[10] After this letter was received, new information arrived that in Beijing not only details were still being discussed, but the probability of Chinese military intervention. The leaders were worried in the Kremlin.

Meanwhile in Beijing all pros and cons were being weighed. Stalin was waiting for the results of the process in an impatient way. Since the Chinese could improve the situation, the Soviet dictator decided that he would employ his own Red Army only at the very last moment if the situation became extreme; this, despite the fact that he already had decided to use Soviet aviation from Chinese airfields adjacent to the North Korean border. By Stalin's order, the Soviet LXIV Aviation Corps with augmented air defense artillery units was operating together with the North Koreans. The majority of Soviet officers, pilots, and artillerymen were veterans of the Great Patriotic War and therefore had a great deal of combat experience.

Finally Beijing responded. Mao agreed to provide direct military support to the North Koreans, as he informed Stalin. The intervention of huge masses of Chinese troops began on October 25, 1950. In the Socialist press they were called "volunteers." Their offensive proved to be long and difficult, but entirely responsive to the request of Kim Il Sung. They saved the day for the North Koreans. United States air superiority was faced with entire companies, battalions, and regiments dug in trenches so deeply that both bombs and incendiaries were ineffective against them. Conditions finally became reminiscent of the western front of the First World War. Soviet military personnel continued to participate in combat against the United Nations forces. They were not only advisers and instructors, but often manned artillery, tank, and aircraft crews.

Desperate fighting occurred over the entire breath of the Korean peninsula as the combined Chinese–North Korean assault threatened to overrun the entire territory of South Korea. Over a period of about two months, United Nations forces were ejected from North Korean territory with Pyongyang, Seoul, and Inchon recaptured. The front gradually stabilized about fifty miles south of Seoul. The Eighth Army commander, General Walker, was killed in an accident in late December and General Matthew Ridgway was appointed to replace him. Ridgway initiated a counteroffensive in late January 1951. This was successfully accomplished after much hard fighting on both sides, and the front was stabilized roughly at the original 38th parallel boundary by the end of March.

We cannot keep from admiring the American General Ridgway, who first commanded the Eighth Army and then later, after President Truman relieved General MacArthur, became the overall commander of United Nations forces. He was an extremely competent commander with rich combat experience in the Second World War. This enabled him to change the course of the war and to save the world from another Communist victory and another foothold in Asia. We see him in the same mold as Eisenhower, Zhukov, Patton, Timoshenko, MacArthur, Vasilevesky, Marshall, and Rokossovsky, one of the great military leaders of the era. He was a true professional but had a common touch, a trait that made him beloved to his men. There's a story about him, reported by eyewitnesses, that as he was riding in a jeep he noticed a marine trudging along a road, heavily laden with equipment but with an untied boot. The general stopped the vehicle, got out, and personally tied the man's shoelaces.

Russian veterans of World War II learned of Ridgway's death on July 27, 1993, with deep sorrow. We felt that this general respected the accomplishments of Soviet soldiers in that war, a feeling reciprocated by them. If he were able to come here today, these same old soldiers would thank him for his bravery and courage in their common fight.

But we must get back to the Korean War. Stalin, having seen that military victory was impossible, lost any real interest in the conflict. He ordered Vishinsky to initiate peace proposals with the goal of achieving the victory on the diplomatic front that had been denied militarily.

In a meeting in Moscow on September 19, 1952, with the Chinese premier, Chou En-lai, they discussed the means necessary to permit the Chinese and North Koreans to maintain the positions they presently occupied and the exchange of prisoners of war. Stalin reminded Chou that the "Americans would try to recruit some POWs for conducting espionage. . . ." He confirmed that he was prepared to provide weapons to China to equip sixty infantry divisions.[11] Conducting peace talks in Korea did not rule out further military operations.

But Stalin failed to achieve either of his goals. The dictator died in March 1953 and the cease-fire ended the war on June 27 of the same year. This fruitless attempt to solve a perceived problem by force cost hundreds of thousands of lives, many billions of rubles and dollars, thousands of destroyed villages, cities, and industrial enterprises, and rendered millions of common people homeless. The Korean War is one of the needless bloody lessons of history, a lesson we do not need to experience again.

This chapter not only demonstrates the role of the leaders of the Soviet Union in unleashing the Korean War; it also discloses the degree of Soviet military involvement there. It also shows the danger of the presence of any totalitarian regime, ready to resort to any kind of bloody aggression to appease its egotistic interests, ignoring the victims, deaths, and the vital interests of the people. We are presenting documents to help the reader learn the complete truth of the Korean War which was, up to now, hidden in the archives of the former Soviet Union.

We would now like to describe in more detail the extent of Soviet involvement in the Korean War and how it affected the outcome of the conflict. As we have described, the North Korean leader, Kim Il Sung, desired greatly to unify the entire country under his rule. We have also shown that the Soviet Union aided and abetted Kim's ambitions. But some of the reasoning on the part of the Soviet leadership for their actions has been obscure. We have learned that Stalin received some very bad advice from his subordinates, advice that caused him to act in an irrational manner during this period. To a person with any degree of intelligence, it was obvious that North Korea could not wage successful war on South Korea by itself; it needed help in the form of Soviet support. But Stalin began to get some disturbing information. The following came to him from the Central Intelligence Department of the General Staff of the USSR Armed Forces on April 4, 1948:

Reliable information shows that South Korean troops are being concentrated near the 38th parallel. Troop formations are advancing forward. Construction of fortifications is taking place along the border. There is talk among both soldiers and civilians that South Korean troops are actively getting prepared for combat action and are awaiting orders to go on the offensive. American advisers and instructors are arriving. Their number is growing noticeably.[12]

Citing this document, provided here in a condensed version, Defense Minister/Marshal of the Soviet Union Alexandr Vasilevsky reported to Stalin his views on the military-political situation on the Korean peninsula. In a coded message in early 1949, he requested that special attention be paid to the possible consequences of South Korean military preparations. He warned of the menace of South Korea taking over its northern neighbor with the help of the United States, a possibility that should not be ruled out.[13]

Especially zealous in painting the situation even more gravely was the chairman of the State Security Committee (KGB), Lavrenti Beria. Exploiting Stalin's love for himself, his ambitious nature, and his extreme mistrustfulness, Beria sought to implant in his mind the ideas of machinations by American "imperialists" and their desire to expand the sphere of their influence by approaching as closely as possible the borders of the Soviet Union. Beria used reports from his KGB agents for this purpose. In a coded message of May 24, 1949, for example, he stated: ". . . The USA, supported by reactionary elements in South Korea , are spreading militarist slogans and propaganda aimed at preparing the population for a war with North Korea. Such a war may begin in the near future."[14] In another coded telegram of June 3, 1949, a description of the so-called American occupation of South Korea was discussed in every possible detail. The order of battle of the South Korean armed forces to include the army, navy, and air force was detailed, as were the fortifications around principal cities like Seoul and Inchon.

To show how well reports like these affected Stalin's thinking, the Soviet government declared on July 4, 1950, after the war began, that the notion of aggression in a civil war could not be justified; aggression could occur only when a foreign state was involved. In this specific case, the United States was the culprit, as it had interfered in the internal conflict in Korea.

Obviously everything was upside down at this point. The American side had nothing with which to start the hostilities and thus accusations like those just stated were absurd. What was actually happening was quite vivid, as the USSR was busily encouraging the North Koreans in their aggression.

Several groups of Soviet experts went to North Korea late in 1949 and the first part of 1950 to conduct reconnaisance, help in the plans for the future war, provide tactical and operational training, and conduct staff training for the Korean Army and the attached Chinese military representatives. Various versions of the offensive actions to come were studied together, as was the nature of Soviet military assistance, which was discussed in every possible detail.

At the start, Col. Gen. Pytr Batitsky commanded the Soviet forces sent to Korea. He was replaced in July 1950 by Lt. Gen. Sergei Slusarev. Aviation and air defense units were headed by generals who reported to the overall Soviet commander.

The following table[15] details the numbers of Soviet personnel in combat action in Korea from 1950 to 1953:

QUALIFICATION	1950	1951	1952	1953
Fighter pilots	253	212	256	128
Aviation technicians	812	542	410	286
Radar operators	144	186	146	94
Aviation engineers	184	212	97	58
Radar maintenancemen	50	74	82	71

There is no doubt that Soviet military specialists were participating actively in the rearming and retraining of Korean servicemen for combat as well as acting in combat roles themselves. Due to these efforts, the level of training and the combat efficiency of the North Korean Army improved considerably.

North Korea was flooded with weapons and other necessities of combat. The following table[16] provides some data on what was shipped to Korea during the period of the war:

ITEM	1950	1951	1952	1953
Aircraft	212	142	176	94
Radars	93	84	103	60
Target acquisition complexes	74	80	94	62
Air defense guns	160	134	175	98
Small arms*	44	76	81	54
Artillery ammunition*	84	117	112	82
Small arms ammo. (cases)*	91	98	114	67
Food (tons)	310	318	384	246
Fuel (tons)	84	97	114	89
Medical (tons)	34	42	16	10

*In thousands

It is evident from this table that Soviet supplies to North Korea were plentiful and constant. This bothers us because the Soviet economy in 1949 and 1950 was just beginning to recover from the ravages of the Great Patriotic War. To help the North Koreans in their aggression, our own people had to do without many of the necessities of life.

At the start of the war the North Korean Air Force had only about 150 obsolete aircraft, which naturally were not ready for combat. In addition, practically all the airfields in North Korea were in poor condition, some virtually destroyed. All this was well known to the Soviet General Staff. And Korean pilots were not trained to modern standards. Therefore, the First Deputy of the Chief of Staff, Col. Gen. Sergei Shtemenke, in his directive of January 17, 1951, assigned Soviet pilots the mission of active defense against enemy aircraft on land and in the air, as well as protecting important strategic objectives, railways, highways, communications junctions, and troop formations in rear areas.[17]

On November 1, 1950, the Soviet defense minister, Marshal
Alexandr Vasilevsky, assigned the 28th and 151st Fighter Aviation
Divisions the mission of defending the most important administrative and industrial facilities of North Korea from the air. While
Korean troops advanced to the south, pilots were assigned another mission, protecting North Korean communications lines
within the depth of the fighters' operational radius, but not less
than 75 kilometers from the front lines. These restrictions caused
great complications in organizing combat operations and reduced the effectiveness of the air arm, a situation the United Nations pilots were quick to exploit. They conducted many combat
operations near the seashore, and if they found themselves in any
kind of trouble, they could head out to sea and later resume their
attacks.[18]

One can appreciate the peculiarities of this air combat by the
following transcript:

> After the takeoff, the regiment assembled and assumed a
> combat formation en route to the combat area at an altitude
> of 9,000–11,000 meters. This usually took about fourteen to
> sixteen minutes. Approaching the combat area, the regi-
> ment split into two groups, assault and cover. The cover
> group followed the assault group at a higher altitude. The
> combat formation depended on the number of air crews
> available at the time.
>
> In combat Soviet pilots operated in sections, by six or eight
> and mainly in pairs. The fighting was along vertical lines and
> the entire group tried to remain in visual contact with one
> another and in the same area. This allowed them to main-
> tain constant and efficient coordination among all groups,
> sections, and pairs. The main tactic was to attack from a high
> altitude and return there for further attacks.
>
> The fighters would leave the combat area in pairs and sec-
> tions along the horizon, gaining altitude at greater distance
> and speed. The average time of an air combat mission was
> eight to thirteen minutes. After returning to the home air-
> field, the regiment landed by single planes with twenty-to
> thirty-second intervals.[19]

By a decision of the Soviet government late in November 1950, the LXIV Fighter Aviation Corps was deployed to North Korea, forming the basis of Soviet troops there. It was composed of the 29th, 151st, and 50th Aviation Divisions and was 26,000 men strong. At different periods of the Korean War, the number of its aircraft varied from 170 to 240.

The corps also had air defense troops assigned, two Air Defense Artillery Divisions. They were equipped with 85mm guns and 57mm automatic weapons and had both target-acquisition and director-type radars and computers. There was also an aviation technical division, a separate aviation regiment, a searchlight regiment, a naval aviation regiment, two military hospitals, and other support and logistics units.[20]

Generally, the corps was replenished by replacing entire units, but frequently the new troops were not up to the standards of their predecessors. This was reported to Moscow by the corps commander. The following table[21] gives some statistics on combat operations of the LXIV Aviation Corps:

Stage of War	Friendly Sorties	Enemy Aircraft Destroyed	Friendly Losses Aircraft	Friendly Losses Pilots
1950–51: Air Force	19,203	964	34	71
1952: Air Force	23,539	394	51	172
1953: Air Force	18,152	139	25	76
1951–53: Air Def. Arty.	—	105	—	—
Totals	60,894	1,602	110	319

These figures are shown in the report of Gen. Sergei Slusarev to the defense minister of the Soviet Union.

As the Korean War progressed, the experiences of actual combat showed that the organization of aviation regiments did not meet the demands of the situations placed on them. For example, we examined a report from the headquarters of the 28th Fighter Aviation Division to the commander of Soviet troops in North Korea, dated June 18, 1951. This document indicated a shortage of pilots in that they were unable to keep pilots in reserve, necessary so the pilots would be able to react quickly to combat situations. The great tensions of combat flying exhausted them to the point that many could not fly any longer. They needed lengthy rest periods, but this was practically impossible because of the missions given them. Every pilot was precious, and many had to fly combat missions for up to six months in a row.

In addition, higher headquarters should have taken into account the inescapable fact that air fighting produces losses of pilots and aircraft as well as injuries and wounds. Pilots had to eject from damaged aircraft and were subject to infections from a variety of diseases. The job was harder because of the complicated weather conditions in North Korea that our pilots had never experienced.[22]

By fall 1951 recommendations from the operating headquarters were acted on. Reserve pilots were added to each regiment to replace those who needed rest. Other problems were investigated and taken into account. The revamped organization of the regiments looked like this:

The 17th Fighter Aviation Regiment consisted of 319 men. There were 63 pilots, including a reserve of twenty, 104 officers, 123 noncommissioned officers, and 29 other ranks. The regiment was equipped with MiG-15 bis aircraft. In another regiment, the 117th, the strength was a little different. It consisted of 72 pilots (reserve of 22), 115 officers, 160 NCOs, and 12 other ranks, a total of 359.[23]

Combat experience showed that a structure like that shown above met combat needs best. In such a small territory of operations with its inherent restrictions, it would have been a poor idea to deploy larger, more bulky regiments. They would have been more vulnerable to attack while on the ground in the limited airfields available. Furthermore, there would have been extra restrictions in conducting aerial maneuvers with a greater number of friendly aircraft in the air because of problems in command, communications, and control. Air combat in Korea was very different from that experienced by Soviet pilots in, say, Europe, with its vast expanses.

The airfields available to Soviet units were few in number. With this limitation and the necessity to train both Korean and Chinese pilots and ground crews, only a part of the LXIV Aviation Corps was able to perform combat duties. At the start, only about 60 aircraft could be committed to combat. With another airfield becoming operational in July 1951, the number increased to 120–150. At the same time, still another airfield was being readied for use which would make it possible to better the situation further.

The weather affected flying time of the two adversaries in roughly the same degree. The following report gives an indication of this: "Of 229 days of the deployment of the 17th Regiment . . . during 71 of these no flight was possible, 30 percent of the time."[24]

To Russians, the periods of bad weather seemed extremely peculiar, the reverse of the pattern normal to us. The worst flying times were during the summer months, which is the best period in Russia, good, sunny, and stable weather. More fruitful weather conditions in Korea were in fall and winter.

It was not until June 1951 that Soviet air-defense artillery units began to operate more actively. Many of the fire missions were accomplished by the 87th and 92nd Antiaircraft Artillery Divisions. Each division consisted of five regiments. A regiment consisted of four batteries with six 37mm guns and four batteries of eight 85mm guns.

At first, their primary mission was the defense of airfields. In fulfilling this objective, fifty percent of the personnel had to remain in constant combat readiness. During nighttime hours, all means available to them were used: guns, radar, searchlights, etc. Batteries of the 87th Division, during the period September through December 1952, fired in 1,039 engagements and estimated 50 enemy aircraft destroyed.[25] Daylight surveillance was conducted from several coupled and radio-equipped observation posts. They provided information to all echelons of command, as did the radar/searchlight posts at night. They preferred to use telephone land lines for their reports because these were more secure than radio from enemy eavesdropping.

In evaluating the combat success of the air defense weapons used in Korea, Soviet authorities could not give them a very high mark. The guns and control devices were of World War II vintage, not having been upgraded since the end of the war. They were simply not good enough to counter the modern enemy aircraft being sent against them. More modern and sophisticated equipment was needed, including guided missiles. The Korean War clearly convinced Soviet leaders that the air defense means of the Soviet Union were in need of major revamping and modernization.

Like other Soviet troops sent to Korea, the air defense units had an additional mission of training and supporting their Korean and Chinese counterparts. They taught both command and control techniques to officers and NCOs and the use of the equipment to all personnel. In addition to this training, Soviet artillerymen were responsible for the repair of Korean and Chinese guns and other equipment. Records show, for example, during the period, February to October 1952, Soviet soldiers repaired sixty-two 85mm guns and thirty-six 37mm guns as well as other weapons and other equipment. for their Communist comrades.[26] All these training and repair duties had a deleterious effect on their own unit training and readiness for combat.

By the end of 1951 a reevaluation of the command and control of the air force units was conducted. At that time, it was determined that the situation had to be watched closely. Was the highly centralized method of control restricting the initiative of commanders, denying them the opportunity of making rapid and independent decisions? As the year of 1952 unfolded, it became apparent that this question should be answered in the affirmative. Therefore, by the end of 1952, a general decentralization of command and control was happening. Commanders were granted much more independence and the use of their own initiative during operational situations. This caused their sense of responsibility for the outcome of their actions in combat to grow.

At this same time, a joint air army was formed, comprising aviation assets of both the Soviets and Chinese. This new organization had a good supply of aviation units and was able to respond to massive enemy air raids as well as make strikes against enemy targets in the air and on land and water.

Many experienced commanders took part in the Korean War,

men who had received their experience in World War II. Among them was Col. Ivan Kozhedub, three times awarded the prestigious Hero of the Soviet Union. During the war against the Fascists, he completed 330 sorties and in 120 air fights he destroyed 62 enemy aircraft, including one jet plane. Like all his fellow Soviet servicemen, his activities were restricted to certain geographical areas, but on occasion these restrictions were removed and Soviet pilots flew over South Korean territory. They flew reconnaissance missions and even engaged in bombing and strafing operations against deep enemy targets.

The following stories of individual actions should prove interesting:

On June 26, 1951, at 1350 at 6,000 meters altitude an interception was attempted against a B-29 bomber formation escorted by fighters. The situation became highly complex. During the attack of the flight leader, Sr. Lt. Victor Agranevich and the other pilot, Sr. Lt. Vladimir Fokin, they were fired on by the escorting aircraft. As a result, Agranevich's plane was destroyed and the pilot killed.[27]

Among the most successful of the Soviet pilots was Maj. Nicolai Artemchenko. For the period, June 1950 through January 1952, he participated in 152 sorties, managing to direct fire from the three on-board guns of his plane with great effectiveness. He was able to prepare his plane quickly for combat, taking off and landing with only a short turnaround time. It seemed that his plane was practically invulnerable. It was not unusual that his plane returned from an engagement with more than 100 bullet holes in it.[28]

In another mission, ten enemy fighters were detected, so Soviet fighters rose to intercept them. The air fight lasted between twelve and fifteen minutes. Three F-86 jets were destroyed in the air battle; three Soviet aircraft also were lost.[29]

The Soviet high command determined that based on the combat action in the Korean War, the significant losses could be explained by serious deficiencies in command and control under the different conditions of that new theater. Many of these were covered in a high-level conference of the Soviet Air Force convened in Moscow on April 7, 1953. It was noted that planes were too slow in taking off for missions and were unable to gain the necessary altitude in time to give them an advantage over their adversaries. There was a lack of coordination among squadrons, groups, elements, and pairs. Often, firing from the planes was conducted at too great a distance from their targets, diminishing the effectiveness of the fire. Some pilots were unable to attain suitable positions for attacks because of a lack of surprise.[30]

The commander of LXIV Fighter Aviation Corps reported on August 18, 1952 that Soviet aircraft were subject to attack at airfields during takeoff and landing. Also, they had suffered attacks while the planes were located in parking spaces. Losses were quite severe. During the first six months of 1952, the corps had lost twenty-six aircraft in this manner.[31]

The commander of Soviet Forces in Korea reported to the general staff on February 12, 1953 that serious shortcomings had been discovered in the operations of Soviet pilots and that he had concluded that they had insufficient flight, tactical, and gunnery training. This was especially obvious in aerial combat with high-speed fighters like the F-80 and F-84, and even relatively slow aircraft like the B-29. By this time in the war, many more young pilots were replacing the more experienced combat veterans. They were much less capable in conducting aerial warfare against a determined enemy.[32]

Losses of Soviet air crews and planes caused a very negative effect on the morale of all personnel. Commanders had to devote much time in trying to improve the morale of these highly important pilots who in many cases were irreplaceable.

At the start of the Korean War, Stalin and the party leadership were convinced that the conflict would be concluded in much the same way as World War II, with Communist arms victorious. He believed that very soon the Soviet-led troops would demonstrate to the world their overwhelming strength and power. But week after week, month after month, the news from the battlefront became more and more discouraging. As Stalin read the secret and accurate combat reports, he became annoyed. He could not understand how the troops were stymied around the 38th parallel, prevented by the enemy from attaining operational success. He convened a meeting of the Politburo on December 12, 1951, where the Korean War and its problems were discussed at length. The following conversation was recorded:

> STALIN: What is the reason that our troops look so help-less in Korea? Maybe our generals have lost their qualifications or become so lazy that they are unable to accomplish their missions.
>
> VASILEVSKY: The theater of operations is very difficult, geographical conditions are complicated, and the enemy is displaying stubborn resistance. Nothing can be done here with tanks and armored personnel carriers. Everything is decided in local fights.
>
> S: You, Comrade Vasilevsky, always manage to justify your passiveness. Maybe it is time for you to retire; or can you reverse the course of the war?
>
> V: I am ready to retire if you think I am out of place.
>
> S. The war should be ended. Don't you see how deeply involved we are now? We are ready to take any measures, to replace the entire command element, to increase military supplies by two or three times if need be. We shall do anything necessary. The problem must be solved. Decisive success must be achieved in the near future.[33]

In the highest echelons of the armed forces, the general staffs began feverishly to obtain answers to Stalin's questions. The military leadership was well aware of the fact that it was a good idea to take Stalin seriously in whatever he wanted. Unwanted changes were certainly possible. Series of meetings and conferences involving high authority in Moscow along with representatives from the field in North Korea were held in this period to try to satisfy Stalin.

A key part of the unfolding drama was played by Air Force Lt. Gen. Georgii Agheevich Lobov. He had been ordered to report to the Vladivostok area in August 1950. At that time, American aviation was attacking targets close to the border of the USSR, a situation that bothered the Soviet command. One problem they had was the lack of the latest MiG-15 fighter aircraft to neutralize the threat.

Early in November 1950, Lobov and part of his 303rd Fighter Aviation Division moved from Soviet territory to Antun airfield in northeast China near the Yalu River, the northern border of Korea. This put Soviet aircraft quite near the bridges over the river and other key communications points in North Korea. Initially only thirty-three older MiGs were assigned to Lobov. Only after his personal appeals to Moscow was their number increased to about 150, and these the more sophisticated MiG-15.

Discussing the Korean War with a historian from London University, D. Halliday, in June 1993, Georgii Lobov recalled:

> I reported to the Moscow leadership that we were in a very dangerous situation. The enemy was eight to ten times stronger than we were. We could not deny air superiority to the Americans, nor could we attain this ourselves. We had to sweat in our cockpits for many hours on alert and simply wait. The Americans could always choose the most advantageous moment. When we would receive a report of Americans in the air, I could just count seconds to alert my pilots. It was very difficult to plan operations beforehand. We rarely managed to intercept the first wave of the enemy aircraft.[34]

It is very difficult for us to provide in this book a true picture of the Soviet-American air war. It is a long time ago, but the main obstacle is the veil of secrecy placed over the events as they were happening. Stalin did everything he could to deceive the world on our involvement. Soviet identification markings on the aircraft were replaced by those of China. Pilots were deprived of any Soviet identification and they were warned to be silent. At first they wore Chinese uniforms and later some were disguised as Koreans. They wore no shoulder straps, putting on only badges with Stalin's and Mao's profiles on them. To avoid capture, they were prevented from flying over the sea or close to the front lines, although, as we have described above, in emergencies they sometimes did not keep to these guidelines. One of the rules that annoyed our pilots most was the prohibition of speaking in Russian over the radio. They were given notes with Chinese or Korean phrases written in Russian. But as one of the veterans put it, "Who will look for the necessary word during combat?"

Very soon, American pilots started to report that they were hearing Russians talking to each other by radio and had even seen Caucasian faces in the cockpits. So Washington was well aware that the Soviet Air Force was performing operations in Korea. Why did American officials keep silent?

Paul Nitze, who headed the Policy Planning Division of the Department of State, prepared a secret document on the subject. He analyzed all the pros and cons of disclosing to the world the facts of Soviet participation in the war. The officials felt that such disclosures would be harmful. He said that "if we started to disclose these facts, the American public would demand retaliation and we did not want war with the Soviets."[35]

The Eisenhower administration maintained the same approach as Truman's. They did not acknowledge the facts they knew. Both sides restricted themselves to the Korean Peninsula. This was a cynical game for both countries, as it was based on deceiving the public. If losses of as many as one thousand American pilots to Soviet air operations were disclosed, public outrage might have precipitated World War III.

The war on the ground provoked many statements of opinion on the part of Soviet advisers to the infantry, artillery, and armor troops. From one of these individuals we quote the following:

> Combat operations of the Korean People's Army reminded us of the seashore when the waves gradually arrive and advance until they meet some obstacle and again and again retreat, being unable to cross that border. Indeed, despite the concentration of rather significant forces, including almost all branches—aviation, infantry, tanks, artillery—they could not manage to penetrate deeply across the 38th parallel. The troops of South Korea (and the United Nations), supported by US aviation, tipped the balance and our class brothers found themselves in the same old positions, and sometimes had to retreat.

As a rule, their combat actions were of unsteady success.
The same villages and cities were in each other's hands several times during the same short time period. This was probably because they were unable to consolidate any success
achieved by preparing a good defense of the captured position, and to create a reliable system of delivering fire at the
enemy.[36]

One characteristic of the North Korean soldiers was excessive
delight in achieving some success, a tendency that Korean political workers tried to accentuate by any means. Failures produced
the contrary effect, as one might think. The political personnel
tried to keep such events secret or represent them as preplanned
maneuvers. Soviet advisers, however, told the truth to their colleagues, that such misrepresentation of the actual frontline situation was unacceptable.

They found that the Koreans were very sensitive to any critical
comments that tended to disparage their fighting ability or
courage. After battle, critiques had to be conducted with great
tact, patience, and diplomacy, while sticking to the actual facts.
Col. Valeri Aksyonov, reported the problem to his superiors:

My directions on the necessity of detailed and comprehensive analysis of operations as well as presenting to the
troops true information by political workers about the outcome of hostilities are often ignored. This negatively affects
the accomplishment of combat missions. Also, these same requirements of mine cause dissatisfaction in the Korean command, making me sometimes avoid the question in the first
place.[37]

Both sides in the Korean War used modern combat weapons
and equipment such as self-propelled artillery and armored personnel carriers. That used by the North Korean Army came
largely from the USSR or China. Although operations of armored vehicles were somewhat limited in comparison with aviation because of the terrain and undeveloped roads, they were ef-

fective enough in supporting the infantry and when massed could be used to good effect.

Korean Army units suffered heavy losses in personnel and material, especially at the beginning of the war. Col. Pyotr Koval reported: "For the period of hostilities in the first six months of 1951, the division lost almost one-quarter of its combat equipment. . . ."[38] But these losses were quickly replenished by shipments from the Soviet Union.

The following is taken from the transcript of a meeting at the Defense Department of the USSR, November 3, 1951. Colonel General Dmitri Ustinov reported:

> The government of the Korean People's Democratic Republic is requesting additional shipments of combat weapons and equipment, especially of tanks and artillery. The Politburo and Comrade Stalin personally are desirous of a quick solution to this problem. They have ordered our department to ensure complete fulfillment of the request of our Korean comrades. . . .[39]
>
> From the combat report of adviser Col. Pyotr Koval, December 20, 1951: "During September–November 1951, the units of the division received: sixty T-34 tanks, fourteen 122mm guns, twelve 85mm guns, twelve 57mm guns, fifteen 82mm mortars, and nineteen 120mm mortars."[40]

Obviously, success depended not only on the amount of combat equipment supplied, but also on the level of training of those handling it. The training proficiency of Korean troops did not meet the demands of modern combat, especially at the initial stages of the war. Soviet military personnel received frequent and strong exhortations to upgrade the training of the Koreans. Apart from short courses of instruction in units with the use of Soviet interpreters, Korean military personnel received on-the-job training with Soviet soldiers immediately available.

In one combat operation on May 21, 1952, Soviet Sr. Lt. Yuri Yashkin was the tank driver. The other crew members were Korean soldiers. The crew operated in a completely co-ordinated way. This was demonstrated vividly when the tank was damaged by a shell. The soldiers under the guidance of the lieutenant immediately replaced the damaged track and the tank was returned to combat. Yashkin's concept was to have other crew members drive the vehicle to train them in this skill before the next combat operation.[41]

Many of the difficulties experienced by Soviet advisers were caused by the necessity of using translators to impart the sense of the instructor's comments. This was especially true with practical training in such subjects as vehicle driving and artillery firing. It was not only that the instructor's words had to be interpreted as well as manuals written in Russian, but the interpreters themselves frequently translated incorrectly, perhaps not really understanding the technical aspects of the lesson. An entry in the diary of Soviet Colonel Dortsov is interesting in this regard:

The gunners in the Korean People's Army could, in general, manage to fire direct at targets, fire in mine fields to clear them, and support the infantry with direct fire. But when firing from covered positions, the results were more modest. Training conducted by Soviet instructors with Korean artillery crews did not solve the problem. Difficulties have to do with the language barrier and the Koreans' lack of imagination. When they fire from an open position, seeing the target, they do well, but when it is necessary to imagine the target's location and to perform the calculations correctly to hit it, their weakness is obvious. Mistakes are made both at full and reduced preparation of firing data. Things get worse in more complicated firing conditions and longer periods of fire adjustment. Soviet instructors are blamed for all this, as though they could not explain, demonstrate, and control. Major Chichev was even sent home with a reduction in grade.

On October 12, 1952, because of incorrect target acquisition data, one of the Korean artillery batteries fired at friendly troops, resulting in losses of personnel and combat equipment which are now being counted. Major Chichev relied on the training level of the Korean artillery crews and was not able to control them; such a sad outcome.

Working with Koreans demands complete selflessness. Lieutenant Colonel Asker Abdullayev serves as an example. Day and night he trained his counterpart, commander of an artillery regiment, until he learned to control artillery fire. It was more difficult with battery commanders and leaders of fire control and firing battery platoons. But Abdullayev was successful here also. He hoped that they would pass on their knowledge to their subordinates. Combat operations by this regiment were so successful that they were noted personally by Kim Il Sung. This was not only due to his professional qualifications, but to his fluency in the Korean language, which he was able to gain in the short time of six months.

In combat on July 16, 1952, a Korean regiment whose adviser was Lt. Col. Anatoi Gribov suffered heavy losses in personnel and materiel. On the eve of a planned offensive, there was a war game in the division. Soviet advisers warned the Koreans of the possibility of the enemy using these maneuvers to cut off the main body of the attacking forces. This is why a general attack along the front was senseless. Regimental or even division attacks on a narrow front seemed to be more fruitful, especially with active support by tanks and aviation. Something similar was studied during the war game. On the maps, everything was done as recommended by Soviet advisers. But in the field when real combat began and a penetration of enemy lines had been achieved, the Korean command group forgot all the lessons of the war game and began to widen the captured sector with regimental units being dispersed from ten to fifteen kilometers. Anatoli Gribov saw the danger immediately and tried to persuade the Koreans not to broaden the offensive zone. He wanted them to consolidate what had been gained and establish defensive positions temporarily until other units from the division could arrive, to include armored vehicles and other combat and service support. In answer to Gribov's arguments, the Korean regimental commander nodded in a sign of agreement and smiled, but took no corrective action. The enemy did not let them wait for long. With major forces they conducted a counterattack supported with artillery, aviation, and armor. Without much effort they were able to destroy the Korean platoons scattered along the front line that had not yet taken time to consolidate their positions. What remained of the regiment and the staff managed to escape with great losses. The Korean regimental commander was quickly relieved. Anatoli Gribov was called to be disposed of by the personnel department of the USSR Defense Ministry.[42]

An important role was played by Soviet specialists in ensuring reliable communications both within and among units. They demonstrated to the Koreans how telephone and telegraph lines should be established to prevent delays in communications when forward units move. This is so necessary to guarantee stable control of the troops. In another medium, it took great effort to train the Koreans in the most effective ways of radio communication.

There are many anecdotes, some amusing, when Soviet and Korean personnel found themselves trying to communicate on the same radio net. When interpreters were available, most problems could be solved without complications developing. But when a Soviet soldier was without an interpreter, neither party could understand a word. In one such instance, Sr. Lt. Vladimir Drosdov was called by an infantry commander who wanted to explain the tactical situation to him and get some advice. But Drosdov could understand nothing. It was as if two dumb men were trying to talk with one another. In the heat of heavy combat, at the moment of peak mental, physical, and psychological tension, both the Soviet and Korean officers forgot that they could not speak together without assistance.[43]

Another significant combat support function was that of the engineers. Again, Soviet specialists helped train the Koreans in their duties under fire. They became able to overcome strong enemy defensive structures and well organized positions, mine fields, and barbed wire entanglements under difficult terrain conditions. These engineer pioneers cleared trails, constructed crossings, and restored roads, In addition, under the guidance of the Soviet engineers, Korean soldiers learned how to construct strong defensive positions of their own.

Unfortunately, for unknown reasons the Koreans did not rely enough on engineer construction work, seemingly failing to appreciate their significance. The Soviet engineers tried their best to show them the consequences of underestimating this very important function, but often to no avail. Major Dmitri Vorontsov recalls:

> An infantry company had moved to an open sector of terrain and did not bother to consolidate its position. They had no foxholes for the soldiers or bunkers and camouflage for the vehicles. The company commander ordered the troops to break for a meal. But hardly had the soldiers taken out their mess kits than enemy aircraft appeared and bombs began to explode. In just a few seconds, the company lost almost every third soldier. To make matters worse, their two vehicles were destroyed, depriving the company of any kind of transportation. This debacle became a lesson that Soviet instructors used in their arguments with their Korean counterparts on the proper organization of terrain.[44]

Success in combat depended to a great extent on the capability of service troops to provide necessary logistics support. Colonel Yuri Ventsov recalls that one of the biggest problems encountered by all troops was that because of the road network and difficult terrain, there were immense difficulties in supplying food and ammunition. Sometimes they had to requisition horses from the local populace and resort to air resupply of these essential classes of supply. Ventsov remembers that most Koreans were undemanding in their food requirements. They could go without food for long periods. Soviet soldiers, on the contrary, became nervous and indignant when the field kitchens were late or if rations were not issued at the expected time. If Koreans could get by with lower ration levels, resorting to eating insects and plant roots, this was not satisfactory to Soviet soldiers at all. Russians are accustomed to the regular three meals each day and could not accept some of the reasons for being deprived of what they were used to. In fact, most of the problem was due to poor performance by those serving in support and supply units.[45]

The Korean War was Stalin's last military adventure. After his death, his successors blamed him for the failure of his policy in Asia, and for committing numerous sins. But these same leaders failed to learn as much as they should from Stalin's great error. Military and diplomatic personnel were cashiered and replaced, but the same policies were retained and in many cases expanded. The next attempt was to be in the jungles and mountains of that lush little country, Vietnam, that became infamous to a whole generation of Russians and Americans.

Chapter V

Vietnam Proving Ground

The surrender of Japan on September 2, 1945, following the cease-fire of August 15, made for closer relations between the USSR and the United States after the cataclysm of World War II. People everywhere in the Western world saw this event as the chance for cooperation between the two great powers in achieving peace and developing the spirit of freedom, democracy, and understanding throughout the world. Nowhere else was this possibility more hoped for than in Asia. Unfortunately the USSR had other ideas. Stalin wanted to bring to Asia the Communists' own "European liberating mission." The newly liberated Asian countries like Korea and Vietnam were among them. We have already seen what happened to Korea in 1950. Now let us look at Vietnam.

As the documents of surrender were being signed by the Allies and Japan, Communist guerrillas in Vietnam under the leadership of Ho Chi Minh were waging active war against the Japanese occupier. His forces were called the Viet Minh and were successful by this time in having brought a great portion of the northern part of their country under their control. They were aided in this endeavor by the United States and Nationalist China, on the basis, we suppose, that any enemy of my enemy is my friend. In the months that followed, a singularly uninspired policy was followed by the Allies. They saw to it that the French were reinstated into the country despite the fact that they were almost universally unpopular with the people and that Ho Chi Minh had become something of a folk hero because of his successful fight against the Japanese occupiers.

This made it easy for the USSR to gain influence in all of Indochina. Ho declared himself the president and premier of Vietnam and proclaimed a people's republic. This fit beautifully into the Kremlin's plans. Stalin could see that with some encouragement, all of Indochina could be brought into the Communist family of nations. This was the agenda proposed to "Vietnamese comrades" by Kremlin advisers along with promises of support during a visit by a Vietnamese delegation to Moscow in November 1947. The Vietnamese Communists needed support to achieve their goals. They could not depend much on their fraternal brothers from China because of their fight with the Nationalist Chinese and their lack of modern weapons. The Soviet Union, on the other hand, was armed to the teeth after World War II and was in a position to contribute significantly.

Diplomatic relations between the Soviet Union and the Democratic Republic of Vietnam (DRV) were established on January 30, 1950. After that date, close contacts between them in economic, military, political, and ideological matters took place. Joint meetings, consultations, and other communications became regular. One main topic was the method for providing military aid to the DRV. The purpose of the Soviet Union in providing aid was much like their attitude to Korea. They were not especially interested in the good of the peoples of Asia. They merely wanted to strengthen their influence in the Asian region. The immediate problem was the presence of the French in Indochina. Although the USSR and other Communist bloc powers had recognized the DRV, this does not mean that the new country had dominated the territory of Vietnam or the other two countries of Indochina, Laos and Cambodia.

The French recognized their own puppet regime, the Republic of Vietnam, as a member state in the Indochinese colony. They sought to reestablish their control over the entire country, so during the next several years the French war against the Viet Minh raged from north to south, but especially in the northern sectors. French troops along with their Vietnamese counterparts fought valiantly to subdue the insurrection of the Viet Minh, but with limited success. They had a worthy foe in Gen. Vo Nguyen Giap, a genius in the art of guerrilla warfare who maintained great pressure against the French. The war went on for years and finally ended with the great set piece battle of Dien Bien Phu, a siege that lasted from November 1953 to May 1954. The French met with a resounding defeat as they were outgeneraled and outfought by the wily Giap. The surprise of this defeat rocked all of France, and marked the true end of the first Vietnamese war.

The war finally came to a close with the signing of the Geneva Accords on July 20, 1954. This agreement between the major powers temporarily divided Vietnam into two countries at the 17th parallel of latitude, similar to the situation in Korea. The southern part of Vietnam became a French-oriented country under the rule of a member of the old Vietnamese monarchy, Emperor Bao Dai, with rising star Ngo Dinh Diem as premier. In the north a Communist state was organized under Ho Chi Minh. The southern regime was recognized by France and the United States, and aid to this new nation began to flow from both countries. In October 1955, as a result of an election, the new Republic of Vietnam (RVN) was formed with Ngo Dinh Diem as its first president.

Pressure on the RVN began almost immediately from their northern cousins, as the Communists fought to complete their conquest of the country. The United States in response supplied the South Vietnamese government with various kinds of military and economic aid and in training and organizing the Army of Vietnam (ARVN). The United States sent a military assistance advisory group of American officers and other specialists to supply and train the army. Again we can see parallels to the war in Korea.

Ngo Dinh Diem was overthrown and assassinated in a coup in November 1964. Succeeding governments came and went and the struggle against the Communists, now known as the Viet Cong, continued to escalate.

Aid supplied by the United States was being matched by the Soviet Union to its ally, the Democratic Republic of Vietnam. Many reports and requests from the DRV arrived in Moscow, validated by the armed forces' intelligence department (the GRU). The thrust of this intelligence supplied by the GRU was that the United States was sending ". . . the most modern weapons, including incendiaries, missiles, and artillery shells of great power."[1] Ho Chi Minh reinforced the reports of the GRU by requesting the necessities for waging modern war from his big sponsor in Moscow. He wrote as follows to Leonid Brezhnev:

Within the framework of these agreements, I request that small arms and artillery and associated ammunition should be sent at first, as well as specialists capable of taking part in combat actions. We are thankful to learn that a large food shipment is on the way.[2]

The State Security Committee of the USSR (KGB) supported Ho Chi Minh's appeal for help from the Soviet Union. The chairman of the KGB, Victor Shelepin, prepared a detailed report for Brezhnev in which he explained the necessity for immediate aid in Vietnam:

. . . Some trustworthy sources report further escalation of the Vietnam War is expected because of direct American participation in this military conflict. It is necessary to provide urgent help to the DRV and to meet Ho Chi Minh's request for military and material support. . . .[3]

Similar reports were prepared by the Foreign Ministry of the USSR headed by Andrei Gromyko and sent to Brezhnev. They coincided in their opinions with those of the KGB. After reading them, Brezhnev called for their discussion at a meeting of the Presidium. The general secretary of the CPSU Central Committee who replaced the deposed Nikita Khruschev was faced with a serious problem.

What should our reaction to developments in Vietnam be?

What steps should be taken to demonstrate toughness, resolve, strength, and international solidarity and at the same time prevent the transformation of a local guerrilla-type conflict into a global military confrontation between the two great powers? The recent crisis in the Caribbean when the world was on the brink of nuclear war was in the minds of the masters in the Kremlin. This is why Brezhnev did not dare to act in as blatant a manner as had Stalin in Korea in 1950.

A meeting of the Presidium of the CPSU Central Committee took place on November 17, 1964. Its record is short. The participants listened to information from Foreign Affairs Minister Gromyko and Defense Minister Malinovsky on the situation in Vietnam. Those who spoke were Suslov, Mikoyan, Polyansky, Shelest, Kunayev, Mzhavanadse, and Ustinov. The discussions were summarized by Chairman Brezhnev. It was decided to provide material, technical, and military aid to Vietnam. As for sending military specialists there, the defense minister was charged with reporting recommendations to another meeting of the Presidium on December 17.[4]

Based on decisions of the CPSU Central Committee and the government of the USSR, Vietnam received fighter aircraft, air defense systems to include rockets, artillery, radars, communications means, fuel, ammunition, small arms, and numerous other material and equipment. The following table[5] shows details of this support provided from the Soviet Union to Vietnam, 1965–1972.

Type	1965	1966	1967	1968	1969	1970	1971	1972
Aircraft	82	63	57	44	36	26	18	14
Radars	31	—	43	16	22	18	16	10
FA guns	127	116	114	177	119	90	78	—
AD rocket systems	10	12	14	—	14	10	10	10
Small Arms ammunition	17	18	12	12	12	13	10	10
Artillery ammunition	29	16	16	17	19	16	11	8
Small arms	16	17	22	18	14	18	16	10
Food	124	116	137	122	118	113	106	110
Medical supplies	3.5	4.2	6.3	5.0	8.0	11.0	10.0	5.0

Note: ammunition is in thousands of cases; small arms in thousands; food and medical supplies in tons.

Actually, shipments of various kinds of equipment took place before the dates shown in the table, going back to the 1950s, during hostilities with the French and later against the Army of Vietnam under Ngo Dinh Diem and his successors. For example, during the fight for Dien Bien Phu mentioned above, the Viet Minh used for the first time the Katyusha multiple-rocket system made famous during the Great Patriotic War against the Germans. These and other weapon systems were supplied by the Soviet side along with the crews that trained the Vietnamese in handling the new weapons.

Shortly after the end of World War II, when the USSR recognized the new DRV, the CPSU Central Committee studied the problems of providing military aid to their Vietnamese comrades. They began in those early days to send weapons and other combat equipment, accompanied by large numbers of advisers, the same as was done in Korea, to train the Vietnamese in the use of the arms supplied and also to teach them tactics and staff work, to better enable the field commanders of the DRV formations to control their troops. In 1955, for instance, 160 military specialists with wartime experience were sent to Vietnam.[6]

In addition to the training conducted in Vietnam, many Vietnamese were brought to the Soviet Union to learn the intricacies of managing a modern army and to learn combat specialities. Upon graduating from schools and academies in the USSR, the students were assigned to command positions at various levels in the DRV's army. Trainees gaining proficiency in performing specific complex jobs like piloting jet aircraft were, of course, assigned wherever they could do the most good. The following extract from the journal of the V. I. Lenin Military-Political Academy (now called the Humanitarian Academy of the Russian Armed Forces) illustrates these students and their curriculum:

From 1968–1971 there were Vietnamese officers studying at our academy. They were exposed to the entire course of military and political training and learned Russian. At seminars, the future political workers of the Vietnamese Army have not only grasped the essence of Marxism-Leninism, but have also studied techniques to train their subordinates. After they graduate and return to their motherland, their ties with the academy have stayed intact. Most of them continue to write letters to the director of the academy and instructors in which they express gratitude for the training they received and provide accounts of their military duties. Analyzing these letters, one can conclude that the majority of our graduates are now at high-level command and political posts in the army, successfully guiding the training of their soldiers, inspiring them for the struggle of liberating their motherland.[7]

Many top commanders of the North Vietnamese Army graduated from command academies of the armed forces of the USSR, "At present, almost 20 percent of the commanders of the Vietnamese Army have studied in our academy." This is a quotation from the Frunze Military School.[8]

Even before he became the CPSU secretary, Leonid Brezhnev spent a great deal of time studying the questions concerning party, state, and military ties with the DRV. On many occasions he met with Vietnamese leaders, including Ho Chi Minh. Now that he was the leader of the USSR, he devoted more attention to the assistance provided to Vietnam. At the Politburo meeting of the CPSU Central Committee on December 13, 1966, Brezhnev pointed out the necessity of intensifying military aid to the DRV, which faced massive escalation of American forces in the war in Vietnam. He underlined the fact that the Soviet people would not abandon their Vietnamese brothers to face disaster. He ordered the defense minister to prepare for him information on providing new shipments of weapons and other combat equipment to the DRV very rapidly, as well as sending more military specialists there.[9]

Although he was giving the impression that the USSR was sending most of the combat goods received by the DRV, he should have mentioned that other countries in the Communist bloc were also providing a great amount of material too. According to data kept in the USSR Foreign Ministry, the value of annual shipments to the DRV, expressed in U.S. dollars, was 450 million from the USSR, 180 million from China, and 190 million from other Communist countries.[10]

At the conference of the Political Consultative Committee of the countries of the Warsaw Pact held in Bucharest in July 1966, the question of joint coordinated military to DRV was a separate item on the agenda. It was pointed out that the Soviet Union was providing the greatest part of the aid. In the official declaration, the participants of the conference expressed their readiness to provide "volunteers" for Vietnam. But the whole world already knew that the DRV had long been supported by "volunteers" from Communist countries, especially the USSR, although this was officially denied categorically by the leadership of the Soviet Union. During the war in Vietnam, more than 15,000 Soviet servicemen participated in combat actions there as military advisers.[11] The following table shows year-by-year participation of Soviet military personnel in Vietnam from 1965 to 1972.[12]

PERSONNEL	1965	1966	1967	1968	1969	1970	1971	1972
Pilots	102	148	152	136	171	128	84	64
Aviation technicians	96	87	84	82	54	32	27	19
Radar operators	74	68	92	81	87	54	38	14
Aviation engineers	54	41	35	44	19	14	—	14
Infantry	117	108	92	87	—	63	39	28
Artillery	37	68	84	52	39	34	26	16
Armor	56	28	—	27	43	21	17	13
Engineers	72	137	124	118	—	19	34	18
Admininistrative troops	48	32	17	21	43	14	16	14

Note: Dashes in the above table mean that the information was not available.

During the association of the two countries, many official visits between them occurred. The number of these meetings increased over time, and tended to focus on military matters. In 1966, for example, there were twelve such visits of Vietnamese to Moscow and ten Soviet visits to Vietnam. The following official communique reflects the scope of these meetings:

By invitation of the Central Committee of the Labor Party of Vietnam and the government of the Democratic Republic of Vietnam, a friendly visit was paid between January 7–13, 1966, to the Democratic Republic of Vietnam by delegates of the Soviet Union. They were: a member of the Presidium, Secretary of the CPSU Central Committee A. N. Shelepin, alternate member of the Presidium Central Committee of the CPSU D. F. Ustinov, First Deputy of the Section Head of the Foreign Affairs Ministry A. S. Chistyakov, Col. Gen. V. F. Telubke, and the USSR Ambassador to Vietnam I. S. Scherbakov.

The two delegations discussed the grave situation evolving from the escalation of the aggressive war in Vietnam and Southeast Asia by the American imperialists. Also covered were problems of Soviet-Vietnamese relations, the international situation, and a number of other problems of interest to the Soviet Union and the Democratic Republic of Vietnam.

During the time the Soviet delegation remained in Vietnam, a new agreement was signed, envisaging the provision of additional support by the Soviet Union to the Democratic Republic of Vietnam.[13]

A special briefing was conducted for a restricted number of officials at the regular plenary meeting of the CPSU Central Committee on January 16, 1966. This was a follow-up to the visit of the Soviet delegation to Vietnam described above. The Secretary of the Central Committee, A. N. Shelepin, reported as follows:

> . . . In accord with the agreement between our delegations, it was decided to send an additional large group of our military specialists to Vietnam, consisting of aviation engineers, radio technicians, air defense artillery and communications specialists, and engineers. As coordinated with the Defense Department, two air defense units staffed with excellent specialists will be sent to Vietnam. . . .[14]

Information concerning specific figures of the tonnage and numbers of military shipments to Vietnam were concealed care-

fully from the Soviet people. Even the documents that we have
been able to find in the archives classified "Top Secret" contain
shorthand descriptions and records that were condensed and do
not give a complete picture of the situation of those times. Training provided and the dispatch of our soldiers to Vietnam were
kept absolutely secret. Servicemen and their families were forbidden to tell anyone about the special "tour" they were taking,
the name of the destination country, or the reason for their departure. The soldiers heading for Vietnam, regardless of rank or
posting, traveled there in civilian clothes designed for working
and living in the tropics. They wore no insignia. Soviet soldiers
knew their commanders only by their facial characteristics.

Preparing the troops for duty in Vietnam and sending them
there was performed by the General Staff of the Armed Forces of
the USSR, the senior staff of the Air Force's Air Defense Troops,
and the headquarters of military districts. The units were airlifted
by military cargo planes that departed from secret military airfields with an intermediate landing facility in Beijing. Military
equipment, food, and weaponry not going by sea went by railway
across China. After 1968, when relations between China and the
Soviet Union worsened, these planes flew across Afghanistan, Pakistan, India, and Burma, with landings in Karachi and Calcutta.
After their arrival in Vietnam, the Soviet servicemen lived in field
camps and wore Vietnamese uniforms.[15]

The following extract from the memoirs of Lt. Col. Alexei Li-
hevitsky illustrates the lives of Soviet soldiers in Vietnam. Perhaps
this will bring back some memories in the minds of American veterans of their own Vietnam War.

It was difficult for the Soviet personnel to become accustomed to the climatic conditions, to the hot and humid tropical climate which was so different to them, coming from Europe. The temperature was up to 35–40 degrees Celsius and
the humidity 80–100 percent. We lived in small huts made
of bamboo and palm leaves or in tents hidden in the jungle.

We often had to march at night which was very hard because of the wet dirt roads which were frequently flooded.
Besides, we were subject to constant enemy fire.

It was no easier for those who worked in the vans associated with the air defense rocket systems where the temperatures were up to 50 degrees Celsius. Some fainted because of the extreme heat, particularly those soldiers who had not been there long enough to become acclimated to the terrible climate. Their bodies had not yet managed to get used to the heat.

Apart from the weather, huge numbers of a variety of insects and poisonous snakes were threats to our health and well-being.

The nutrition of Soviet servicemen performing duties in Vietnamese units was in accord with food supplied to corresponding indigenous troops. The food was cooked in the Vietnamese way and it was very modest, consisting of low-calorie items of perhaps a single course, but expensive. Many Soviet soldiers were not satisfied with the rations and turned to what was available from the local people, although such purchases were strictly forbidden.

The Vietnamese people are in general very enterprising. Despite the hostilities, the local people, mainly farmers, did not miss a chance to sell or buy things. Very often small groups of them would appear in the midst of units, offering to sell or barter fruit, vegetables, rice, and fish or other seafood, advertising their goods in every possible way. When the Russians bought from them, they did it in a covert manner. They knew very well that the KGB representative was nearby and could compromise them. When caught, they were subject to punishment by their commanders.[16]

The Soviet military specialists were under the command of a senior official who was assisted by a rather small staff. He received his orders from the General Staff of the Armed Forces in Moscow. He sent written and other reports to the same authority through the regular communications means. From time to time he was summoned to Moscow to present his reports personally on the work accomplished in Vietnam. The work of all military advisers and technicians was coordinated by the Ambassador Extraordinary and Plenipotentary of the Soviet Union to Vietnam, Ivan

Scherbakov. He was in constant contact with the leadership of
Vietnam, particularly Ho Chi Minh. He passed on to Ho the views
of the Soviet Union on the course of the hostilities and received,
in turn, views on the struggle from the Vietnamese viewpoint.
They discussed the overall military and economic situation and
the problems that needed solution by both sides.[17]

The Soviet Union responded rapidly and constructively to the
ambassador's recommendations, because there was a sincere desire on the part of Soviet officials to alter the situation in Vietnam
in favor of the DRV. They were looking toward the elusive day of
unification of the entire country under, of course, the patronage
of the USSR with its Marxist-Leninist ideology. They not only were
enlarging and strengthening the overall socialist group of countries, but were doing so in Asia, a long-desired objective. Additionally, successes in the Vietnamese jungles were a boost to the
reputation of Soviet arms. So each new request from Ambassador
Scherbakov to Moscow received expedited treatment, sometimes
even by Brezhnev himself. Sometimes rosy pictures were painted
for the leadership like this briefing note by Brezhnev:

> . . . during the first three months of 1965, the Presidium
> of the CPSU Central Committee has discussed questions con-
> cerning our provision of military aid to the Democratic Re-
> public of Vietnam on four occasions. Thanks to our ambas-
> sador and information from the military, we have a complete
> picture of the situation in the theater of operations in the
> region. I am pleased to state that we control the situation
> there. . . .[18]

Vietnam, like Korea, apart from political considerations presented an obvious opportunity to be a kind of proving ground for
the Soviet military-industrial complex. Combat equipment produced in secret plants of the Soviet Union—aircraft, tanks, armored vehicles, artillery, and small arms, as well as associated ammunition and other equipment—was tested in Vietnam.

For example, let us consider the secret plant at Barrikady that
produced the famous SS-20 missiles. During the years of the cold
war, no one was allowed to approach even the checkpoint outside

the plant. But in 1989, military inspectors from the United States were permitted to visit the plant. With them were members of the press, including one of the authors of this book, Maj. Gen. Oleg Sarin of *Red Star*, the Russian armed forces newspaper. During their tour of the facility, the delegation was briefed by officials from the facility, the chief production engineer Vladimir Sobelev, and a representative from the Department of Defense, Sergei Frolikov. These men told the guests that the factory had been producing modern military equipment that was used on the battlefields of the Great Patriotic War and later in Korea, Vietnam, Africa, Israel, and Afghanistan. On the date of the visit, however, the plant had already been converted to the production of civilian oriented goods such as washing machines. They were able to use the design of the SS-20 missile launcher for a variety of civilian applications. The American representatives expressed pleasure at this conversion from wartime production to civilian.

But let us return to the Vietnam War. The Vietnamese Army was equipped mainly with what was left over from World War II. This was largely true for the first few years of the war. Generally, their adversaries from the south were armed with newer and better equipment that came from American aid. But beginning in 1964, the Soviet Union began to supply better and more modern armaments in greater quantities. The MiG-21 fighter aircraft replaced the older MiG-15 and MiG-17 models, the T-54 tank replaced the T-34, and so on. These were a better match for the latest American models. At first this new equipment was operated by Soviet servicemen. Later, as necessary training was received and the Vietnamese demonstrated their proficiency, the new items were integrated into Vietnamese Army and Air Force units. The following excerpt from the memoirs of Maj. Nikolai Zhuravsky illustrates this transition:

Initially, the crews were composed entirely of our specialists, who operated rather successfully against the enemy. But we were ordered to give the equipment to the Vietnamese after training them for a month. Together with our interpreters, we organized the crews, primarily from those who had already fought with T-34 tanks. Training often took place in combat conditions. On the one hand, this made the task more complex, as often one man had to be the driver and the gun layer simultaneously. On the other hand, the training done this way was very effective. When the training was conducted in combat, accompanied by the thunder of artillery and the noise of bullets hitting the tank, soldiers learned everything quickly. The training courses lasted not months, but weeks, and sometimes even days.

The process looked like some kind of conveyor belt. A number of new vehicles arrived. Our people tested them, and only a few days later, the whole crew became Vietnamese. Even tank commanders were Vietnamese officers. Certainly, not every Vietnamese soldier was capable of handling a new Soviet tank. This demanded more than the qualifications necessary for the old T-34 tank. Physical fitness, combat experience, and repair skills (especially in combat) were important in this kind of accelerated training. That is the reason for our request to the Vietnamsese authorities to select soldiers with this kind of experience on the older equipment in order to prepare the crews for combat in a cohesive way.[19]

The first chief military adviser in Vietnam was Lt. Gen. Alexei Dzyza, who had his headquarters in Hanoi. His deputies were both major generals, Gregorii Belov and Alexandr Trombachev. He was succeeded by the following officers:

Maj. Gen. Gregorii Velov 1966–67
Lt. Gen. (AF) Vladimir Abramov 1967–68
Lt. Gen. (Arty) Valentin Stolnikov 1968–70
Lt. Gen. Nicolai Maksimenko 1970–72
Maj. Gen. Alexandr Hyupenen 1972–74
Chiefs of Staff of the Soviet military group were:
Col. Nikolai Valkovich 1965–67
Col. Valentin Veronov 1967–69
Col. Sergei Medvedev 1969–71
Col. Ivan Tatarchuk 1972–74[20]

These officers commanded and directed the activities of all the Soviet servicemen in Vietnam—aviation, air defense, field artillery, infantry, communications, ordnance, medical, and so forth. The largest contingent of Soviet troops was in air defense. They were assigned to practically all the air-defense regiments of the Vietnamese Army. Colonel Vasilii Batov recalls:

I arrived in Vietnam accompanied by a group of Soviet military specialists in May 1964. I was previously stationed in the Baku Air-Defense District, where I had commanded an air-defense brigade. The Vietnamese Army had been equipped with our rocket systems, but, as we learned, they were poorly utilized. There were cases of self-launching as well as inaccurate controls being set in the equipment, so targets were missed frequently. The Vietnamese high command tended to blame these failures on supposedly outdated equipment that could not compare favorably with similar models of American air-defense systems. We were ordered to investigate everything concerning these "accidents" in place and to take the necessary corrective measures. Special attention was paid to developing clear-cut and highly professional training curricula for the Vietnamese air defense crews. We had no reason to doubt that the causes of the failures were because of poor training of the individuals in the crews and the units themselves. We Russians were armed with the same equipment. We fired live missiles during our own tactical training and with good results. Our missions normally were successful, so why was the reverse true in Vietnam? As we supposed, the primary cause of their failure was connected with the handling of the combat equipment. Primitive knowledge and the overall poor qualifications of the Vietnamese soldiers reduced the effectiveness of the system's firepower.

We designed programs for training the crews and discussed them with our higher headquarters as well as the Vietnamese high command. They approved and we began to implement them. Their essence was to create training cadres in all air-defense regiments where the Vietnamese crewmen could be trained intimately by Soviet specialists on the job not currently performing in a combat mission. We spent about two weeks in accomplishing the training task, with Soviet specialists actually performing the jobs during combat so that the Vietnamese soldiers could see at first hand how the work should be done. Within a month our work brought favorable results. The offensive of a Vietnamese motor rifle division supported by air-defense rocket artillery was successful. We reported all this to the general staff.[21]

As stated by Colonel Batov, reports of this successful training and the results gained therefrom were sent to the highest levels of the Soviet military. This prompted Defense Minister Marshal Radion Malinovsky to send a coded message to General Dzyza suggesting that a two-month training course be established in Hanoi for Vietnamese air-defense officers. This idea was discussed with the high command of the Vietnamese military, but the concept was never implemented. The Vietnamese evidently had no enthusiasm for Malinovsky's idea. This is described in General Dzyza's memoir, which we excerpt below:

We developed the training program literally detailed by hours and tried our best to prove its importance, but for a long time there was no response whatsoever from the Vietnamese general staff. Later they said that this delayed answer was because of the frequent bombing of Hanoi. They felt it was not safe to implement such centralized courses, and, instead, favored the immediate establishment of training where the air-defense units were located.

Without doubt, such hasty training in the units could do little good for really professional training of air-defense specialists. Besides, we had to disperse the numbers of our officer-instructors which also lessened the effectiveness of training. . . . We should admit that Soviet military specialists were not advisers and instructors in the direct meaning of these terms. In the majority of cases, they themselves took part in combat and often their jobs as instructors were somewhat secondary.

For example, Maj. Gregorii Ljubintsky was a technician in a Vietnamese air-defense rocket unit and took direct part in combat as an integral member of the crew. His Vietnamese colleagues praised his combat skills and good adaptation to the difficult conditions in the jungles. Surrounded by tropical trees, he was able to exploit the peculiarities of the landscape for camouflage. . . . Together, Vietnamese and Soviet soldiers planned ambushes at points where enemy aircraft habitually turned back after their bombing runs. . . .

In preparing air-defense positions on rocky soil under difficult conditions, local people, including the elderly, women, and children, worked together with soldiers. . . .

In one air-defense battalion there was a group of Soviet technicians under Lt. Col. Fyodor Il'inych. They made a suggestion which was adopted to make the unit more mobile, altering firing positions more frequently. This made it difficult for the enemy to detect their launcher positions and hence to destroy them.[22]

The air-defense rocket systems sent to Vietnam significantly increased the fire power of Vietnamese artillery. For example, the S-75 rocket system, called "Dvina," was composed of a radar and associated computer, a two-stage rocket (the booster used liquid fuel, while the sustainer stage was of solid fuel), six launchers, and other associated equipment. The system could be deployed in four to five hours and dismounted in four hours. Speed along the roads was up to twenty kilometers per hour. It could engage targets traveling at a speed of 1,500 kilometers per hour and up to an altitude of twenty-two kilometers. During a ten-minute period, the system could engage up to five targets at intervals of one and one-half to two minutes. To destroy one target, two to three missiles were required. Its weak point was its lack of capability to engage low-flying targets below three kilometers in altitude. It also had trouble engaging very high-speed targets, 1,800 kilometers per hour or more in velocity.

Modernization of the air-defense rocket systems took place during the conduct of the war with the ZRK-75 "Desna" and "Volhov" modifications to the basic systems. "Desna" could destroy targets at an altitude of thirty-four kilometers, while "Volhov" could reach up to forty-three kilometers. "Volhov" could engage targets up to 2,300 kilometers per hour. This information was contained in a report from the chief engineer on the modernization project, Maj. Gen. Anatoli Rumyantsov, to the technical committee of the General Staff of the Armed Forces of the USSR on August 27, 1965. He stressed the necessity of Soviet participation in the coordination and control of these air-defense missile systems.[23] The air-defense systems and their limitations were discussed in a report from Col. Alexandr Stolyarov, a senior adviser:

> On July 24, 1965, in the area northeast of Hanoi, some rockets were launched at low-altitude targets, using the S-75 system. As this "Dvina" system is not designed for the destruction of low-flying targets, it failed to engage the enemy aircraft successfully. This significantly undermined the confidence of Vietnamese air-defense personnel in the reliability of the weapon. Our Vietnam command was aware of the technical and operational features of the "Dvina," but it often failed to provide the information to the units equipped with the system. In addition, it was necessary to increase the number of Soviet personnel available, so that at least one of them could operate in each crew. . . .[24]

This problem was solved relatively successfully and just a year later, the same Colonel Stolyarev was able to report with satisfaction:

> . . . For ten days between October 24 and 27 and between December 14 and 19, 1967, we launched 63 successful rockets. Soviet military specialists took part in all of them, not only helping the Vietnamese, but fulfilling specific duties as members of the crews.[25]

All was not progressing entirely satisfactorily in other parts of the Soviet mission to Vietnam, as reported by Col. Boris Arzamastsev in his memoir of his service in Vietnam:

> Vietnamese higher commanders, staff officers, and officers in units could not keep operational plans secret due to information leaked out of the various headquarters. In addition, ground units in preparing for offensive action did not use wisely and sufficiently well-tested measures such as camouflage, covert concentration of forces, and deception. As soon as planning for an operation started, the enemy learned about it and undertook countermeasures to ruin the plan. We reported these problems to the General Staff, and therefore the information was addressed to the Vietnamese leadership.
>
> On our advice, a special conference was held between high level commanders of the Vietnamese forces and our advisers in September 1967. This was followed by staff training that emphasized measures that would ensure secrecy in implementing operations. Problems were studied that were connected with the nature of staff correspondence, the preparation and storage of classified papers, radio communications techniques, and personnel qualifications for those in staffs who were responsible for operational and organizational matters. Later such conferences and training sessions were conducted several more times. In general the results from them were positive.[26]

Among the Soviet personnel in Vietnam there were staff officers who were oriented toward operational matters. They participated with their Vietnamese counterparts in developing combat plans. But this joint planning did not always accomplish the desired objectives. Maj. Gen. Ghennadii Belov discussed these failures in a report to the General Staff on February 7, 1964: ". . . Lack of clear coordination between the arms as well as the difficulties in support and supply of units on the offensive, especially with fuel, sometimes cause failure of operations."[27]

Moscow was annoyed with such reports, recalls Lt. Gen. Alexei Dzyza. He said that as a rule in such cases the high party leadership reacted with "thunder and lightning," responding to Soviet advisers something like this: ". . . And where were you? What do the Vietnamese have to do with all that? You will be to blame for any failures."[28]

At the same time, Soviet leadership should be applauded for the measures that they put in motion on the basis of information from the field. Actions taken were usually in the form of additional shipments of equipment, supplies, and weapons to Vietnam. In March 1964 the same General Belov reported the results of such shipments:

> To conduct a combat operation near Vinh, great amounts of materiel had to be transported along poor roads for about 700 kilometers. This included: Artillery ammunition—6.5 tons, aviation ammunition—4.6 tons, fuel—12 tons, food—5 tons, and other items—8 tons. To transport this cargo, 1,200 vehicles and trailers were employed. These had come from the Soviet Union in response to our requests.[29]

The above data confirm the great scale of the work of the combat and logistics support units in the rear. Vietnamese officers operating with the help of their Soviet counterparts did their best to support and supply the troops conducting combat actions along the entire front line.

In the last years of the Vietnam War, starting with 1970, the quality of the Vietnamese Army began to improve. This was happening because of the active participation of Soviet military specialists and Vietnamese personnel who had graduated from schools and academies in the Soviet Union. This trend permitted the USSR to reduce the numbers of specialists assigned to units and let them return home with their missions completed. This is illustrated in Col. Vasilii Batov's memoir:

> In December 1970 I was summoned unexpectedly to the office of Lieutenant General Maksimenko at the headquar-

ters of the People's Army of Vietnam. The general himself was away visiting some units and I was met by his assistant. He told me that I had to leave for Moscow the next day to report to the personnel department of General Staff of the Armed Forces. I packed everything quickly, and at the appointed time I flew to the Motherland on a military plane. On it I found another twelve people who had been ordered to leave Vietnam on an urgent basis.

As it became clear later, the reduction of the Soviet military contingent in Vietnam took place at Moscow's initiative. This was a way for the USSR to exercise pressure on the Vietnamese government to make it ease its stance at the prospective negotiations between Hanoi and Saigon. The Kremlin saw that the war should be stopped, as it demanded enormous materiel resources as well as bringing to the people of Vietnam great hardship and suffering that aroused indignation of the people of the world, including those in the Soviet Union. Additionally, continuing the Vietnam War ruled out any possibility of improving the international situation, particularly relations between the Soviet Union and the United States. All this compelled the Soviet government to redesign its own policy.[30]

Although the truth about the Vietnam War was being carefully concealed, the fact of Soviet military participation in this region was becoming more and more widely known. Information kept leaking from official bodies, but more from our servicemen themselves who were returning to the Soviet Union, both unharmed and suffering from wounds and disease contracted in the war zone. These men were strictly forbidden to disclose any details of their roles in Vietnam, but keeping the truth from seeping out was next to impossible. The dark curtain over the war was beginning to be lifted. It became apparent to one of the authors of this book, Oleg Sarin, as a military journalist, that Soviet pilots were participating actively in flights of the Vietnamese Air Force in countering American raids into North Vietnam. Other people were also aware of facts like this despite the severely curtailed information available.

At a meeting of the Political Bureau on December 13, 1966, Vladimir Soherbitsky asked why our people in Vietnam could not influence the course of combat on land and in the air. Defense Minister Marshal Radion Malinevsky replied: "I regularly receive reports on the activities of our specialists, including pilots. I am constantly aware of combat developments including the air situation. At any moment, necessary measures can be taken."[31]

Soviet pilots lived close to one another in small groups ordinarily located near the airfields where their combat equipment was located. The airplanes, painted with Vietnamese insignia, were maintained principally by Soviet engineers and technicians. Colonel Alexei Vinogradov recalls:

> We were based near Hanoi in hastily constructed wood huts. Sometimes we participated in two or three sorties each day. Our aircraft were maintained by Soviet specialists. There was a Vietnamese pilot in every crew who also flew sorties. The Americans knew only too well that Vietnamese planes of Soviet design were often flown by Soviet pilots. In one combat fight, both the American and Vietnamese planes were seriously damaged, causing both pilots to eject. As it happened, the Americans landed in territory controlled by the North Vietnamese Army and our pilot, Anatoli Gribov, found himself in the midst of South Vietnamese troops. The next day there was an exchange of prisoners. Gribov did not complain. On the contrary, he said that the Americans, who took charge of him, treated him in a relatively friendly manner. They gave him cigarettes and asked him for information, such as the duration of his service in Vietnam and the number of people who had come with him from the Soviet Union.
>
> Anatoli refused to answer their questions. They laughed and told him that they knew everything without any evidence from him. Then they offered him a rather large reward if he wanted to fly an American aircraft and to test its qualities in air combat. This seemed to Gribov as a joke to check on his reaction. Gribov answered in a highly negative manner. The

day after his return to his squadron, Gribov was summoned to the headquarters and sent back to the Soviet Union.[32]

As a rule, fighter pilots with combat experience were sent to Vietnam. These included highly experienced instructors who were capable of training other pilots. The newspaper of the Baku Air-Defense District, *Na Strazhe* (On the Vigil), published a series of articles by Pilot 1st Class Col. Nicolai Storezhenko, whose duties included the training of Vietnamese pilots on site in their country. It was impossible, of course, because of censorship, to disclose the full combat biography of this officer or to admit the truth, that it was the Vietnam War being described. In the article the author dwelled only on the techniques for training pilots under combat conditions and in a short period of time.[33] It was evident that the matters discussed in the article were connected directly to combat actions in either Korea or Vietnam. Military readers were, after all, better informed than the average member of Soviet society, being basically well educated and well informed. Such officers with recent combat experience were often selected as the authors of professional military articles and other works. The experience they had gained in Korea and Vietnam was especially interesting to the officer class as a whole because these were medium-scale wars as opposed to the giant cataclysm of the Great Patriotic War.

Beginning in 1970, information about the Vietnam War appeared in civilian newspapers and other publications. Prior to 1970, early articles on the war were remarkable only because they criticized "American imperialism" and justified completely the actions of the North Vietnamese as the victims of aggression. But now new voices could be heard, calling for a cessation of hostilities and for negotiations. Letters were published openly such as the following:

Valerie Nikolskii, a worker from Volgagrad— . . . It's time to stop this insanity; to return peace and calm to the land of Vietnam severly mutilated by bombs. This has been done by the two great powers, the USSR and the USA.

Retired Sgt. Sergei Zamyatin— . . . I had to live through the entire Great Patriotic War and I know the price of frontier battles where every hour hundreds and thousands of my comrades perished. The same is taking place today in Vietnam. Couldn't two brotherly sectors of the Vietnamese people agree to solve their problems by peaceful means when the lives of millions of common people are at stake? Let them recall the Second World War; let them recall the disaster and death that this war brought to almost every home. Isn't this lesson instructive?

Valentina Kushnir, engineer in a Moscow textile plant and mother of three— . . . It is a tragedy when in peacetime bombs and shells explode. It is not only soldiers, but also children, elders, women, residents of cities and villages, who are dying. I am speaking about Vietnam. It's fearful to listen to the radio and to watch television programs showing us the war in Vietnam. What's the use of blaming and exposing the enemy when everything should be done to stop this horror: to give peace to the suffering people of Vietnam?[34]

The editor in chief of *Pravda*, Academician Victor Afanasyev, addressed a conference of the principal directors of the mass media at the Central Committee of the Communist Party of the USSR on January 26, 1971. He said in part:

Daily, hundreds of letters arrive at our newspaper from people of different ages and professional orientation concerning the war in Vietnam. We publish many of them, but there are some letters that we cannot publish. The letters express indignation and surprise at the fact that this war continues to be waged. . . .[35]

At a Politburo meeting on April 15, 1971, Foreign Affairs Minister Andrei Gromyko, Defense Minister Marshal Andrei Grechko, and chairman of the CPSU Leonid Brezhnev spoke. The following are excerpts from the meeting's record:

GROMYKO: We wrote letters and met with our Vietnamese comrades, as well as with the Secretary of State of the United States. I think we are approaching an agreement, although today Vietnam isn't ready so far to begin negotiations.

GRECHKO: I think that the DRV has an advantage in forces. They will be able to reach their goals only by force. We are ready to provide them with the necessary support in the future. . . . At the same time, following the directives of the Central Committee, we have reduced the scale of military shipments a little.

BREZHNEV: We will not leave the Vietnamese in a troublesome state, but our own capabilities are not unlimited. A meeting should be planned with their leaders and steps aimed at solving the problem should be discussed. . . .[36]

The meetings referred to by Gromyko in the discussion reported above continued later in the year. One, for example, was held in Hanoi, where the foreign minister discussed with the Vietnamese important problems of getting better Soviet-Vietnamese relations. This was reported in the press. Later in Moscow at the end of the year, Leonid Brezhnev received a delegation from North Vietnam headed by Le Suan, the First Secretary of the Central Committee of the Labor Party of Vietnam. Nothing was reported on the contents of the negotiations except for the usual clichés like "guarding humanity' and "ever-strengthening friendly relations."

For more that two years after that meeting, the Vietnam War continued. The Soviet Union continued to provide much military and material support to North Vietnam, although not on the same huge scale as furnished previously during the initial years of the conflict.

Brezhnev made a report on March 30, 1971, to the 24th Congress of the CPSU on the Vietnam War that contained many condemnations against the "aggressive war unleashed by American imperialists against the freedom-loving Vietnamese people." He covered the assistance that the Soviet people had been providing the North Vietnamese as well as support planned for the future. But in the report an important paragraph was omitted: the necessity for ending the war and that the USSR and the USA were already meeting with each other on a peaceful solution. When discussing the report at a Politburo meeting, it was decided to omit this paragraph so as not to annoy the Vietnamese. They wanted to enhance their cherished friendly relations.[37]

During American president Richard Nixon's first term of office, he sought to extricate the United States from the Vietnam War. We have referred to statements from Gromyko on meetings that had taken place concerning the war with United States officials. This was part of Nixon's desire to reduce American participation. The Soviet leadership wanted the same thing, but both powers had trouble in getting their Vietnamese friends to cooperate in making concessions. Both big powers began to reduce the numbers of their personnel in the country. In the case of the United States, their troop withdrawals were tied to a process of "Vietnamization," whereby the South Vietnamese Army would take over the bulk of the fighting, aided by air and naval support. By early 1972 this program had gone a long way.

The process was shattered, however, by a massive conventional attack across the 17th parallel by North Vietnamese divisions against defenses of the South Vietnamese on March 30, 1972. Attacks were widespread in the country. The fighting was confusing, but the offensive was ultimately unsuccessful. The South Vietnamese Army fought well, aided by considerable United States air power and naval gunfire bombardments. Counteroffensives by South Vietnamese troops were generally successful.

Response to this offensive from the American side consisted of even more massive air strikes against North Vietnam and the mining of the harbor of Haiphong. The purpose of these actions was to induce the North Vietnamese to the negotiating table. This seems to have been successful, because the American Secretary of State, Henry Kissinger, and North Vietnam's Le Duc Tho initialed a cease-fire agreement on January 23, 1993.

Finally, after a tremendous amount of further negotiation, a peace settlement was signed in Paris on January 27, 1973. It called for all foreign troops to be withdrawn from the territories of both North and South Vietnam under international control and the repatriation of prisoners of war. On March 29, 1973, the last American troops left Vietnam.

The signing of the peace treaty, unfortunately, did not lead to a peaceful solution to the long war. Fighting continued as before, except that the South Vietnamese were now more and more on their own. They could not stand up to the well-disciplined attacks by the North Vietnamese Army throughout 1974, and eventually collapsed with the surrender of the South Vietnamese government on April 30, 1975. So this is how the reunification of the country of Vietnam happened, through the force of arms, not by the peaceful means envisaged in the 1973 accords.

The reunification of the country under a Communist regime has not brought to the Vietnamese people the expected hopes for material prosperity and democratic reforms. The Soviet Union and other nations in the Soviet bloc continued to provide economic aid, but this was undermined by the United States, which imposed a trade embargo on the newly formed country. Food has been rationed, small businesses have been discouraged, and the Marxist-Leninist ideology has been imposed. This has turned people into zombies who adhere to the cult of leaders. These policies all contributed to dissatisfaction among the people, resulting in a mighty flood of emigrations to neighboring countries.

The collapse of the Soviet Union and the Warsaw Pact nations of Eastern Europe made economic conditions even worse in Vietnam, a country that could build a "bright Communist future" only with help of the Soviet Union and other Communist countries. Under these new conditions, Vietnam has had to try to join the family of nations and especially has been trying to gain concessions from the United States. As we prepare this text, great strides are being made between the two countries with normalization of trade and investments by American business there. President Bush began the process and this has been extended by

President Clinton, who has extended full diplomatic recognition to Vietnam. Vietnam is now a country where tourism is encouraged by the government, creating a situation where many American veterans of the war are visiting the country with their families. Other western countries have begun trade with Vietnam, also leading to diplomatic recognition. We think membership in the United Nations will follow.

Russia and other former Communist bloc nations have lost interest in their former ally. They are all too poor to help Vietnam, asking the question, "What can Vietnam do for us?" The answer is, of course, nothing. Instead, Russia is looking for aid from their former adversaries and has reduced greatly its armed forces, having withdrawn them from adjoining countries.

So what did the Soviet Union gain from its participation in the Vietnam War? Some have held that it was a good "proving ground" whereby weapons were tested and our troops seasoned. But did we gain a friend there? Obviously not. The negative consequences of the war were great, just as for the United States. Both sides lost men for no good reason and depleted their treasuries of funds that could have been used to ameliorate the living conditions of their own peoples. Further, the Soviet Union lost prestige in the world and faced the ever-present danger of the cold war turning into a hot war. We must keep in mind the obvious fact that the real purpose of Soviet involvement in Vietnam was to spread world Communism and strengthen its influence in the world, not to upgrade the lot of the poor people of Vietnam. The final outcome of this war and the Korean War did not provide the lessons that should have been apparent to our leadership, as we shall see in the chapters to follow.

Soviet Army armored crewmen in formation before leaving for Spain, 1937.

Soviet airmen commanded by Maj. Alexii Senetorov getting prepared for the war in Spain, 1937.

Soviet ski troops operating in Finland, 1939.

Finnish artillery seized by the Red Army, 1939.

Communist commissar "inspiring" troops prior to battle, 1939.

Red Army sniper, Finland, 1939.

Meeting in 1939 between the USSR and Nazi Germany during which the infamous nonagression treaty was signed. From the left: German Foreign Minister Von Ribbentrop, Soviet Marshal Stalin, and Soviet Foreign Commissar Molotov.

Soviet pilots in Korean War were dressed in Chinese uniforms. Second from right is Ivan Kozheduv, future Air Force Marshal and four times "Hero of the Soviet Union."

Soviet tank under attack in Budapest, 1956.

Destroyed Soviet tank in Budapest, 1956.

Orientation of Soviet troops in Czechoslovakia, 1968.

Damage to Soviet truck in Prague, 1968.

Soviet troop convoy in Prague, 1968.

Soviet military advisers in Angola, 1975.

Soviets teach small arms techniques to troops in Mozambique, 1976.

Soviet armor operating in Afghanistan, 1982.

Soviet infantry deploying in Afghanistan, 1982.

Soviet Army medical corpsman administers first aid during Afghan War, 1983.

Iosif Vissarinovich Stalin and Mikhail Suslov, Communist Party ideo-
logue.

Marshal Georgi Zhukov reviewing his victorious troops in Red Square
at the end of World War II.

Soviet soldiers parade in Red Square after their victory in World War II.

Captured Nazi banners and standards captured when Red Army overran Berlin in 1945. They currently reside in the Russian military museum.

Nikita Khrushchev, the architect of the Cuban missile crisis, makes a point.

Leonid Brezhnev in a happy mood, perhaps when things were going well in Afghanistan.

Chapter VI

Middle East and Africa

The victory of the Allies over Nazi Germany, Fascist Italy, and Imperial Japan did not lead to a stabilized worldwide situation. So far, we have discussed the role of the Soviet Union in spreading its ideology in Europe and Asia. In this chapter we shall present our view on Soviet actions in the Middle East and Africa.

The Second World War spelled the end of colonialism as it was known in the client countries all over the world. In rather rapid succession, Britain, France, Portugal, Spain, Belgium, and Holland lost the colonies they had enjoyed having in their spheres. In some cases, such divestiture happened by a kind of mutual arrangement. In most, however, independence came about as the result of armed struggle, lasting in some cases several years. New states appeared in both the Middle East and Africa. Logic tells us that the victorious nations should have cooperated fully to aid emerging countries in working toward democracy, peace, economic security, and creating proper infrastructures in these new countries.

Unfortunately, such was not to be the case. Powers holding colonies, such as Britain and France, wanted to retain them, as France tried to do in Indochina. The Soviet Union made its contribution to this instability also. The USSR added its Communistic ideology to this most explosive situation. It did not use common sense and truly accept responsibility for the destiny of its own people. Instead, the Communist Party leadership lost any realistic base they could have had and moved to fanaticism as they sought to expand their spheres of influence. The leadership sought out places where there might be friendly regimes in power with conditions present that might be favorable to socialistic orientation. The attitude of the Soviet Union to Israel and the Arabs is illustrative of this policy.

The British protectorate over Palestine, a land claimed by both Jews and Arabs, persisted until November 29, 1947, when a resolution was adopted that created a Jewish state, Israel, out of this disputed countryside. Open warfare broke out after the British withdrew its troops from the area. The Arabs were determined to drive the Jews into the sea and erase the state of Israel as a political entity. After a ferocious struggle, Israel prevailed in 1949. As a member of the United Nations, the Soviet Union had voted on the resolution that brought Israel into being, as did the United States. Thus it was logical that the USSR recognize the new state and exchange ambassadors. An Israeli embassy was established in Moscow, as well as in the capitals of many other countries. But the USSR also began to support the various Arab states.

The leadership in the Kremlin needed time to determine where their sympathies lay. They wanted to know which side would be the eventual winner. As was happening concurrently in Korea and Vietnam, the United States was present, providing support to Israel. This support and that from other nations was helping make Israel into a viable state, increasing its economic and military potential. On the other hand, the Arab states had the wealth of the oil contained under their desert sand and therefore were extremely important to the rest of the world. The Soviet Union saw penetration into the Middle East as a top priority and part of its plan for global political expansion. Therefore, the Kremlin gradually began to support radical "antiimperialist" regimes in Arab countries, thus opposing Israel. This shift of political focus happened especially after Gamal Abdul Nasser came to power in Egypt in July 1952.

As we mentioned in connection with Soviet aid to Korea and Vietnam, there was plenty of arms and military equipment available to be sent to new friends in the Middle East and thus keep the pot boiling between the adversaries.

One of the major Soviet objectives in those days was the Egyptian coastal city Port Said because of its strategic location on the Mediterranean Sea near the Suez Canal. This desire on the part of the Kremlin masters caused some coolness from the Egyptians because the Soviet efforts were too persistent. They did not want to see the Soviet marshals and admirals turn Port Said into a Soviet naval base.

Former Commander in Chief of the Soviet Navy Adm. Sergei Gorshkov stated in his memoirs that during Soviet-Egyptian talks in Moscow in February 1954, the Kremlin insisted on being granted special status and other benefits in Port Said by the Egyptians. Later this issue was raised more than once, and the USSR's claims were getting more and more ambitious. According to Egyptian diplomat M. Kamfil at talks in December 1966, the subject of Port Said was raised vigorously during negotiations about the Egyptian purchase of wheat from the Soviet Union.[1]

This port became the trump card for then Defense Minister Andrei Grechko. His Egyptian counterpart, Marshal Amer, was willing to allow Soviet ships to enter Port Said and to supply the crews with food and the ships with oil. But Grechko's demands were far greater. He wanted to turn Port Said into a base for strategic intelligence in the region. As part of the deal, Soviet leaders promised to share the information obtained with their allies. The Kremlin was actively trying to show the Egyptian leaders that the situation in the Middle East was far more dangerous than the prevailing thought in Cairo. They tried to convince Egypt that it would be better for that country to hide under the Soviet defensive umbrella than try to go it alone or ally itself with one of the Western democracies.

The USSR, as we have seen in other instances, sent not only military and economic aid to Egypt, but also supplied them with advisers in many disciplines. By 1957 many Soviet specialists had been sent to Egypt. For example, a unit of military technicians called Pozharsky's Group, named for the Soviet general heading it, was in Cairo (actually Zemalec Island) at that time. Its purpose and mission was to provide technical support to the Egyptian military and to serve as trainers for Egyptian soldiers using their new Soviet equipment.[2]

Soviet influence in the area tended to increase as the new state of Israel became more self-sufficient. The Israelis were surviving and strengthening themselves, with Western aid to be sure, and were becoming better able to defend themselves and their territory. From the time of their initial success in 1949, the neighboring Arab states did everything to inconvenience and threaten Israel. There were frequent clashes along the borders, with the Israelis responding vigorously to Arab raids, while continuing to maintain an overall defensive posture.

On October 29, 1956, the Israelis launched an attack against inept Egyptian troops in the Sinai region, penetrating the lines almost as far as the Suez Canal. This was a clear victory for Israel that was accelerated when Britain and France intervened on the side of Israel. In combined operations, troops of the three countries decisively defeated the Egyptian forces after fighting that lasted until November 6. The United Nations demanded a cessation to the hostilities which was observed, the British and French having achieved their objective of seizing the Suez Canal. Shortly thereafter, on November 15, the United Nations established peacekeeping forces in the area to attempt to safeguard the rights of all parties. From then until 1967, a kind of armed truce prevailed with both Arabs and Israelis building up their strength.

During these intervening years, Soviet-Egyptian relations were developing. On May 13, 1967, an Egyptian delegation headed by a prominent leader in the parliament and future president, Anwar Sadat, visited Moscow on the way home from a trip to North

Korea. He had a brief meeting with the chairman of the Presidium of the Supreme Council of the USSR, Nicolai Podgorny. Their conversation centered on the overall situation in the Middle East. Podgorny shared with his guests information of "extreme importance." Soviet intelligence had determined that Israel had concentrated its troops on the border with Syria and intended to inflict a decisive blow at the Arab nations during the period of May 18–20, 1967.[3] This friendly warning played a decisive role in turning the ongoing Arab-Israeli confrontation into a dangerous military crisis.

As soon as this word reached Cairo, the various Arab states, particularly Egypt, began large-scale military preparations. Egypt concentrated troops near the Sinai frontier and blockaded the Strait of Tiran. Other Arab states like Syria, Iraq, and Jordan followed suit. Israel viewed these actions of the Arab states, fully supported by the Soviet Union, as menacing to its national security. Since it had warned the world that it would react stringently if the actions the Arab nations were taking actually occurred, what happened next should not have come as any surprise to the Arab world.

On May 30, 1967, the Soviet government announced:

> Israel is playing dangerous games in a region which is quite close to the borders of the Soviet Union. . . . [Perhaps it would have been more accurate to phrase this "in the sphere of strategic interests of the Soviet Union."] No one should doubt the fact that whoever would unleash aggression in the Middle East would encounter not only the unified power of Arab nations, but also the decisive counteraction by the Soviet Union and all peace-loving states [i.e., the armed-to-the-teeth Socialist camp.][4]

At dawn on June 5, 1967, Israeli fighter aircraft, in a preemptive and massive attack, bombed air bases in Syria and Egypt, destroying practically all the aircraft available to these nations. These attacks from the air were followed immediately by a concentrated ground offensive against Egypt and Jordan and later

Syria. Israel did this, of course, because it had good reason to believe that the Arab states were poised to attack first. The war finally ended on June 10 when a cease-fire was arranged. The overall result was a tremendous Israeli victory that resulted in their occupying several important strategic regions: the Sinai Peninsula, the Golan Heights, the western area adjacent to the Jordan River, and the ancient and important city of Jerusalem. The Kremlin immediately characterized the Israeli attacks as acts of "blatant aggression," and ceased diplomatic relations.

The governments and public in Western countries treated the situation differently. The declaration of the United Nations following the brief conflict did not even use the word "aggression." Why? Experts on international law consider these events to be only replies to the chain of aggressive steps taken by Arab states against Israel. In particular, they cite the demand of Nasser to withdraw the UN peacekeeping force, the closing of the Strait of Tiran, and the dispatch of Iraqi forces to Jordan as acts so provacative as to practically require some kind of retaliatory action on Israel's part. So this time, as compared with Israel's strike against Egypt in 1956, world opinion was clearly on the side of the Israelis, except, of course, the Soviet Union and its allies within the Communist camp. Even today, many years after this war, Egyptian and other Arab researchers and historians do not use words like "Israeli aggression" or slogans such as "The plot of world imperialism against freedom-loving Arab nations."[5]

The quiet coup that happened in the Kremlin tended to be obscured by the war in the Middle East in 1967. The Politburo of the CPSU decided that Nikita Khrushchev had been pursuing a course of management of the country, and his relations with other nations were far too liberal to suit the hard-liners in the party. Further, he had become something of an embarrassment to them. They remembered the Cuban missile crisis and the loss of prestige that had accompanied it. Much of his authority had been undermined already by the CPSU Central Committee, the Ministry of Defense, and the Foreign Affairs Ministry. So, the most reactive elements of the party and government got the man they wanted, Leonid Brezhnev, and the "thaw" in the cold war with the Western powers ended.

As a result of the regrouping of the political forces in the Kremlin, the decisive role in both internal and foreign policy began to be played by the most militant and uncompromising wing of the military-industrial complex and various party functionaries. The Minister for Foreign Affairs, Andrei Gromyko, acknowledged that the disruption of relations with Israel was ". . . the bone thrown to the hard-liners to avoid further escalation of the crisis."[6]

The mobilization of "Brezhnev's fist" in the Middle East immediately affected the situation in the USSR. Two new enemies abroad appeared: "Israel, agent of imperialism" and "international Zionism." These phrases and accompanying sentiments were trumpeted in the state-controlled media and naturally affected the public of the Soviet Union. They had been inured to such attacks on the Jews during the Stalin days, so in short order, the three and one-half million Soviet Jews were considered by the ordinary Soviet citizen as some kind of "fifth column" of international imperialism and a threat to the state. Unfortunately, there has always been anti-Semitism in Russia and the Soviet Union, but now this had been advanced to the level of official Soviet governmental policy. So there was reaction to it, both in the Soviet Union itself and also in other countries sympathic to the USSR.[7]

Tens of thousands of scientists, teachers, doctors, and other cultured people found themselves closely observed by the KGB and the police, with ominous results for Jews openly stating positions like a desire to move to Israel, or even discussing that Jewish state. The expansionist philosophy of the new Soviet leadership was reflected in a propaganda boom in the country, as the KGB sought out "enemies of the motherland" and persecuted them.

Soviet influence in the Middle East began to accelerate. For example, in 1970 ships with Soviet flags began to appear in the port of Alexandria with rather peculiar cargoes. Many came and the intervals between them were short. Their decks were crowded with various kinds of "agricultural products." Tourists walking along the decks, surprisingly only male, were joined by "sportsmen" from below decks. If asked, they would have had trouble explaining what kind of competetion they were to engage in or with whom.

These guests were not received by the Egyptians in accord with standard procedures for foreign tourists. Hospitality was so broad that these newly-arrived Soviet citizens were issued Egyptian military uniforms devoid of insignia. They were given no papers to process. The goods they brought with them certainly seemed strange to any observer: military vehicles, air-defense missile systems, small arms, camouflage netting, and other equipment and supplies of war.[8]

Unloading was chaotic because people directing had had no sleep for three days. Apart from fuel, the equipment was painted in desert-type camouflage markings. When the unloading was finished and the tourists and sportsmen were married up with their assigned equipment, the vehicles were organized into columns and proceeded into the desert without any maps or plans. Some people had routes drawn on cigarette packs. Their destination was west of Cairo from Alexandria on roads designated only for military transport. The desert winds were blowing, pelting the convoys with sand that penetrated vehicle compartments and clothing alike.[9]

Egypt was extremely short of a real air-defense capability, which made it extremely vulnerable to both reconnaissance and attack by Israeli aircraft. Since the 1967 war, aircraft sporting the Star of David had unbridled access to the skies over Egypt, an intolerable situation to both the Egyptians and their Soviet friends.

A high-ranking Soviet military delegation arrived on a coordinating visit. It was headed by the Commander in Chief of Air Defense of the Soviet Union, Marshal Pavel Batinsky, and the young Gen. Alexei Smirnov. Very soon thereafter, Smirnov was appointed commander of the air-defense division in Egypt and was posted there. At approximately the same time, a group of Egyptian air-defense specialists were sent to the Soviet Union to learn the intricacies of the most modern air-defense system, the model 125. This system was capable of destroying low-altitude targets. The old model 75 system installed by the USSR in the late 1950s in Egypt was no longer capable of countering Israeli aircraft.[10] The 125 system was called the "Nikolayev" and referred to by NATO and the Americans as "SAM-3." The deployment of these Soviet servicemen and the equipment came about, in part, because of representations by Gamal Abdul Nasser himself to the Politburo.

To counter the Israeli threat, it was deemed expedient to move whole Soviet air-defense battalions directly to Egypt, attempting to disguise the soldiers as we have just seen. Leaders of both countries felt that they did not have sufficient time available to conduct adequate training of Egyptian personnel to meet the stringent time schedule devised. These battalions defended airfields, ports, principal cities, and major troop units and military depots and dispositions. Also, the Soviets had an interest in the mighty Aswan Dam, which had been one of their pet projects. In the event of future hostilities, an event more likely than not, a high level of air defense would be necessary if the terrible losses of the 1967 war were not to be repeated.

An event of far-reaching importance occurred on September 28, 1970, when President Gamal Abdul Nasser of Egypt died. It was he who had negotiated the friendly arrangements for personnel and equipment with the Kremlin, so the Soviet Union lost a real friend in this region so vital to its interests. He was succeeded in office by Anwar Sadat, who was appointed to the post by parliament. In 1971 he conducted a purge of opponents who were violently pro-Soviet and anti-Israeli, so in a short time he felt secure enough to sign a treaty of friendship with the Soviet Union that guaranteed him continued Soviet support but which safeguarded his government from a coup by the extremist elements he had purged.

A disturbing element in relations between the two countries was that before he died, Nasser was thinking about a negotiated peace with Israel through secret talks umpired by the American Secretary of State. But on learning of this development, Leonid Brezhnev turned on the "red light" and the proposed talks were aborted. So despite the treaty that had been signed as described earlier, it probably came as no great surprise when on July 18, 1972, President Sadat ordered the Soviet advisers out of the country. The equipment remained, as well as some Soviet technicians. The Soviet specialists left Egypt in a hurry.

The Soviet Union had considerable interest in the other coun-

tries in the region and provided support of equipment and supplies to countries like Syria, Iraq, Lebanon, and Jordan. But
Egypt was the most important in size and capability and therefore
was able to get more from the Soviet Union in terms of all kinds
of military and economic support. So any cooling of relations between the two countries of any size had to disturb the Kremlin.

By October 1973, Anwar Sadat believed that Egypt had
achieved a sufficient military posture with Soviet help to again
challenge Israel on the battlefield. We cannot tell from our research if he expected to win the next war that he unleashed, but
he had reason to be at least somewhat confident. His resources
and those of his allies in the region were far stronger than they
were six years earlier. In particular, his air defense and air units
were at a high state of readiness, as were his armor, artillery, and
infantry troops. No longer could Israeli fighters and bombers fly
with impunity over Egyptian soil.

In meetings between the Egyptians and Syrians in September
1973, a coordinated attack on the nation of Israel was decided on,
to occur in the next month. Early in October, as a prelude to the
impending conflict, a number of Soviet technicians and depen-
dents were ordered out of the country. Troops began maneuvers
near the Israeli border. This should have alerted Israel to an impending near-disaster, but the Israelis were too complacent, and
were terribly surprised when they found themselves at war again
on October 6, the sacred Yom Kippur holy day.

The Egyptian and Syrian attacks were brutal and delivered with
unexpected professionalism. The easy time the Israelis had had
in the 1967 war made them doubt the fighting qualities of their
adversaries, a near-fatal lapse. Both of the Arab offensives in the
Sinai and Golan were initially successful and put the Israeli defenders in a very dangerous position. They mobilized hastily and
after surviving several setbacks, they were able to counterattack
over the next couple of weeks and eventually encircle large troop
elements of the Egyptian Army and destroy most of the Syrian armor. In the air they lost many of their best planes when they tried
to penetrate Egyptian air space. The Soviet air-defense systems
and their Arab students were very effective, preventing the Israelis

from supporting their ground forces to the degree necessary in the initial stages of the war.

Eventually, a cease-fire was arranged with help from the United States and the Soviet Union and the war came to an end on October 24, 1973. The Soviet role in this was more than that of mediator, however. The General Staff in Moscow had alerted several divisions of paratroopers to be ready for expedited movement to the fighting front. They were alarmed that the Israelis would continue the war up to sending armored columns as far as the capitals of Egypt and Syria, producing an impossible political situation. Knowing this, the United States did not want to see Soviet troops on the ground in the combat zone. Perhaps this was a bluff, but nobody could take the chance of an escalation of the conflict. The United States, therefore, used its good offices to influence the Israelis to agree to a cease-fire. The Soviets did the same with their allies.

Both sides suffered grievous losses in the intensive combat, with the Israelis losing many irreplaceable soldiers and airmen. They also gained a new respect for the combat capabilities of the Egyptian and Syrian troops, who were well-trained, -led, and -motivated, and who came close to winning the war. The final result restored the borders and the territory won by Israel in the 1967 war. After the shooting ended, the United Nations supplied a strong peacekeeping force in both the Sinai and Golan areas.

A kind of armed peace, punctuated by many border raids over the years, settled on the area. After a long period of negotiations, Egypt and Israel agreed to a formal peace treaty on March 26, 1979. This historic event was arranged in many particulars by then-President Jimmy Carter of the United States at the Camp David negotiations between Sadat and Israel's prime minister, Menachem Begin, in September 1978. This treaty prevented any possibility of continued influence of the Soviet Union in Egypt and effectively in the rest of the Middle East. Arms and other support continued to be provided to Syria and Iraq, but as subsequent events would prove, this equipment was no match for the latest materiel obtained by Israel from the United States. Israel fought Syria in Lebanon during this period with great success against the best aircraft and armor the Soviets had provided. Later, the United States defeated Iraq's best troops and equipment, all supplied by the USSR, in the decisive Gulf War of 1991.

We cannot help observing that this adventure of the Soviet military into the affairs of the Middle East ended with the loss of millions of rubles worth of equipment and supplies to no particular purpose. Worse yet was the inescapable loss of prestige in the world. The Soviet Union was again basing actions on illusions of expanding Soviet influence throughout the world, only to find its surrogates defeated and the arms supplied bested by those coming from the United States and other Western countries.

In other chapters of this book we have included reminiscences of Soviet servicemen who served in our various alien wars. We think it would be interesting for the reader to know what some of our soldiers said of their experiences and their ideas on the conflict in the Middle East. We received many letters at the *Red Star* newspaper. Because of censorship of everything in those days, we could not publish them then, but now we are free to do so.

Lieutenant Colonel Andrei Belousiv: On June 30, 1973, the surface-to-air-missile (SAM) battalion commanded by Lieutenant Colonel Komyaghin was the first to be involved in combat and repelled two air raids. . . . During these raids the following Soviet soldiers were killed: Lt. Sergei Sumin, Sgt. Anver Mamedov, Pvts. (brothers) Ivan and Nicolai Dovgalyuk, Alexei Zabuga, and Pavel Velichko. Later in December of the same year, an air-defense-missile battalion commanded by Lt. Col. Konstantin Popov was emplaced in Ismalia.

Major Georgii Lopatov: Combat formation of an infantry battalion was composed of two echelons. They were supported by tanks, mortars, artillery, and engineers. To contain and destroy forward positions, three to four assault groups were employed, depending on the number of positions attacked. Usually such assault groups were composed of an infantry platoon reinforced with three or four guns of different calibers, two or three mortars, an engineer section, and communicators. The most experienced officers were assigned to command these assault groups.

While preparing the units to break through defensive points, Soviet advisers paid great attention to ensuring the mobility of artillery and its coordination. In acquiring targets, signal flares, tracers, and smoke shells were recommended.

On one occasion, a reconnaissance in force was used to detect the enemy's fire support system as recommended by a regiment's Soviet adviser. Two infantry companies were utilized. But this action was unsuccessful. Restrictive and indecisive execution by Egyptian commanders and staff officers caused the attack to be aborted at its very beginning after a great deal of preparatory work. The enemy directed flanking fire at the attacking force as well as direct fire from the front. But still the information was somewhat useful because some targets were acquired for further offensive action.

Major Anatolii Nosov: Egyptian servicemen neglected their combat equipment that was sent to Egypt by the Soviet Union. Even with the smallest repairs, they became desperate, not trying to do the necessary work. They remained this way until the Soviet specialists arrived. They threw away entire assemblies that could still be used. Soviet technicians could return equipment to working order after Egyptians called it inoperable. When this happened, they would be ashamed, but still blame their troubles on the equipment or on the Soviet technicians. It was especially difficult to work with the so-called intelligensia, sons of local officials. They were utterly indifferent to events and were scared to death of the Israelis. It was quite futile to try to command such people, to teach them discipline and their duty.

Colonel Vladimir Sosnovsky: During the 1973 war, Egyptian troops found themselves in a very difficult situation although they continued to hold the bridgehead on the eastern bank of the Suez Canal. Under the guidance of Soviet military advisers, particularly engineer Col. Vasilii Kushnikov, a defense sector eighty kilometers long was designed.

A first echelon of 800–2,500 meters wide contained 40,000 men in reliable shelters. Embankments two to four meters high were constructed along with antitank ditches three to five meters wide filled with water. Barbed wire and mine fields also were used. In our opinion, such a well-constructed defensive position should have hindered Israeli assaults, but everything went wrong. Israeli troops penetrated to the depth of the system quite easily. The Egyptians failed to organize their fire systems and stop the enemy at the forward edge of the battle position. Three Soviet advisers were taken prisoner and later the USSR had to undertake a great diplomatic effort to free them. The Egyptians tried to blame their Soviet advisers for their own failures and shortcomings. The fact is that they lacked both combat experience and skills, as well as physical and moral strength. [11]

We hope that we have provided some interesting information on the history of Soviet involvement in the several conflicts that occurred in the post–World War II years between Arabs and Israelis from our point of view. We would like now to discuss Soviet involvement in the conflicts that were happening on the dark continent of Africa during essentially the same time period.

During the period from 1945 through 1987, there were over sixty military conflicts in Africa. Of these, forty-two ocurred because of political matters, six for economic reasons, and thirteen as a result of ethnic rivalries and animosities having historical bases.

Much of the trouble in that backward region had its genesis in the fact that major European powers had colonized the region and exploited the various native people shamelessly for many years. When, after World War II, many of these countries and ethnic groups were able to throw off the yoke of the colonists' oppression, they found themselves with poorly conceived infrastructures and governing bodies. Most of them were unable to fend for themselves politically and culturally, and were certainly not in any condition to compete as equals with modern industrial states. Their colonial governments had been staffed by experienced Europeans such as British, French, Spanish, and Portuguese, who made the decisions and did not share much of the actual governing with the native people. Therefore, when the Europeans left, vacuums were created with hardly anybody available from the indigenous populations to take over the high-level positions in government. The same was true in the rudimentary armed forces of the new countries. Then add to this confusion the fact that many of these ethnic groups had despised each other for centuries, making conditions ripe for unrest throughout the entire continent, a situation greatly to the liking of the leaders in the Kremlin.

The Soviet Union was directly involved in some twenty conflicts in Africa and indirectly in nineteen of them. Our involvement in these military actions was matched in many cases by other foreign states trying to minimize the influence of the USSR in the area, from both political and ideological viewpoints. During this period, the African states spent over $140 billion on military requirements, including equipment and supplies. This huge sum amounted to two-thirds of their collective foreign debt.[12]

The state policy of the USSR regarding Africa was that it could be an important strategic opportunity in expanding the Soviet power base, very promising in its probable future socialist orientation. The Soviet Union took highly practical steps in these emerging countries to make them dependent on the USSR in both political and economic areas. This also provided a heaven-sent market for the great stockpile of arms and ammunition and other military supplies to be donated or sold to the breakaway colonies of the Western powers.

To illustrate this, let us consider the developments in Ethiopia and Somalia, how the USSR viewed the territorial disputes between these two countries, and how we came to participate in them and exploit the situation wherever possible. The disputes between the Ethiopians and the Somalis had been going on for centuries, as were disputes in other parts of the continent. These conflicts were often accompanied with bloody confrontations.

On one hand, the USSR adhered to the plans of the Organi-

zation of African Unity that had been adopted in 1963. The pronouncements and agreements of this body provided for the stable nature of borders between countries in Africa and proscribed
the use of force in border disagreements. This is the reason for
Soviet support of Ethiopia in its territorial dispute with Somalia
in 1977 and later years.

Things were not all that simple because, on the other hand, the
USSR had been wooing the Somalis for years before this latest dispute. As time went on, the situation in that part of Africa became
more and more complicated. Somalia had been an Italian colony
before World War II and after the war it was assigned to the British
for administration. The country gained independence in 1960
and began to exert pressure for territorial concessions in Kenya
and Ethiopia. After a military coup in 1969, Siad Barre seized control of the government and began to orient his policy toward the
USSR. In 1971, a treaty calling for friendship and cooperation was
signed between the very large Soviet Union and tiny Somalia. But
the Somalis had something very important to the Soviet Union,
an excellent port at Berbera. By 1975, when a Soviet naval base
was established at this port, the Soviets had significantly helped
the Somalian government in organizing and equipping its armed
forces.

As with other involvements of this era, the Soviets sent soldier-
technician-specialist teams to Somalia to train the army on how
to use its new equipment from the USSR and how to employ the
newly-trained troops. It was necessary to train commanders and
staff officers as well as logistics specialists and other technicians.
Virtually the same pattern of support went on as was happening
simultaneously in other countries around the world. Wherever the Soviet Union perceived an opportunity to extend its influence, it did so. Between 1970 and 1976, the USSR spent
1,970,000,000 rubles in Somalia.[13]

Soviet military advisers and specialists functioned at all levels
of the Somalian Army. On January 1, 1970, the number of these
men in Somalia was 1,500.[14] In addition to the trainers and planners, interpreters and administrators were present directly at battalion and regimental level.

As we indicated above, the Soviet Union was also busy in Ethiopia. That country changed its political structure as well as its philosophy. In October 1976, the nation's leadership announced the program of "national-democratic revolution," another way of saying that the country was becoming Communist. In December of the same year, Ethiopia and the Soviet Union signed an agreement for the provision of military aid to the small African country.[15] The local press in the Soviet Union applauded this treaty as they wrote about this new friendship and how the Soviet Union had gained a stable and reliable ally, an arrangement that would last for centuries.[16]

Students from Ethiopia joined other communist comrades at various high-level military schools in Moscow and Leningrad. Here they were trained for their subsequent duties in their homeland. During 1978–1979 more than ten thousand Ethiopian students received instruction in Soviet military schools.[17]

After a bloody battle in the capital in February 1977, Lt. Col. Menghistu Haile Mariam seized power in Ethiopia. He announced that on a priority basis he would strengthen ties with socialist states. In furtherance of this statement, shortly after this coup he paid a visit to Moscow. Other documents concerning friendship and cooperation between the two countries were signed during this trip. A secret protocol was also signed by both powers on the export of large quantities of war materiel to Ethiopia on a scale to permit a high level of combat readiness. Covered were aircraft, armor to include tanks and infantry fighting vehicles, small arms, engineer equipment, and many other types of military impedimenta. Again, as with Somalia, Soviet military specialists were to be sent to Ethiopia under this agreement. These officers and soldiers were to function at the top of the military establishment and down to battalion level. By the end of the year, Soviet soldiers were arriving in Ethiopia. The senior adviser and commander of the Soviet contingent was Lt. Gen. Vasilii Pirogov, a soldier of great distinction.[18]

Thus was created a bizarre situation in which the Soviet Union was actively supporting two small African states with men and materiel that were opposing each other on the battlefield. During this period, Ethiopia was having trouble with Eritrea, so Somalia saw a chance to invade the Ethiopian province of Ogaden, a sparsely populated desert area that had already started, earlier in the year, to break free from Ethiopia. Some 70,000 Somalian troops entered Ogaden in July 1977, supported by a great mass of Soviet equipment with which they had been supplied. Soviet intelligence reported that the force consisted of twelve mechanized brigades, 250 tanks, 350 armored vehicles, 600 artillery pieces, and forty combat aircraft.[19]

The Soviet military advisers found themselves in a strange and dangerous situation. In fact, they were fighting on two sides of a conflict not of their own choosing. We cannot think of a similar situation in all of recorded military history, short of a civil war. Colonel Fyodor Bogdanov, who worked in the General Staff of the Armed Forces of Somalia as their principal military adviser, recalls how difficult it was to plan operations, knowing that just a short distance away his classmate at the military academy, Col. Konstantin Akopyan, was in the Ethiopian command post studying the very same maps at the same time. Their instruction and practical exercises at the academy did not cover this type of situation.[20]

In another case of a military adviser, Lt. Col. Robert Polosov recalls that he once mentioned to his Somalian counterpart that it was unnatural that Soviet soldiers were fighting on both sides of a conflict. This Somalian disagreed greatly with Polosov and reported to President Siad Barre himself that Polosov was unreliable. The president evidenced his displeasure on this to the Soviet command and Polosov was forbidden to take part in operational planning and soon was sent back to the Soviet Union.[21]

But Somalian President Siad Barre took care of the problem. Flushed with early success in his campaign with Ethiopia, he expelled his Soviet military advisers in November 1977. He apparently was greatly disturbed about the help that was coming from the USSR to his foe, so he changed his allegiance from Communism to capitalism. This was not the only occasion when a country like Somalia changed sides, but it certainly was an embarrassment to the USSR.

The mass media in the USSR that had been lavishly praising Siad Barre a day before switched its story line, accusing him of ingratitude and betrayal, obviously because of a directive from the Kremlin. Learning of this, the Soviet populace began to ask themselves why it had been necessary to help Somalia and waste huge resources since our problems at home were far from being solved. No one dared, of course, to speak out. We could only think about it and know that it was safe only to outwardly praise the wise policy of the Communist Party and the Soviet government. Everyone knew that the Party and the State were wasting national wealth sending the nation's sons to foreign countries, God only knew in the name of whose and what values.

We cannot state that the USSR did not try to achieve a reconciliation between the two hostile neighbors, Somalia and Ethiopia. Visits and summit meetings were devoted to this goal. The leadership even resorted to bringing Fidel Castro from Cuba to attempt to bring peace between the two nations. He came in 1977 to meet with Siad Barre and Menghistu Haile Mariam. He proposed the establishment of a federation of East African states to consist of Somalia, Ethiopia, and Djibuti, a compromise and solution of the political and military problems. But the Somalian leader, Siad Barre, resolutely opposed the idea and so nothing came of these negotiations. He was so offended by the Soviet Union's playing both sides against each other with the aid now flowing to Ethiopia that there was no reasoning with him. Having severed his ties with the USSR, Siad Barre began a full-scale war against Ethiopia and severed diplomatic relations with Cuba.[22]

The Soviet government then threw all its weight behind the Ethiopians against the Somalis. Another peculiar situation occurred. When the Soviet advisers were expelled from Somalia, some of the more senior officers were sent to the Ethiopian capital, Addis Ababa, to advise the military there. Two of these, Lt. Cols. Andrei Filatov and Semyon Nezhinsky, who had been in positions of authority advising the Somalian General Staff and planning operations there, found themselves on the other side of the fence. They had excellent knowledge of the strengths and weaknesses of the Somalian Army, as well as details of the operational plans, and the combat readiness of the various troop units. All this information was of priceless value to the Ethiopians in subsequent campaigns.

By the summer of 1978 there were 100 Soviet advisers in Ethiopia, but by the end of the year, 3,000 were present for duty. Increased shipments of Soviet combat equipment began to arrive daily. Starting in November 1977 and lasting until January 1978, the Soviet high command organized an air bridge between the two countries. Some 225 cargo planes, mainly the AN-32 type, airlifted military cargo to Ethiopia worth one billion dollars. By sea, major shipments of T-54 and T-55 tanks, 135mm artillery guns, air-defense weapons systems, MiG-21 and 23 fighter aircraft, small arms, and many military vehicles were shipped.[23]

In this connection, the Soviet Union was not the only nation supplying weapons and equipment to Ethiopia and Somalia. Cuba, East Germany, Czechoslovakia, South Yemen, North Korea, and Libya were also providing such aid. The flow to Somalia ceased in 1977 and was diverted to Ethiopia. But, as in other cases we have already described, the Soviet Union was providing the bulk of these shipments.

The actual fighting against the Somalian Army was not conducted only by Ethiopian troops. The Cuban government at the urging of the USSR sent large contingents of soldiers to Ethiopia and other countries in Africa where unrest was present, like Angola. Starting with only a few hundred Cubans in Ethiopia, the numbers increased to 3,000 and then 18,500 men by the end of 1977. These were regular troop formations that arrived with organic weapons and combat equipment mainly of Soviet production like T-62 tanks and infantry fighting vehicles. These Cubans formed the main striking force against the Somalians. By early 1978, they were achieving real success in battles with the Somalian Army. Eventually, the combined forces of Ethiopians, Cubans, and Soviets were able to decisively defeat the Somalian Army and restore the province of Ogaden to Ethiopian control. But President Menghistu was not content to let well enough alone. He directed his forces against the dissident Eritreans and Tigreans with unfortunate results. For more than a decade, Ethiopia was at war with its neighbors, the Soviet Union supplying the most modern equipment to a losing cause. Finally, in 1991 rebel forces deposed Menghistu and set up a government in Addis Ababa.[24]

In our treatment of Soviet involvement in the affairs of foreign countries in other chapters, we have included experiences of Soviet soldiers. We have one from the Egyptian-Somalian experience that we would like to quote, a remembrance of warfare in Africa from Col. Albert Sevtsov:

> Together with Cuban comrades we worked out a plan for the Ethiopians envisaging a breakthrough at the front separating the Somalians and the Ethiopians. The unit having the primary mission was the 10th Infantry Division whose backbone was composed of Cuban soldiers. These Cubans had been trained by Soviet instructors at training bases in the Soviet Union and Cuba.
>
> On the morning of February 15, 1978, the 10th Infantry Division equipped with Soviet tanks and artillery attacked Somalian positions in the Marda and Shebele mountains. The route of advance was chosen to avoid Somalian positions in the pass between the mountain ranges. Instead, we proceeded along mountain paths. Our attack was successful to the point that Ethiopian forward units were able to engage in a pursuit of the enemy. In all, we were able to destroy six enemy brigades of a total strength of 6,000 men. After this action, Ethiopian troops launched a general offensive to the northeast so that by March 16, 1978, the entire territory occupied by Somalian troops was liberated.[25]

Because of this African war, the USSR suffered great losses in material and supplies. Recently, the Moscow press stated that as of November 1, 1989, the Ethiopian debt amounted to close to three billion rubles, most of it associated with military expenditures.[26]

In other parts of Africa, similar patterns were evolving, with Soviet arms and men becoming involved in the affairs of the emerging African states. One of the most important of these was the former Portuguese colony of Angola, where in early 1975 surrogate Cuban troops followed shipments of Soviet arms and other equipment in support of the Popular Movement for the Liberation of Angola under Agostinho Neto. These insurgents managed to overthrow the provisional government, but were surprised when South Africa intervened later in the year. They finally left Angola in the spring of 1976. But civil war continued with the primary antagonist against the Communist faction being the UNITA faction led by Jonas Savimbi, who was supported by South Africa and the United States. Fighting went on for years despite the presence of many thousands of Cuban troops and profligate expenditure of Soviet military supplies and equipment. Finally, Savimbi's forces were victorious and the Cuban forces left Angola in 1991. Again, this was an unsuccessful projection of Soviet power in a foreign fight.

Soviet participation in this and other parts of Africa brought the Kremlin leaders no political gains. The loss of our military equipment and the lives of our servicemen who were sacrificed on the altar of unbridled ambition hurt the Soviet Union in many ways that are still with us. In the long run, the Soviet Union failed to involve these African states in our zone of influence despite our support of supposedly friendly nations and direct military interference in their affairs. As we see it, history has had it its own way.

The military adventures we have been describing unfortunately placed our country on frequent collision courses with our former allies from World War II, particularly the United States. Nowhere else was this confrontation more fraught with danger than in the very backyard of the United States, the Caribbean. In the next chapter we will turn our attention to Cuba.

Chapter VII

The Caribbean Crisis

Many outstanding politicians and military leaders, prominent journalists, and current affairs observers of the world consider the year 1962 as perhaps the most dramatic of the complex and difficult years following World War II. This was the time when the crisis in the Caribbean occurred, an event that brought the world to the brink of a nuclear disaster. We do not intend to discuss what caused the crisis. Much has been said and written about that. Our task is different, since our aim in writing this book is to present our views and information available to us on the numerous times that the Soviet Union participated militarily in foreign conflicts. The primary concern in 1962 was in the small island nation of Cuba.

Although there was no combat action in Cuba at that time, the USSR sent troops there with representatives of all arms of the service, including surface-to-surface-missile (SSM) units, ready for war. The leadership in the Kremlin must be held responsible in part, at least, for bringing the threat of a nuclear exchange so close. The Soviet troops sent to Cuba seemed to have taught the world the most dangerous lesson of the twentieth century.

Let us look back to the history of the Soviet Union in 1953. This was the year of the dictator Iosif Vissarionovich Stalin's death. This momentous event produced a lot of confusion on the actual governance of the Soviet Union. Chief contenders for Party chairmanship and premier were Georgi Malenkov, Lavrenti Beria, and Nikita Khrushchev. Beria was a sinister figure as head of the KGB and evidently aspired to replace Stalin as dictator. This did not sit well with the other two politicians and the rest of the Politburo, so he was deposed and executed later that year. Over the next few years, Khrushchev consolidated his power base and eventually realized his ambitions as the primary politician of the USSR, not the unquestioned dictator that Stalin was, but still possessing immense personal power. His job and that of other leaders of the government was to arrive at a different policy for settling international disputes.

This period of our history can hardly be described as cloudless. The aftermath of the Great Patriotic War was horrible. Grief and devastation kept haunting the country. People could not put out of their minds that 28 million of their countrymen had been lost in the war. The postwar years failed to bring a fresh breath as the nation began to fall into the vortex of the cold war. Instead of peace, various local wars all over the world drew the people of the Soviet Union into participation in them, most in areas where there was no earthly excuse for Soviet involvement. Conditions of life in the country caused our leaders to take a look around, to try to find new approaches to pressing international problems.

We have already seen the effects of Soviet involvement in the affairs of foreign states, both before and after Stalin. While these other important events were occurring, a development that would have far-reaching effects on the Soviet Union was taking place in Cuba.

Starting in 1952, an unpopular regime was in power in Cuba, that of Fulgencio Batista, who had seized the reins of government in a coup. He was opposed by a revolutionary movement headed by Fidel Castro and his brother, Raul. The situation gradually deteriorated over the next several years for the Batista dictatorship, with a full-fledged rebellion occurring in 1958 and Castro seizing power in 1959. The United States recognized this new regime immediately thereafter. The next year, Cuba joined the Soviet bloc and began to make threatening gestures toward the U.S. naval base at Guantanamo. So the United States cut off diplomatic relations with Cuba and sponsored the Bay of Pigs invasion by Cuban nationalists in 1961. This was a badly flawed action planned and executed by the American Central Intelligence Agency (CIA) but not backed by American military might. The invasion, as a result, was rebuffed by Castro's Cuban forces, causing great embarrassment to the United States and a deepening of bad feelings between the United States and the Soviet Union.

By the spring of 1962, the Cuban government had reason to believe that the United States had not abandoned its desire to overthrow the Castro regime. They asked for increased support from the Soviet Union, which was forthcoming, not only in the form of supplies and economic help, but in the political area also. In September the Khrushchev government warned the United States that it would intervene if the Americans were to stage another invasion.

By the end of May 1962, the Cuban Revolutionary Armed Forces consisted of three field armies and four army corps. Included in these major units were fourteen infantry divisions, five at full strength, and a separate tank brigade. Air-defense units were scant, and consisted of antiaircraft guns and automatic weapons only. There were just four squadrons in the air force, and the navy was very weak and in the process of formation. These Cuban units were equipped with Soviet IS-2m and T-34 tanks, self-propelled SAU-100 vehicles, 76 to 152mm artillery guns, 82 to 120mm mortars, BM-13 "Katusha" rocket launchers, 25 to 100mm antiaircraft guns, MiG-15 and 19 fighter aircraft, and various small naval vessels. All in all, the armed forces numbered about 100,000 men.[1]

The Cuban high command divided the country into three military zones to defend against a possible American invasion. They saw the three districts of Havana, Cienfuegos (south), and Banes (east) as likely invasion areas and established naval and coast defenses in these places. They also identified possible airborne

drop zones in the regions of Havana, Santa Clara, and Cam-
aguwaya. But Raul Castro and his general staff were realistic in realizing that with their weak forces they would have trouble defending the island against the mighty United States armed forces.
They needed more than revolutionary zeal and therefore turned
to the east European nations for help, and particularly to the Soviet Union.

The Kremlin saw the need for help as realistically as did the
Cubans, but also considered this as a grand opportunity to gain
a strong Communist foothold in the Western Hemisphere, a
short distance from its nemesis, the United States. So, aid was immediately forthcoming. We should stress in all candor that the
military aid accorded the Cubans was defensive in nature, not
equipment and supplies that would enable them to attempt an
offensive action against the United States. If we believe this as fact,
how do we explain the ballistic missile systems sent to Cuba? We
have the same trouble as the reader in answering this question.
If the medium-range R-12 and 14 ballistic missiles were not placed
in Cuba for offensive action, then why were they sent all the way
from the Soviet Union to Cuba?

We believe that this escalation happened because of all the international tension over the several years before 1962. It is certainly true that the Soviet side could have tried other remedies
and acted quite differently, such as through diplomatic channels.
But with the mood prevailing in the Kremlin, we believe that this
kind of reasoned action was virtually impossible. The deployment
of the missiles was seen in Moscow as a credible response to what
they saw as provocations on the part of the United States.

A victor in the Great Patriotic War, the Soviet Union had no intention of losing its status as a superpower. It exploded its first nuclear weapon, and between that date and 1962 had been on a
crash program to match the United States in this area and in
guided missile development, as well as in other modern armaments. By the time of the Vienna summit in 1962 between
Khrushchev and President John F. Kennedy, the USSR and US
were approaching parity. This was a new factor in the strength
equation between the two giant powers. While Soviet military doc-

trine of the time was defensive in nature, the nuclear warheads and the sophisticated missile delivery systems gave the Soviet Union the potential of crushing an aggressor in its own territory, using the considerable offensive power available.

Logic tells us that it was not very sensible to place the missiles in Cuba, aimed at the United States, when the Soviet Union had missiles in the motherland fully capable of firing directly at targets from Washington to San Francisco. However, logic alone has not always played a main role in political gambling.

We must not overlook the situation within the USSR itself. Much propaganda was devoted to reports on overfulfillment of plans and leaders' plans to overtake and surpass the United States in all areas, and even to be too strong for the United States to contend with, and thus bury imperialism. This propaganda had nothing to do with reality, designed only to distract the Soviet people's attention from the absence of social rights and the economic recession in the country.

We have evidence enough to believe that Khrushchev had discussions with Politburo member Anastas Mikoyan after the latter had visited Cuba in 1959. The information gained from these conversations provided the genesis for the decision to provide help to the fledgling new Communist government. Mikoyan had met with Fidel Castro, Che Guevara, and other Cuban revolutionaries and became greatly sympathetic to their goals and aspirations. Khrushchev's opinions were strengthened by stories told him by his close relatives who had also visited Cuba. After the Bay of Pigs affair, he became convinced that the United States would inevitably attempt to invade Cuba with a larger force. He did not believe that it was possible to secure Cuba's defenses with conventional weapons. He came to the conclusion that nuclear weapons were required and that the two missile systems, R-12 and R-14, were the answer to the problem.

Late in April 1962, he shared his ideas with Mikoyan, arguing that it was the only way to guarantee Cuba's security. He followed up on this at meetings with the military high command and then later with Radion Malinovsky, the Soviet defense minister. Malinovsky told him that American missiles deployed on the other side of the Black Sea in Turkey could strike the Soviet Union's vital centers within ten minutes' time, while Soviet missiles would take twenty-five minutes to reach American territory from the confines of the USSR. This gave an edge to the Americans.

Therefore, the decision to deploy missiles in Cuba was largely unilateral, Khrushchev's alone. The candidates and members of the CPSU Central Committee's Presidium, various ministers, and the military were invited to discuss the plan, but, in fact, they were asked to support it. In his reminiscences, Khrushchev wrote that it was a collective decision. His idea of a collective decision must have been a Stalinesque one: "We support."

Early in June 1962 at a meeting of the Defense Council with CPSU Central Committee members, CC secretaries, and the Defense Ministry leaders present, Khrushchev proposed the provision of aid to friendly Cuba. The problem of delivering Soviet troops, missiles, and other equipment topped the agenda. The assemblage present had no doubts that this kind of move would trigger a sharp reaction from the United States and might threaten the world with a nuclear catastrophe. Mikoyan spoke out against the idea of deploying the missiles to Cuba. The debate was heated and took a long time, but it was finally decided to deliver to Cuba both troops and missiles. The Council of Ministers, Defense Ministry, and the Maritime Ministry were ordered to organize a clandestine delivery of troops and combat equipment to Cuba. The process, once started, began to pick up speed in lower echelons of the military high command.[2]

Major General Vladimir Statzenko was directed to take to Cuba a missile division that was to be under his command. The division consisted of five surface-to-surface-missile (SSM) regiments containing some forty launching units, twenty-four R-12s with thirty-eight missiles having a range of 2,500 kilometers, and sixteen R-14s with twenty-four missiles of a greater range—4,500 kilometers. Three regiments were to be deployed in the western porions of the island and two in the center to increase the threat by appearing to be ready to use the missiles. A special missile regiment called "Sopka," having an effective range up to eighty kilometers, with six launchers, secured the defense of the coast in the areas of the most probable landing sites. The locations of the tactical "Luna" SSM battalions were chosen in advance so that they could attack the enemy as they were approaching the coast or when they concentrated on the beachheads. Their fire was tightly controlled by higher headquarters. Targets would be specified by the appropriate infantry regimental commander.[3]

In addition to these SSMs, two surface-to-air-missile (SAM) divisions with 144 C75 launching units were sent to provide air defense for the island and for the troops there. To determine the number of air-defense units needed for the mission, Moscow made a simple calculation: The perimeter of the entire island was divided by double the missiles' range. This produced a solution of about 150. Also specified were their locations in Cuba. One division, under the command of Air Force Maj. Gen. M. Tokarenko (replaced later by Col. S. Melihov) was to defend the western part of Cuba. The other division, commanded by Col. G. Voronkov, would cover the eastern half of the island. The area's depth covered the entire territory and measured 40 by 200 kilometers. SAM density was to be higher in the western and central parts, where the medium-range SSMs and the bulk of the troops were located.[4]

A fighter regiment comprised of forty MiG-21 aircraft, commanded by Lt. Col. N. Shibanov, was located in the center of the island. This enabled the aircraft to operate both in the direction of Havana and eastward. The regiment was assigned to destroy airborne targets between the effective zones of the SAM complexes and to patrol around Cuban territorial waters. They were aided by the radio-technical troops who provided early-warning radar and signal support to both the Cuban armed forces and the Soviet air-defense units, both missile and aircraft. Other Soviet forces assigned to the island also profited from this electronic support.

The Red Army was also well represented with four separate motorized infantry regiments in Cuba. Each regiment had a tank battalion attached to it. For artillery support, there were battalions of tactical SSMs having a range up to forty kilometers. These missiles were called "Luna" by the Soviet troops. The primary mission of these strong forces was to protect and defend the Soviet missile and air force units as well as the communication, electronic, and other specialist troops. They would, of course, have been valuable in defending against an invasion from the powerful northern neighbor, had such been attempted.

In case of an invasion, each motorized infantry regiment would be assigned to a combat area up to 200 kilometers wide and 30 to 150 kilometers deep from the north to the south coasts. In coordination with Cuban forces, their task was to prevent the landing of enemy troops, either by sea or by air. Two of the regiments, commanded by Col. V. Nekrasov and Col. A. Tokmachev, were deployed in the western part of the island, the area where most SSM regiments were located. In addition, this area contained the headquarters of the missile units and numerous engineer, supply, and other support troops. The Cuban capital, Havana, was also in this zone. A third regiment, under Col. V. Kovalenko, was deployed in the central part of Cuba in the direct vicinity of two SSM regiments. The fourth regiment, commanded by Col. D. Yazov, was located in the eastern part of the island. Colonel Yazov later became famous as the Defense Minister of the Soviet Union during the attempted coup against Mikhail Gorbachev. He was arrested when the coup failed and only recently have he and the other coup plotters been released by the Russian parliament.

These regiments were required to provide a battalion for local defense of each missile regiment, paying special attention to the defense of the launching sites and command and control facilities. Generally, the defense was circular, with strong points along the perimeter of the defense. Patrol units using armored personnel carriers were assigned to cover the areas between the strong point outposts.

A helicopter regiment was given multimission tasks. Included among them were the transportation of a variety of special cargo on a priority basis, movement of the wounded to hospital facilities, reconnaissance of the coastline, and transport of troops from one place to another as necessary to exert command and control and to protect important installations.[5]

The naval forces available in conjunction with the air-and-ground-based resources were to attack combat ships of the enemy and attempt to neutralize beachheads as they might occur anywhere on the Cuban coast, particularly in the Havana, Banes, and Cienfuegos areas. The navy was to receive protection from the infantry regiments and Cuban Army troops, air force fighters, and air defense missiles.[6]

Logistics units had the mission of providing whatever the troops needed. Stocks of food, fuel, and other supplies were planned for a three-month basic load. Troops who arrived before the assistance treaty between Cuba and the Soviet Union were issued civilian clothes as a kind of disguise. After the treaty was publicized, Soviet soldiers wore tropical-weight uniforms. In all, troop strength was about 44,000 men. Seventy to eighty ships from the Soviet Maritime Ministry were assigned to transport the troops and their equipment from the USSR to Cuba.

This intervention of Soviet troops and equipment in Cuba was code-named Operation "Anadir." The final order setting it up was signed on May 24, 1962 by Soviet Defense Minister Marshal Radion Malinovsky and the Chief of the General Staff, Marshal Matvei Zakharov. The deployment of the forces and their transportation was planned in three echelons.[7]

The first echelon (June-July) consisted of the movement of a squadron of surface ships: two cruisers, *Sverdlov* and *Mikhail Kutuzov*; two guided missile frigates, *Boikiy* and *Gnevniy*; two destroyers, *Skromniy* and *Svedushiy*; eleven attack submarines; and associated maintenance and support ships.

The second echelon (July-August) consisted largely of merchant ships to transport missile launchers and maintenance materials along with seven missile-capable submarines and eighteen small missile-capable patrol boats.

The third echelon (August-October) consisted of a large number of freighters to transport aircraft with associated maintenance means, mobile radar stations, and various maintenance and repair vessels.

The movement of these ships was accomplished under conditions of strict combat readiness with the pretext of a two-to-three-day naval exercise south of the Bermuda Islands in the Caribbean Sea. Ships stopped at several ports along the route to refuel and take on additional necessary provisions.[8]

Prior to the movement of these ships, a military delegation headed by Marshal S. Biruzov, the commander of Soviet missile forces, went to Cuba by air. Accompanying him were Air Force Lt. Gen. S. Shakov, who had visited Cuba previously, and Maj. Gen. P. Aggeyev. Their function was to perform a preliminary reconnaissance of the ports, airfields, and missile deployment areas in Cuba set aside for use of Soviet troops when they arrived.

Upon their arrival in Havana, the delegation was received by Fidel and Raul Castro. The Soviet officers briefed the Cubans on Nikita Khrushchev's plans and ideas. At the meeting, Fidel Castro told them that Cuba was ready to take necessary risks and assume a share of responsibility to serve the cause of world socialism and the struggle of oppressed peoples against American imperialism. Marshal Biruzov later remarked that he received the impression that it was not the Soviet Union who stretched out a helping hand to Cuba, but that it was the Cuban revolutionary government that was helping the Soviet Union to reach its own goals. The delegation soon returned to Moscow to an early session of the CPSU Central Committee Presidium, where the talks with the Cubans were discussed and approved.[9]

Later in June, Raul Castro, Cuban Minister of Defense, traveled to Moscow as his brother's confidential emissary to discuss the details and basic principles of the treaty between the two countries. The talks between Castro and the Soviet leaders were strictly secret with attendance severely restricted. Attendees from the Soviet side were Khrushchev and Marshals Malinovsky and Biruzov. Four Soviet officers were selected to prepare the treaty: Maj. Gens. A. Gribkov, G. Yeliseyev, and P. Aggeyev, and Col. V. Kotov. They all came from the Soviet General Staff. In addition to offering military protection to Cuba, the treaty stipulated cooperation with one another in their countries' defenses.

The treaty provided that each country's military units would remain under the command of their respective governments. Soviet troops in Cuba were to abide by Cuban laws. Residence in

Cuba by Soviet troops was to be only on a temporary basis. The treaty was to last for five years, after which it could be renewed if both sides desired. It was to be made public in November 1962 during a planned visit by Nikita Khrushchev to Cuba. The draft treaty was initialed by Raul Castro and Marshal Radion Malinovsky.[10]

Later that month, Malinovsky, Col. Gen. S. Ivanov, and some other officers were summoned to the office of the deputy chairman of the Council of Ministers, A. Kosygin. This meeting was arranged to discuss issues concerning the fulfillment of the provisions of the treaty, particularly the movement of troops and missiles to Cuba. The timing of the movement of convoys and measures to ensure tight security were discussed at length. It is interesting to note that Leonid Brezhnev also attended the meeting.

Meanwhile, the planning, preparation, and organization of the troop transport was already under way in conformity with the "Anadir" schedule. Lists of tasks to be accomplished, dates of goal fulfillment, and people to do the work were formulated. The schedule was approved by Malinovsky on June 4, 1962. All this planning was done by a select and small number of people to avoid security lapses.

In compliance with the directive of the CPSU Central Committee of June 10 and the instructions of the defense minister, a General Staff team headed by Marshal Zaharov completed the detailed plan under conditions of tight security and submitted it to Malinovsky, who approved it on July 4, 1962. We find it interesting that Marshal Zaharov shifted the lion's share of the work to General Ivanov, an officer of the highest reputation and ability. He knew all the details of the operation as secretary of the Defense Council. It was primarily he who briefed the CPSU Presidium and others in the government on the progress of Operation "Anadir." Further details involving specific troop units were worked out by a special group headed by Gen. A. Gribkov.[11]

The real burden of transporting the Soviet troop units to Cuba fell to the officers and men of the Soviet Navy. Over a very limited time period, June 15 to November 15, cargo amounting to

230,000 tons and over 40,000 passengers were to be transported by sea to Cuba. Seven dozen large capacity ships were to make 115 to 120 voyages. The first ships were to arrive in Cuban ports as early as August 1, provided that the cargo and troops were ready by then. When the loading time came, Marshal Malinovsky delegated special emergency authority to a group of eight generals headed by General Gribkov to supervise the deployment of the troops and to control the situation on the ground, both in the Soviet Union and Cuba. General Gribkov was given a coded message to send to Marshal Malinovsky when the troops were ready to perform their missions. The message was "Sugar cane harvesting is going on successfully." Only two people knew the code, Malinovsky and Gribkov. Fortunately for all concerned, events at a very high level intervened, making its transmission unnecessary.[12]

There was a problem in the selection of the commander in chief of the Soviet forces in Cuba as well as the creation of the staff. The fact that missile troops constituted the majority of Soviet personnel to be sent there was an important consideration. The original decision was to form the command as one of the Soviet missile armies. Navy, air defense, and air force elements would be attached to the basic missile command. In effect, it was a unified command of all components of the Soviet armed forces in miniature. General of the Army Issa Pliyev was appointed the commander of this multiservice force.

His appointment occurred at the very last moment because "missile fumes" had intoxicated many minds. The original plan was to appoint Air Force Lt. Gen. P. Dankevich, a missile expert, with the staff being largely that of a missile army. But then other considerations were brought forward. Many believe that Issa Pliyev was designated to conceal the high percentage of missile troops in the package. This may have been true, but we think that Nikita Khrushchev must have been guided by far more serious factors. A very strong personality was required to manage such an acute political issue should events in Cuba take some unexpected turn.[13]

It appears, however, that appointing Pliyev was something of a mistake. Pliyev was a highly decorated veteran of the Great Patriotic War, a soldier's soldier with a somewhat peculiar personality. He certainly was a strong man, but he was no diplomat. This caused a problem, because the use of tact and the usual ability of a diplomat to compromise when necessary were the talents that the commander of the Soviet force needed. This was an intensely complicated situation which was aggravated by the proximity of the United States. General Pliyev failed to establish a close and confidential relationship with Fidel Castro.

The principal subordinate commanders and high staff officers were approved by Nikita Khrushchev personally on July 7, 1962: Lt. Gen. P. Dankevich—first deputy, Maj. Gen. P. Petrenko—military council member, Lt. Gen. P. Akidinov—chief of staff, Maj. Gen. (Armor) A. Dementyev—deputy commander, Lt. Gen. (Air Force) S. Grechko—air defense deputy commander, Vice Adm. G. Abashvilli—navy deputy commander, Maj. Gen. N. Pilipenko—deputy commander for logistics operations, and Maj. Gen. L. Garbuz—deputy commander for training operations.[14]

With these appointments, things began to accelerate. A new TU-114 airliner, serial number 76479, took off from Vnukovo Airport at about 2:00 P.M. Moscow time on July 10, 1962. This was a historic flight for this new plane because it opened a new civil aviation route with a direct flight from Moscow to Havana.[15]

Few people knew that there was a large number of "agricultural specialists" aboard, sent to Cuba to carry out "large-scale land reclamation projects." The group was headed by a man named "Pavlov," who looked like a true native of the Caucasus. In fact, it was the commander in chief of Soviet troops in Cuba, General of the Army Issa Alexandrovich Pliyev. This deception was only one part of a carefully contrived plan for the entire gigantic operation. The timing of plane and ship departures along with loadings on one end and unloadings on the other were all meticulously scheduled. The actual transportation of the troops and equipment to Cuba was executed by the Maritime Ministry using the extended resources of the North, Baltic, and Black Sea Fleets.[16]

The motor ship *Marina Ulyanova* was the first to arrive in the port of Cabanyas on July 26, 1962. During the period July 27 to July 31, nine more ships with personnel and weaponry arrived.

Their arrival, unloading, and transit to the emplacement sites were coordinated by the officers of the advanced strategical group. The majority of the group's commanders and staff arrived on July 29 on the motor ship *Latvia*. They plunged at once into their meticulous work. The Cubans greeted these new arrivals warmly, sending delegations to the various western ports the night before the ships were to arrive. From the Soviet side, the bulk of the work was performed by the commanders' and staff chiefs' deputies and chiefs of sections.[17]

The Cubans appointed port commanders, who were charged with meeting all ships, facilitating their arrival, unloading the cargo and safeguarding it, and arranging for transportation to eventual destinations. The Soviet group's headquarters was located near the country's eastern ports, only 600 to 1200 kilometers away. In addition, the Soviet commander established a team of thirteen men at Camaguay to work with the port commanders.

Unloading the cargo from the arriving ships was mainly accomplished by the use of on-ship equipment because most of the ports did not possess large floating and pier-based cranes, either wheeled or on tracks. Only the ports of Havana, Mariel, and Casilda had this type of heavy and versatile equipment. There were special problems related to unloading military equipment that needed to be concealed from aerial and other surveillance. Tanks, missiles, and other such equipment were unloaded only at night, whereas the rest of the equipment and supplies could be unloaded at all hours. Unloading of weaponry was done by the crews of the freighters and the military personnel who had come with the ship. Tight security over the ports was maintained by the Cuban armed forces while the Soviet troops guarded the ships in port. Cuban patrol boats protected the ports from any incursion of any curious citizens or intruders. Special firing points were placed around the harbors for the same purpose.

Convoy commanders tried to transport equipment unloaded at night off the piers and start it to its destinations before first light of morning. If this were impossible, the equipment was covered by screening until nightfall. Routes from the ports to the interior were well guarded by outposts and ambush points, and mobile squads of the Cuban Army accompanied the convoys to prevent any interaction along the roads. On long marches, rest stops were set up along the route with extra security measures taken there. The Cuban troops attempted to deceive any observers by pretending to be on tactical field exercises while guarding the convoys. Soviet soldiers escorting the columns were dressed in Cuban Army uniforms. During the march, all commands were spoken in Spanish. Any identification of the units and formations as well as the ranks of officers and noncommissioned officers were not mentioned in the presence of strangers.

All these precautions no doubt produced at least some of the desired effect, but as always occurs in situations like this, there were a few amusing episodes. One happened when a column of a motor-infantry regiment was moving through the suburbs of Havana. A tractor-trailer carrying a 120mm mortar fell behind the rest of the convoy. The driver, a Kasach by nationality, stopped at one of the coffee shops along the street and inquired of a Cuban policeman the route to his objective. They obviously could not communicate. While they were gesturing at each other, some local citizens became curious at what was contained under the tarpaulin on the trailer.

Seeing that he had attracted entirely too much attention, the driver returned to his vehicle and left in a great hurry. The policemen became convinced that something was wrong with all this and started in pursuit, stopping the truck in a short time. Continuing to have language difficulties, the Cubans were able through sign language to learn that this was a *companiero Sovietico.* Their solution was to take the truck to the Soviet embassy in Havana. The Soviet ambassador was surprised when the errant truck and driver with police escort were delivered to him along with the 120mm mortar. We think that Comrade Alexeyev did not find the situation as hilarious as other bystanders did. The driver explained that he thought that the Cubans at the coffee shop wanted him to sell the mortar, so as a result he hurried away to rejoin his comrades.[18]

Secrecy of the operation was considered so important that many stringent measures were taken by officials at all levels, both political and military. For example, correspondence between the Soviet headquarters in Cuba and the subordinate troop units was restricted greatly. Orders and directives were given in person or by trusted messengers between the various headquarters. This applied to both staff and tactical units in the field. Radio and other electronic methods of communication were banned during the entire period of the troop buildup. When personnel arrived at their tactical locations they were restricted to the immediate area of their positions and billets.[19]

There were two important aspects to the Caribbean crisis, political and military. Both superpowers, the USSR and the US, were heavily involved at all echelons of their political structures. Their military leaders also became players in the deadly game under way, taking their cues as usual from their political bosses.

On September 13, 1962, the United States president issued a special statement sharply criticizing the actions of the Soviet government in Cuba.[20] The American administration's position toughened because its intelligence services had obtained reasonably reliable information about the presence of Soviet medium-range ballistic missiles in Cuba.

The Soviet ambassador in Washington was Anatoly Dobrenin. When responding to questions about Soviet involvement in Cuba, Dobrenin said that he was authorized to assure the American president that neither surface-to-surface missiles nor any other offensive weapons "would be deployed to Cuba."[21] In addition to the ambassador's official statement, throughout September and early October Soviet official and unofficial sources continued to say that there were no offensive weapons in Cuba. Unfortunately for our side, many high-ranking officials, including Nikita Khrushchev himself, diplomats at the United Nations in New York, and Soviet spokesmen in Washington and other capitals were heavily involved in this misinformation campaign.

While all this posturing was going on, the United States was doing everything to uncover the facts. The CIA and other intelligence operatives worked hard to detect missile-launching sites. To provide surveillance on them, high-altitude reconnaissance aircraft such as the U-2 carried out photographic coverage of the island. As a rule, this was done without violating Cuban air space, using optically strong side observation aerial photographic equipment. On October 14, photographs were taken that when interpreted left no doubt that SSM launching sites were being constructed. The laborers doing the construction on the missile sites were unable to camouflage their work in time to avoid the cameras of the American airplanes. Other U-2 flights confirmed information previously obtained on SSM deployment. They also disclosed the fact that Soviet IL-28 medium-range bombers were being assembled at Cuban airfields. The Americans rightly considered them to belong to a family of purely offensive weapons systems, along with the ballistic missiles themselves.[22]

After he made his momentous statement, on October 16, President Kennedy was briefed on the intelligence situation in Cuba by William Bundy and a CIA official. Kennedy was able to see at first-hand the evidence of missile site preparations and missiles themselves. He angrily said at this meeting, responding to Khrushchev's statements to the contrary, "He can't do this to me." He no doubt understood that these SSMs in Cuba could alter the balance of power, shifting a large advantage to the Soviet side. At this time the United States possessed a considerable superiority over the Soviet Union in intercontinental ballistic missiles, in range and numbers and especially in the quality of the delivery means available to both sides. The Soviet Union had nothing to compare with the B-52 bombers, Polaris submarines, and multipurpose tactical fighters possessed by the United States.

We suppose that Khrushchev's motives were to compensate somewhat for the growing strategic imbalance he was facing with the United States. This was, in other words, a quick "fix" to even things up somewhat. Whatever Khrushchev was trying to achieve, President Kennedy realized immediately that nuclear weapons so close to the United States border would cause difficulties for American early warning systems, alter the balance of power, and cause consternation among the American public.

This was the greatest crisis of Kennedy's presidency and therefore produced a very strong reaction. He called for twenty-four-hour planning sessions that went on for the next seven days. Virtually all important officials of the Kennedy administration were involved in these meetings. All other considerations took a backseat for people like Vice President Johnson, Secretary of State Rusk, and Secretary of Defense MacNamara and the joint chiefs of staff of the American armed forces. Participants at the meetings discussed all contingency plans already developed and considered other possible courses of action in response to the Soviet threat.

Two main alternatives were advanced at the meetings: first, to begin military actions to destroy the most important targets in Cuba such as the missile locations. This would be accomplished by massive air attacks followed by a seaborne landing with the view of occupying the entire island. The second idea was a sea blockade to prevent any equipment and supplies from reaching Cuba. This would include offensive weapons, other types of combat equipment, and strategic materials such as food, medicine, etc.

Eventually, the sea blockade alternative gained favor with the planners. This was proposed by MacNamara and supported by Attorney General Robert Kennedy, the president's brother. Adlai Stevenson, the American ambassador to the United Nations, also preferred this course of action. Proponents of offensive action against Cuba pointed at new photographs taken on October 17 and 18 that showed that the work in Cuba was progressing to an advanced stage. They asserted that the blockade would do nothing about the missiles and other offensive armaments in Cuba, but the National Security Council finally advised the president to adopt the blockade.

President Kennedy was beset with other problems with the Soviet Union in addition to those in Cuba. He also had a conversation planned with Soviet Foreign Minister Andrei Gromyko, who was in the United States to attend the United Nations assembly. Things to be discussed were the German peace treaty and the situation in Berlin.[23]

As to the Cuban problem, Gromyko told the young president that the Soviet Union would never play the role of idle observer while the United States was engaged in increasing the anti-Cuba campaign and performing hostile acts against the "peace-loving" Cubans. The Soviets would support the Cubans and respect Cuba's sovereignty. Kennedy did not argue with Gromyko on these points, instead reading him his previous statement of warning about deploying missiles to Cuba. There was no mention of surface-to-surface missiles at their meeting. When asked later about this, Gromyko said that "the president never asked me about them." At the same time, he estimated that the talks with the president were very important in that they outlined, as he put it, "the landmarks for future agreement."[24] We doubt the authenticity of Gromyko's statement in that it lacks documentary record of the occasion. We think that the meeting was totally fruitless, because nothing tangible came of it.

On October 20, 1962, the Kennedy administration decided to impose the sea blockade. Emergency military, political, and economic measures were imposed. The armed forces of the United States, both within the country and overseas, were placed on an alert status just short of actual war. The Sixth Fleet in the Mediterranean and the Seventh Fleet in the Pacific were especially alerted. Polaris submarines took operational positions in accord with contingency plans, threatening the Soviet Union and other Communist states with nuclear attack. Reserves were mobilized in the United States. Plans were perfected to move troops and ships to the southeastern coast of the United States to threaten Cuba itself with invasion. The Strategic Air Command ordered its bombers dispersed around the country with twenty percent on air alert. American troops in Europe were moved to their battle positions.

The invasion force destined for Cuba contained about seven combat-ready divisions and one hundred forty ships, backed up by a strong force of combat aviation from all services.[25] Never since World War II was humankind so close to having one false step cause the annihilation of life on earth.

President Kennedy scheduled a radio-television address for October 22 in which he announced his decision to impose an air and sea blockade, or quarantine, against shipments destined to Cuba. An hour before the address, Dean Rusk, the secretary of state, called in Soviet ambassador Dobrenin to inform him of the president's decision and outline the reasoning behind it.

At a symposium in Moscow in January 1989, Dobrynin was stormed with questions on why he had never mentioned the missiles in his frequent discussions with the Kennedy administration.

He replied that he had not been provided with any information on the subject. Andrei Gromyko, who was in the room hypocritically asked Dobrenin, "Didn't I tell you about them?" Dobrenin answered with a flat "No. No you never told me anything about it."[26]

The official Soviet confirmation of the presence of Soviet ballistic missiles in Cuba emerged during a meeting that Nikita Khrushchev had with an American businessman in Moscow, William Knox. Knox rushed to the American embassy after this meeting to report Khrushchev's staggering statement. This information was immediately sent to Washington.[27]

Khrushchev's admission about the missiles in Cuba was hardly a slip of the tongue. We are convinced that this was a deliberate leak that was sure to be publicized. By October 25, the Soviet leadership surely realized that there was no use in concealing the presence of the missiles inasmuch as the Americans had definite proof of their existence from photographs and other intelligence.

A Soviet diplomat, G. Bolshakov, a member of the Soviet embassy team in Washington, recalls that the news of Khrushchev's confirmation of the missiles' deployment to Cuba came to the Soviets there as a bolt from the blue. The embassy staff had great trouble putting a good face on the whole affair. For a long time they had been denying everything about the missiles. They had been kept in the dark on the situation, whereas the Americans knew the truth and took their denials as deliberate misinformation. Bolshakov wrote that this spoiled the previous good business and personal relations he had had with the president's brother, Robert Kennedy, who had helped to establish an unofficial relationship between Khrushchev and President Kennedy.[28]

President Kennedy and his administration realized that the blockade was a two-edged sword, so he sent a letter to Nikita Khrushchev on October 22, calling on him not to violate the blockade, because it had been unanimously approved by the Organization of American States. Kennedy stated that the United States had no intention of attacking any Soviet ships. The letter closed as follows: "I am sure that we both will have enough sense not to aggravate the situation."[29]

All day long on the twenty-third the White House awaited a reaction from the Kremlin. Finally at the end of the day, the Soviet government issued a bellicose statement that called the concept of a blockade an "unprecedented aggressive move" that violated international laws of the sea and was therefore utterly illegitimate. The statement called on the governments of all countries of the world to condemn the United States for "propelling the world into the abyss of total catastrophe." Moscow stressed that the Soviet Union would not hesitate to retaliate in the event that the United States unleashed a war.[30] On the same day, the chairman of the Soviet Council of Ministers sent a letter to President Kennedy that claimed that the missiles in Cuba were deployed there for purely defensive purposes, regardless what size or class they belonged to.[31]

The two governments continued to exchange letters and messages, using both open and closed channels, during the days that followed. Each side accused the other of aggressive intentions and an unwillingness to be sufficiently prudent to assess the situation clearly. The Americans said that it was the Soviet Union that was to blame for the deterioration of relations between the two countries; that only unilateral Soviet moves could promote normal relations.

During this momentous time period, the United States involved the United Nations on October 23 by demanding in the Security Council that the Soviets cease work on their missile-launching sites in Cuba and begin to dismantle them. On October 24 the UN Secretary General, U Thant, read at a UN session the letters he had sent to the Soviet and American governments, calling on them both to negotiate their positions on this crisis and come to some peaceful solution. Forty-five "third world" countries issued a statement supporting his proposals immediately after the session.[32]

The two sides continued to exchange letters and messages, each sticking to its own stand. This, of course, caused international tension to increase continuously. Soviet cargo ships continued to head toward the Cuban coast, since they had no instructions to return to their home ports. Many of the ships had in their holds only peaceful cargo. But some were carrying all types of weaponry and military equipment, including launching units and R-14 SSMs which in military terms were far more advanced than the missiles already deployed in Cuba.[33]

At the United Nations, U Thant, seeing the situation deteriorate further as each day passed, again appealed to the two countries to settle the crisis peacefully in line with the Charter of the UN. In his appeal to the Soviet Council of Ministers, U Thant asked that Soviet ships on their way to Cuba be instructed to avoid the areas of possible interception and any clashes with American ships. He also called on the Americans to avoid direct interactions of American combat ships and planes with the Soviet vessels.[34]

Kennedy replied that he had received U Thant's message and that he welcomed his efforts at finding a comprehensive solution to the problem. The president promised that the United States Navy in the Caribbean would do everything possible to avoid clashing with Soviet ships.[35] This restrained response did not sit well with "hawks" in the military and political spheres in the United States. The media also had a field day with the subject, causing the people in the United States great apprehension. Many southerners hurriedly left their homes in Florida and the Gulf states to find shelter in other parts of the country. For the first time in many years, common people felt the sinister breath of war at their very doorsteps.

In the meantime, on October 22, the Cuban government ordered a full mobilization of all its armed forces. Within seventy-two hours, all reserves and other forces reported to their battle stations to man their positions and engage in intensive combat training.

Finally, all the diplomatic effort paid off on October 29, when Nikita Khrushchev and the Soviet government backed off and gave in to world opinion. Every minute counted. The usual diplomatic channels in Moscow and Washington simply did not fit the situation. Therefore, when the statement was ready, its full text was broadcast by radio. It was, no doubt, an unprecedented diplomatic act. As Khrushchev stated, "any delay meant death." The document was of such extreme importance that it was delivered to the radio station by the CPSU Central Committee Secretary, L. Ilyichev, who acted as courier. When the document arrived, the radio program then in progress was interrupted and the announcer read the government's statement at about 9:00 A.M. Moscow time.

It was a generally conciliatory paper in which Khrushchev expressed his satisfaction that the American president had demonstrated that he knew how and where to draw the line, realizing his responsibility to preserve the peace. In addition, the statement said that orders had been sent to Cuba to cease all work on the missile emplacements and other construction sites and to dismantle, pack, and return to the Soviet Union all the weapons that the United states had described as offensive in nature.

The statement continued with Khrushchev's satisfaction with a message from Kennedy on October 27 that reassured the Soviets that neither the United States nor any other country would invade Cuba. Khrushchev closed by requesting the Americans to ban violations of Soviet and Cuban air space by reconnaissance flights. In conclusion, the Soviet statement read: "We should be very cautious to take no steps that may prove harmful for the defenses of the countries involved in this matter, steps that may cause irritation and eventually a fatal move."[36]

After he and his advisers had studied the text of the Soviet statement, President Kennedy quickly made a television report to the American people. He said that he was satisfied with the Soviet position for settling the crisis and pledged that after things were back to normal the United States would take steps to lessen the arms race and ease international tensions. He also said that the two superpowers should reach an agreement on nonproliferation of nuclear weapons and the banning of nuclear tests. He proposed that negotiations should begin on these issues without delay. His message to Khrushchev on October 28 was written in the same spirit.

The two countries fortunately found a mutually acceptable solution to this grave crisis. The Cuban issue became a matter of peaceful negotiation. Recovering from the shock, the entire world sighed with relief. The Cuban leaders received no joy from the unilateral negotiations that settled the crisis. They saw that the negotiations served Soviet-American interests, not Cuban. They saw the mutual concessions that resulted from the negotiations as unjustified violations of socialist principles. Their scepticism was such that they trusted neither the American commitments, nor, probably, those of the Soviets. They perhaps had a right to feel "used."

The dismantling of the SSM sites got under way on October 29. Fuel components were transported to special dumps. The large handling equipment was taken to the ports of Mariel and Casilda for loading on Soviet cargo vessels. Nine large vessels were used to take the missiles and associated equipment back to the Soviet Union. Instead of hiding the missile crates below decks, they were placed in full view on the upper decks of the ships so that American ships and planes could see them without difficulty. By November 11, all Soviet missiles had left Cuba.

During the time of the cold war, nothing so grave as the Cuban missile crisis had occurred. It demonstrated vividly how fragile, how vulnerable, human civilization is; how thin the invisible boundary between war and peace is; the acute sense of responsibility that should be always present when heads of state challenge one another over a potential nuclear battlefield. Even the dispatch of troops or military aid to a foreign country should be accomplished only after all other possibilities of settling disputes have been exhausted. In this case, the Soviet Union should not have sent the missiles to Cuba. A war for one country's interests on another country's soil can never bring dividends to its organizers. It tends to bring only grief and suffering to the people involved. In the nuclear age, the potential danger is that a small war can escalate quickly into a nuclear one in which humankind may be annihilated. This is the lesson that the Caribbean crisis has taught us.

Chapter VIII

Eastern Europe in Soviet Terms

There were two dramatic attempts to humanize the totalitarian system of state socialism in the history of the Communist bloc of Eastern European countries. These attempts ended with defeats of Communist reformers. The outcries of the people of these countries were suppressed by force of arms. The scenarios of both invasions were similar.

RUSSIAN TANKS IN THE STREETS OF BUDAPEST

The developments that occurred in 1956 in Hungary were viewed both in Hungary and the USSR as counterrevolutionary by Communist leaders. They considered them as attempts to restore capitalism provoked by Western countries. In reality, it was a complicated and contradictive social process developed by different political forces at different times. Unfortunately, the protagonists have not left notes or memoirs except for some fragments in the memoir of Nikita Khrushchev. In accord with the official party line determined by the Socialist Workers Party of Hungary (SWPH), the following four interrelated factors are to be found in Soviet pronouncements after the military actions were completed: mistakes and criminal activity on the part of the ruling group in Hungary (M. Rakosi and I. Dobi), revisionist and hypocritical political activity by Stalinists and rightists, subversive activities of neo-Fascists and landlords' counterrevolutionary attitudes, and subversion from abroad (international imperialism).

Nothing, of course, was said on the other side. The reasons stated above are far too simplistic. Little was said about the desire of socialists to reform the system or of people desiring to inject some democratic qualities into the equation. Also left out were attempts to build a national model of socialism under the slogans of the Twentieth Congress of the Communist Party, Soviet Union (CPSU), and the striving for partnership with the USSR. Since the time of the uprising until very recently, Soviet researchers were deprived of access to documents on the subject from the archives at CPSU and from the USSR government and had to resort to information from the West and official Hungarian sources. Now the situation is being improved, but quite a few puzzles still remain. During the meetings of the Constitutional Court of the Russian Federation late in 1992, some classified documents on the Soviet invasion of Hungary were declassified. President Boris Yeltsin in November 1992 provided the Hungarian government a number of such documents.

After Stalin's death on March 5, 1953, his successors, along with other party and governmental leaders, sought to overcome the vicious consequences of Stalin's political legacy, both within the USSR and the countries of the Communist bloc. In the summer of 1953, under the initiative of the new leaders, conferences were held with the leadership of these bloc countries to include Hungary. The purpose of the talks was to discuss necessary changes in the way these socialist countries did business and the foment for change emanating from the people themselves. The situation in each country was studied on an expedited basis. Particular attention was given to Hungary.[1]

The situation in Hungary was tense as the power of Rakosi, "Stalin's best pupil," was diminishing. In the Kremlin, he was considered as suffering from "leader's mania," having concentrated too much power in his own hands. He was ignoring historic moments in the development of his country, and it was felt that he was guilty of many violations of the law. Although the fight against Stalinism had not yet begun in Moscow, when the Hungarian leaders arrived in the Kremlin for the talks, they were received rather roughly. Rakosi and other members of Hungary's ruling group were sharply criticized for having monopolized the power structure. Soviet leaders demanded that priorities in economic development be changed and the peculiar situations in diverse parts of the country be taken into consideration. People who had been unjustly condemned and imprisoned were to be rehabilitated, and changes in personnel policy where to be implemented. This information comes from the notes of Hungarian participants at the meetings. Soviet records have not been found to this date. It is ironic that the primary critics of the Hungarian leaders were two devout Stalinists, L. Beria and V. Molotov.[2]

Rakosi defended himself by saying that he had merely been obeying his orders from Moscow. Beria and Molotov put him in his place quickly enough and demanded that older members of the country's leadership be replaced with younger men. Imre Nagy was at that time the deputy head of the government. At this meeting he supported the criticism from the Soviets. He had previously warned about extremes such as forced creation of agriculture cooperatives. Although Nagy was a member of the group of previous Hungarian emigrants in Moscow, he was not a close associate of Rakosi.

At a plenary session of the Central Committee of the CPSU in June 1953, the policies of Rakosi and his allies were severely criticized. In the eyes of the party, Nagy had become the real leader, succeeding Rakosi as premier. Beria was exposed shortly thereafter, and when one of his chief critics left the scene, Rakosi began a fight to restore his power. The records of this plenary session have not been published, but by 1955, Rakosi had convinced Nikita Khrushchev and other Soviet leaders that Nagy was pursuing a revisionist course and promoting nationalism. Malenkov's position became weakened at about this time and this led to problems for Nagy. Former Premier Andras Hegedus, who succeeded

Nagy, writes ". . . that carelessness and some passivity played their role and he underestimated his opponents."[3] The internal struggle within the Hungarian party's leadership ended when Nagy was deposed as premier in the spring of 1955 and was later expelled from the party by the end of the year.

Curiously, Soviet contacts with Nagy continued. The CPSU leaders considered his expulsion from the party a mistake. In fact, in the summer of 1956, M. A. Suslov and A. I. Mikoyan made contact with him. Reports of the British embassy in Budapest confirm this fact.[4]

Although the situation in Poland was most worrisome to the leaders in the Kremlin, they observed that events in Hungary were becoming more and more heated. They could not ignore reports of fomentation in the masses of Hungarian people that came to them from Budapest. In their analyses of the problems in Hungary, they saw that the dissatisfaction in the country could be blamed on Rakosi and his henchman, Farkash. Farkash was in charge of the armed forces and state security. The CPSU party line as developed in its twentieth congress had aroused some favorable expectations for democratic reforms, a process that Rakosi attempted to torpedo. This was contrary to what the people desired, as the local Communist Party recognized. Demands were made that those responsible for failures in political matters and reprisals against the people be punished. In June 1956, the Political Bureau of the Hungarian Communist Party appealed to Soviet leadership in the Farkash case, since it was clear that Rakosi was trying to make a scapegoat of him. The Hungarians requested that Suslov, who was current on the situation and who had taken part in the CPSU plenary meeting in March 1955, be sent to confer with them.

Generally, Suslov supported the measures proposed against Farkash, but recommended that extreme punishment be avoided because this might harm the party's cause and its leadership. At that time there was a proposal on the table to rehabilitate the memory of the old minister of the interior, Laszlo Rajk, who had been executed for supposedly acting like Tito, the Yugoslavian leader. Suslov said that the execution should be viewed as the result of the breakup with Yugoslavia, something not the fault of any

Hungarian, but the responsibility of Stalin and Beria.[5] Suslov wanted to solve the Farkash problem calmly and without hysteria to keep from splitting the party. He stressed that changes in the leadership, in particular changes that would replace Rakosi or split the central committee, would be "an undreamt surprise for adverse forces."[6]

But erosion of the command-administrative system in Hungary continued. Rakosi's name was generating overwhelming hatred. The embassy of the USSR reported to the Kremlin that dissatisfaction was spreading not only among the intelligensia, but also among the working class. The situation was getting explosive. In September and October, the Soviet embassy reported to Moscow that the situation was getting worse; that "our friends" had failed to undertake necessary measures to improve things; for example, improvements in agriculture. The Hungarian leader Erno Gero, returning from vacation in Moscow on October 12, told our ambassador that the internal political situation had worsened drastically, that the situation was serious not only in the party, but in the country as a whole.[7]

Shortly after this report, the kettle came to a boil. On October 23, 1956, in a totally chaotic atmosphere, a large student demonstration took place in Budapest. It was quickly joined by thousands of other people from all strata of the society. There was a total of 200,000 people in the ranks of the demonstrators. The primary cause of the uproar was overall dissatisfaction with the policies of the party and its leadership. The organizers of the demonstration could not have picked a better time for it, since the governmental leadership had just returned from a trip to Yugoslavia. At first the minister of interior prohibited the demonstration, but later lifted the ban.

As with demonstrations of this sort, the various slogans on signs and being shouted called for national independence, democracy, and correction of the excesses of the Rakosi leadership, particularly condemning those responsible for reprisals. They wanted an immediate party congress and appointment of Imre Nagy as prime minister. They also demanded the withdrawal of Soviet troops from Hungary and destruction of the Stalin monument.

The police reacted in a hostile manner which resulted in

clashes with the demonstrators and casualties on both sides. Nagy, addressing the parliament, also failed to calm down the crowds. By evening, a full-scale rebellion began. Armed demonstrators captured radio offices and a number of military and industrial enterprises.

That same night, the party central committee decided to form a new government under Nagy. A state of emergency was imposed. But Erno Gero, who had been removed as party secretary, hurried to the radio station, where he announced over the air that the events of October 23 were a counterrevolution. The next day Gero telephoned Moscow and appealed for Soviet troops to quell the insurrection. He meant the troops stationed in Hungary under the terms of the Warsaw Treaty.

After some deliberation, the Kremlin reacted. The Chief of the General Staff, Marshal Sokolovsky, ordered units of the special corps stationed in Hungary to move on Budapest. This order was received effective local time at 10:00 P.M. They were told to rely on a demonstration of force, but this did not work as the troops encountered resistance from the people.

Imre Nagy, the new premier, was present at the meeting of the Central Committee and did not oppose the use of Soviet troops. He refused, however, to sign a formal letter to the government of the USSR that the Soviet ambassador had presented to him. The former head of state, Andras Hegedus, signed the petition instead. The letter read as follows:

> On behalf of the Council of Ministers of the People's Republic of Hungary, I turn to the government of the Soviet Union with the request that Soviet troops be sent to Budapest to help stop the violence in the city, to rapidly restore order and create conditions for peaceful and constructive work.

The letter was dated October 24, but arrived in Moscow on October 28.[8]

The next day, October 25, the situation became even more complicated as the rebellion continued to spread. Suslov and Mikoyan believed that two events tended to increase the complexity of this already confused scene. First, there was an incident near the Hungarian parliament involving Soviet soldiers who received fire from rooftops of nearby buildings. During this incident, one tank was set afire, after which Soviet troops retaliated with gunfire of their own. Some sixty Hungarian citizens were killed. (We must note that present-day Hungarian historians believe that there were more victims and that the affair was due to KGB provocations.) Second, a detachment of Soviet tankers guarding the Central Committee building fired at a Hungarian Army guard company thinking it was a rebel unit. In the melee, ten Hungarians were killed.[9]

Firefights were taking place all over the city, with Soviet troops responding to small-arms fire from the Hungarians with artillery and machine-gun attacks. At the same time, the situation in Mishkoltz, Seghed, and Pech worsened, with a general strike beginning. Demands for the withdrawal were being voiced still more strongly. Nagy requested that the strength of Soviet troops be increased. This was favored by Hungarian government officials.

As the situation became more and more confused, the old leadership of the party began to make themselves heard. On October 25, Gero resigned his post, making way for Janos Kadar, who became the First Secretary of the Communist Party in Budapest. New members were inducted into the Politburo, many of whom were associates of Nagy's. Two of Nagy's friends, F. Donat and G. Loshonzi, argued that concessions be made to the rebels and suggested that the events should not be characterized as a rebellion, only a democratic movement of the people. The military committee of the party, however, wanted to destroy the main rebel positions with Soviet tanks and military aviation.

Prime Minister Nagy evidently did not desire to associate his name with forceful means of suppression, so he hesitated and finally rejected both alternative courses of action. He was still thinking about reforms from the top on the basis of the program of 1953–1954, although the situation was rapidly getting out of hand. The demands of the people in the streets were escalating. Various revolutionary groups were not content with "improving socialism," but wanted free elections and a coalition government.

The question of Soviet troops operating in Hungary to suppress the revolt was very much under consideration at the top of the government. At one of the many meetings of the Central Committee, a member of the Politburo suggested that the population should be told that after order and calm were restored, the Hungarian government would ask that the Kremlin withdraw Soviet troops from the country. Suslov and Mikoyan, who were present, immediately stated that ". . . it was impossible to raise a question on the withdrawal of Soviet troops, because this would mean the arrival of American soldiers." They suggested that the message to give the populace was that when order is restored, the Soviet troops would return to their normal stations. The proposal for withdrawal of the troops was rejected. But speaking over the radio that night, Nagy said that his government would initiate talks about relations between Hungary and the USSR to include withdrawal of all Soviet troops in the country. Suslov and Mikoyan were astonished at the declaration. "We shall discuss this in the morning," they reported to Moscow.[10]

Recent Hungarian accounts of the uprising contain the information that the officials in the Kremlin who were deciding the fate of Hungary were divided in their opinion of what to do. One faction wanted to solve the problem by force, while the other wanted to find a modus vivendi with the Nagy government. The differences in approach were evident: between Mikoyan and Suslov, between Mikoyan and the ambassador, and between the military and the politicians.[11]

The Soviets in Budapest began to vaccilate, as can be seen from hesitations in the reports of Suslov and Mikoyan from Budapest. At first they spoke only about rejecting all demands of the Hungarian opposition and the revolutionary committees. They advocated leaving the composition of the government intact, relying on the Red Army, and continuing to fight against the insurgents. But as time went on, they began to see that Hungarian authorities risked losing all confidence of the population. New victims would appear and this could well lead to collapse. They started to listen to other suggestions on introducing some prominent democrats into the government as well as representatives of former petit bourgeois parties. They saw this as a risky way that required care in implementation lest more ground be lost. These ideas were also discussed with Imre Nagy, who thought that they should be implemented only in cases of extreme necessity to prevent the loss of power.[12]

The situation worsened as party and local authorities ceased to function effectively. Things came close to becoming critical.

On October 28, speaking over the radio, Nagy told the country that he had changed his assessment of the developments in the country, calling the turmoil a powerful democratic movement and not a counterrevolution. He informed his listeners that the army and the state security forces should be dissolved. He asked for a cease-fire and amnesty for the rebels and to initiate discussions with them. He wanted to form new armed forces using the army and rebels' detachments as a basis. Politicians on the other side of the issue felt demoralized.[13]

On October 30, Suslov and Mikoyan reported the worsening of the political situations in both Budapest and the countryside and recommended that Marshal Ivan S. Konev be sent immediately to Hungary. On October 31, they left for Moscow.[14]

Their recommendations were taken seriously in Moscow. By this time, the Kremlin had decided to restore order in Hungary by force; not to permit losing the country to the West. The leaders saw this possibility as undermining the status quo and strengthening NATO. Another specter was greatly feared, the danger of the remilitarizing of Germany. Further, the collapse of the establishment in Hungary would have negative influences on the other socialist bloc countries. The conclusion was obvious: The Nagy government would have to be replaced. Massive and rapid intervention was necessary to support a new government. The ideological bases were, as usual, proletarian solidarity and the international Communist movement. So Konev was appointed commander of Operation Vihr, and on November 1 he organized his forces to invade the country, seizing key objectives and surrounding airfields, cities, and especially Budapest.[15]

The Soviet leadership in Moscow ,under a spirit of imperial policy and the cold war, relying on the Potsdam agreements, considered that it had ample right to intervene. There was, of course, the possibility that the United States and its allies might react forcefully, but another coincident event played into the Soviet leaders' hands. On October 28, the Suez crisis described elsewhere occurred. When Israel, Britain, and France moved against Egypt, this military action tended to keep the attention of the free world away from the situation in Hungary. Moscow could feel rather calm about the actions the Soviets were about to take, as the West's hands were effectively tied. President Eisenhower was in a reelection campaign, so apart from some impassioned speeches and condemnation in the United Nations, the Americans did nothing substantial.

The behavior of the Soviet leadership in the Hungarian revolt was conditioned a great deal by what had happened earlier in Yugoslavia. It was a blow to the Kremlin when Tito and his special brand of Communism separated his country from the Soviet bloc. Tito and other leaders of Yugoslavia did not hide their sympathies for Imre Nagy and his ambitions. It was not known what Yugoslavia might do to help the separatists in Hungary if Nagy were allowed to go too far. The thinking in the Kremlin went something like this: If we give in, the West will consider us idiots and cowards. We cannot tolerate such an event, either as Communists/internationalists or as a great power, the USSR.

Khrushchev later said that Moscow had concentrated sufficient numbers of troops and decided to put an end to the developments in Hungary. He was in Brioni and was called by the Soviet chairman, Bulganin, who had good news for him: that Munnich and Kadar had managed to flee Budapest and were on their way to Moscow by plane. Allowing capitalism to be restored in Hungary would entail grave consequences in the internal situation in the Soviet Union. Many Soviet citizens would see changes from the way things were handled under Stalin, when everyone was law-abiding and when there were no rebellions. And now, since these new people have come to power (here Khrushchev used some vulgar words describing these Soviet leaders) everything is falling apart. The rebellion in Hungary coincided with the Soviet leadership starting to condemn the Stalin years. Khrushchev said that the first place that such subversive speech was happening was in the Red Army. Clearly, the leadership had to keep the army on its side.[16] The Yugoslavian ambassador wrote something similar, that the army was one of the main reasons that the Soviet Union invaded Hungary.[17]

Initially, between October 23 and 30 five Soviet Army divisions were engaged in the fighting in Hungary. These generally were troops that had been on Hungarian soil before the uprising. Marshal Konev's troops in the Vihr operation consisted of two armies of nine divisions and a special corps of three divisions. Airborne units were also used in key spots. These troops had been assembled hastily from the Odessa and Carpathian military districts and Romania. Many of the troops were unprepared for such a mission, as they had been helping collective farmers bring in the harvest.[18]

Nikita Khrushchev had been in Yugoslavia while the initial uprising was taking place. On his way back to the Soviet Union, he met secretly with Janos Kadar on November 3. They discussed the formation of a new temporary revolutionary peasants' and workers' government to replace the regularly constituted Nagy government. This new political structure was announced by radio, both in Hungary and the Soviet Union.

Early in the morning of November 4, Nagy and his closest associates, fearing arrest by the recently installed Kadar government or directly by the Soviets, fled to the Yugoslavian embassy where he was granted temporary political asylum. He made an announcement that his government was still acting and that units of the Hungarian Army were offering resistance to the invaders.[19]

Shortly thereafter, A. Rankovich sent a telegram to Nagy, proposing that he should resign and support the policies of the new government. Nagy rejected the proposal. Atsel wrote in 1991 that after lengthy talks with Yugoslavian embassy officials, Nagy wrote a draft of a letter of resignation, but members of the Executive Committee of the Party who were with him at the embassy dissuaded him from this course of action.[20]

At about this same time, November 4, Marshal Konev moved vigorously to accomplish his assigned mission: ". . . to help break the resistance of rebels in Budapest and to restore legitimate power and order in the country." This mission was, of course, under the basic direction of his superiors in the Kremlin and by the request of the new Kadar government. We must note here that Konev had begun to move troops into the country several days before the Kadar government had taken office. In November there were about 60,000 Soviet troops in Hungary.[21]

It was decided that the Hungarian Army formations should be disarmed, as they were considered to be unreliable. This was done despite the fact that most Hungarian units did not display organized resistance to the Soviet invaders. The biggest exception to this was in Budapest, where some 15,000 people fought fiercely to gain their objectives. According to information from the Hungarian Health Ministry cited in Soviet military records, in the course of fighting, as many as 4,000 Hungarian citizens were killed. The price of "victory" on the Soviet side was also great. Some 669 Soviet officers and men were killed, 1,450 were wounded, and 51 were missing in action. Such was the bloody result of our policies.[22]

Arrests were made. Hungarian Defense Minister F. Maleter was having a conversation with Soviet General Malinin concerning the withdrawal of Soviet troops. Both he and his official delegation were arrested at 1:30 A.M. on November 4. By November 15 Soviet State Security (KGB) personnel had arrested some 1,372 Hungarian citizens and turned them over to the Hungarian Ministry of the Interior. Large amounts of weapons and supplies also were seized both from the rebels and members of the Hungarian Army.[23]

Janos Kadar and other members of his new government moved to Budapest as soon as it was safe to do so. He immediately swore to bear true allegiance to the chairman of the Presidium of the People's Republic of Hungary, Istvan Dobi. In this way, the problem of legitimacy seems to have been solved. Kadar and his allies enjoyed minimal support in the countryside. The difficult process of a return to normal life began. Kadar sought support from the populace by departing from a hard-line approach, as might seem logical under the circumstances. He continued to blame the previous leaders for the conditions that precipitated the revolt, Matyas Rakosi and Erno Gero.[24]

Gradually, as things stabilized and Kadar's hold on the country became firm, trials were held. In 1985, describing the events to Mikhail Gorbachev, Kadar reported that when the number of death penalties (about 300) among the rebel faction equaled the number of deaths among supporters of the communist government, he asked the Interior Ministry to call a halt to the executions. It is difficult to determine now if this assertion was true and if so how this influenced the course of future events. For example, it is known that Kadar had conversations with two secretaries of the Central Committee of the CPSU, A. B. Aristov and M. A. Suslov, who happened to be in Hungary later in November 1956. He asked them to influence General Serov and the military to be selective about the people they were arresting, especially in outlying provinces. He asked that the real instigators of the revolt be detained for trial, but not those who had become involved by error or circumstance.[25]

In December 1967, at a closed plenary meeting of the Central Committee of the Hungarian Communist Party, Kadar and the Minister of the Interior, B. Bisku, reported the results of the investigation of the rebellion. The documents that recorded the minutes of this meeting were kept secret for a very long time, until the death of Janos Kadar. But neither this meeting nor a second such plenary session in June 1958 on the eve of the trials specified or discussed the nature of penalties. On this subject, the papers say only that it ". . . was necessary to ensure free course of the legal procedure." This means, we suppose, to give a free hand to the judges.[26]

After all evidence had been presented, the judges deliberated and rendered decisions. I. Nagy, P. Maleter, Y. Siladi, and M. Gimesh were all sentenced to death. A lower-ranking member of this group, G. Loshonzi, died in prison in December 1957 before the trials. His health had been undermined and in jail his psychological troubles worsened. The true cause of death has never been released.[27]

Imre Nagy never admitted his guilt as adjudicated by the court. He also refused to ask for mercy, believing that the last word on his activities would be provided by historians after his death. He also thought that he would be remembered by the international workers movement. Nagy was executed at 5:00 A.M., June 16, 1958. The severe sentence aroused wide protests around the world. Nagy kept a diary while in prison that still exists and is in the possession of his daughter, Erzhbet. She does not desire to have the diary published at this time.[28]

The goals of the Hungarian insurrection in 1956 were freedom and independence, doing away with Stalinism, and the elimination of a totalitarian government. To some degree, this eventually happened in Hungary, because once Kadar was in power, he did not repeat many of the repressive policies of the Rakosi administration. Although harsh at the beginning of his reign, he was able to stabilize the internal situation of the country rather quickly and to win the support of the populace. By 1963, Hungary was able to break the kind of international isolation that had existed in the past. Initially, Kadar was not particularly independent, obeying the deluge of guidance he was receiving from our leaders in the Kremlin. But he was an intelligent man with an independent mind and a charismatic personality. He therefore was able to pursue a relatively independent course within the framework of the Warsaw Pact and the attitude of the Kremlin. He succeeded in having three Soviet ambassadors recalled from Budapest who were trying to interfere too much in Hungarian affairs. He was a master of compromise and was able to find common ground with all Soviet leaders, at the same time preserving dignity and independence.

He remained the Hungarian leader for thirty-two years, until 1988. He died in 1989. One can find many errors in this long rule, but many successes also. Over a period of time, Hungary became known as the "iron curtain" country of liberal freedoms and reforms. But the drawbacks of the Communist system, although modernized, prevented Hungary from attaining a true rennaissance of its society. A number of problems were becoming publicized at the end of Kadar's leadership and it was time for someone else. The era of Kadar's "real socialism" ended peacefully in 1989–1990 in Hungary. Its collapse here was the sign of the collapse of the Soviet system. In December 1991, the President of the USSR, Mikhail Gorbachev, condemned the Soviet intervention in 1956 at a reception honoring the new Hungarian Premier, Y. Antall.[29]

As far as the USSR is concerned, the military intervention of 1956 was a mistake because it negatively influenced the internal development of the Soviet Union itself. It froze the thaw after the Twentieth Congress of the CPSU and hindered de-Stalinization. Although this was apparent to our leadership, they used the same logic of imperialistic thinking in 1968 as they had in 1956. Their approach to the problems in Czechoslovakia again stopped reforms in the Soviet Union. The similar policy, or lack of it, led our society to crisis and the *"perestroika"* of 1985–1990 failed to save us from it.

TROUBLES IN PRAGUE

On August 20, 1968, Soviet troops invaded Czechoslovakia. Paratroops took over the principal governmental offices; occupied post offices, police stations and military barracks; and seized the offices of newspapers and magazines. Governmental ministers and even President Ludwig Svoboda were put under tight surveillance. Active participants in the "Prague Spring" movement were arrested. The life of the country was paralyzed.

What happened? Why did the Soviet government, after knowing so well the problems resulting from the invasion of Hungary, decide to adopt such a dangerous course of action? Why were the leaders willing to undertake such a desperate step fraught with the most serious international consequences? And again the victim of this invasion was a country that was a proper member of the socialist community and a loyal member of the Warsaw Pact. Much has been written about this event, most from the West. But many facts are not known to the general public. Many still reside in secret archives and dossiers of the KGB.

Today we have the opportunity to disclose much information previously unknown because one of us authors, Oleg Sarin, was invited to Prague by the Commission of the Academy of Sciences of Czechoslovakia as a representative of the Russian Defense Ministry newspaper, *Red Star* (*Krasnaya Zvezda*). This gave him the fantastic opportunity to work in an archive of over 170,000 documents covering events between 1967 and 1970, including those sent to Prague by the Soviet and Polish governments. We include here the most interesting parts of these documents as well as records of talks among the participants. Reprinted also are secret letters that Boris Yeltsin gave to Czechoslovakian president Vaclav Havel in July 1992.

But first we want to provide a summary of the background that led to the unfortunate actions of the Soviet government.

Czechoslovakia as a country was a product of the Treaty of Versailles after World War I, along with other countries and principalities that were member states of the Austro-Hungarian Empire. Between that time and the mid-1930s it became a relatively prosperous state under Tomas Masaryk and Eduard Benes, despite the fact that it was a combination of two separate and different peoples, the Czechs and the Slovaks, with different customs and languages. It also contained a sizable German-Austrian population. Hitler and his infamous Nazi regime took the country over in 1939 after craven appeasement by the Western European powers led by Neville Chamberlain, the prime minister of Britain. Benes and Jan Masaryk fled to Britain and established a refugee provisional government there.

During World War II, the German protectorate over the country of Czechoslovakia was a brutal one, replete with executions and deportations of agitators to concentration camps. Reprisals were common against the people. The leaders in exile in London and the Czechoslovakian underground looked to the Soviet Union for liberation from the hated Nazis. This occurred gradually in late 1944 and 1945 as the allies swept the German armies from the country. Benes and Jan Masaryk, the son of the late Tomas Masaryk, sought to form a coalition government, uniting the Czechs and Slovaks along with minority Germans, but the majority Communist Party managed to suppress the several other parties. The Communists under Klement Gottwald forced Benes out of office in February 1948. The next month, Foreign Minister Jan Masaryk was found dead in his office. The Communist government announced that it was a suicide, but we have no doubt that he was murdered.

The People's Republic of Czechoslovakia in the twenty years prior to 1968 was formed into a typical Moscow-designed socialist state and became a strong member of the Warsaw Pact. It differed however, from some of the other Eastern European republics, because gradually it became much more liberal politically and attained a better standard of living than others in the Soviet bloc. It was, of course, a loyal member of the Warsaw Pact, with many of its foreign relationships dominated by Moscow. In this, it was not much different from the Hungary of 1956.

A climactic event happened on January 5, 1968, which broke the pattern of former days, when Alexander Dubcek replaced Antonin Novotny as first secretary of the Czechoslovak Communist Party. Dubcek, a Slovak Communist little known outside his country, proved to be more than the doctrinaire Communists in the other countries of the Warsaw Pact could tolerate. He took an even more liberal view of politics than his predecessors and shocked the world by showing a more independent spirit for Czechoslovakia, something like the attitude of neighboring Yugoslavia. He went so far as to publicly extoll the virtues of former respected politicians like Benes and the two Masaryks. Some politicians advocated an entirely independent Czechoslovakia, remaining Communist in form and spirit and loyal to the Warsaw Pact but removing itself from the dominance of the Soviet Union.

Dubcek had meetings with his counterparts in other bloc countries, where reservations were expressed on the degree of liberalization that was occurring in Czechoslovakia. The other countries were afraid that this new spirit might spread to them and cause great mischief. Dubcek did his best to finesse both the Kremlin and his peers, but on July 14, other Warsaw Pact leaders had a meeting that resulted in a letter to Dubcek demanding that his liberal reforms be reversed. Dubcek publicly rejected this ultimatum. The Soviet Union then applied its peculiar pressure in a meeting that started on July 29 on the border in which the Politburo confronted the Czech leaders, again demanding compliance with traditional Communist orthodoxy. Between then and the invasion, Soviet troops in the country that had been conducting maneuvers were withdrawn, but almost immediately new maneuvers were held in the border area and anti-Czech statements were made by Warsaw Pact nations. Finally, the Communist bloc countries invaded defiant Czechoslovakia on August 20.

Recently, top secret documents have been released covering this time period. On July 16, 1992, a personal envoy of Russian president Boris Yeltsin gave two documents to the President of Czechoslovakia, V. Gavel. These came from Special Package 225, classified top secret, bearing the seal of K. Chernenko, with these instructions: "To be retained in the archives of the Political Bureau. Not to be opened without my permission." These papers served as the formal pretext for the military intervention in Czechoslovakia. One of these is quoted below. It is a letter written by an alternate member of the Presidium of the Party Central Committee, Antonin Kapek, who was brave enough to send it direct to Leonid Brezhnev. This was the first appeal for "fraternal help" from one of the Czech hard-liners. Judging by the text, it was probably given to Brezhnev on July 29 or 30 at Chierna on Tissa.

Dear Comrade: I understand that it is unusual to address you like this, but the situation itself in our country is abnormal. This is the specific reason for my writing to you. I am sure you will understand me. . . .

Party functioning at present is paralyzed to such an extent that we cannot stand further unfavorable developments by ourselves any longer. This was proved by the latest meeting of the Central Committee, where the letter of five fraternal parties was being discussed. This was the meeting when the plenary session of the Central Committee, because of outside pressure, was practically deprived of the right to sensible and independent actions.

This is why I address you, Comrade Brezhnev, with an appeal and request to provide fraternal help to our party and our people in repelling the forces that not only are guiding the process of democratization of the socialist society to crossroads, but in essence are creating serious danger for the life of socialism in the Czechoslovakian Socialist Republic. s\ Antonin Kapek

Soviet troops arrested Dubcek and other Czech leaders and took them to Moscow. They were returned, however, because the Czech people did not take kindly to this action and there was fear that a repetition of the debacle in Hungary with the attendant bloodshed might occur. Dubcek and the governmental leaders were forced to roll back most of the reforms achieved and leaders hostile to the Soviets were removed. As the year ended, one new reform was accomplished without opposition. A federal state was inaugurated consisting of three provinces, Slovakia, Bohemia, and Moravia, each having its own subordinate government. Dubcek was finally stripped of all vestiges of power in April 1969. As he left, he was made ambassador to Turkey.

We would now like to provide some excerpts from documents obtained in Oleg Sarin's research into Czech archives as described previously:

Ladislav Novak, former chief of staff of the President, Socialist Republic of Czechoslavakia:

On the night of August 20–21, there was a telephone call in my apartment: "The Russians have crossed the border!" I dialed the number of a house in a garden near Grad, the residence of the president, Ludwig Svoboda. He did not give me the chance to finish the sentence. He said, "I know. Go to Grad and stay at your office." The driver of my car as we drove to Grad told me of the tank columns on the roads, making other drivers blind with their headlights, as they made all the turns in the narrow streets as they approached Gradchany. In the early morning, Soviet tanks, self-propelled artillery, and armored personnel carriers were in the streets and many aircraft were in the air.

Near the gates of Grad, Soviet special forces troops stopped our car with the news: "Passage is forbidden. Only the platoon commander can give you a pass." We protested that the president was expected soon, to no avail. We decided to wait in a little street near Porohovy Bridge for about fifteen minutes, a place that was not filled with troops. We then proceeded along a path through the gardens to the president's house, where we ran into Soviet troops again. While we discussed the situation with these men, a Czech guard opened the gates from within and let us and the car inside. There we met Svoboda outside the house. He said: "At about midnight, (Soviet Ambassador) Chervenen paid me a visit and then Brezhnev called. It was hard to hear him because of the noise in the streets. I told him that there was gunfire in Prague with the arcs of tracer bullets visible from my window. Brezhnev replied that gunfire had not been planned and that he would investigate the situation."

I tried to determine from the Czech guard and the leaders of the Soviet unit how we could get the president into his office. The Soviet officer simply said that he was ordered to let nobody into the house.

Soon thereafter (after being allowed into the offices) at 8:00 A.M., there were new elements of the Soviet Army in old Prague, artillery guns and columns of combat vehicles. I wrote the draft of the president's first address to the people. Svoboda read the text over the telephone for broadcast over the radio. The speech was a call for the citizens to remain calm and not to offer any resistance. Since he was an old soldier who lived in camps in Russia during the war, the President knew only too well that any resistance was futile.

I insistently was calling the Soviet embassy to try to talk them into permitting us to go to Grad. An hour later I was informed by the embassy that the troops would be pullled back from the street near the Porohovy Bridge and that the President and his staff could come to the palace.

There were tanks and guns near the walls of Grad as Svoboda, the hero of the Soviet Union and the hero of Czechoslovakia, by himself was crossing an unusually quiet open space covered with granite. He walked with his grey head cast downward as he passed the Church of Saint Vit, the mausoleum of Czech kings. He continued his walk along the walls behind which foreign troops were clanging their mess kits.

The president's assistants began to call various central headquarters. They learned from the Central Committee that Dubcek, Smrkovsky, Krigal, Cernik, and Shimen were arrested by some unidentified persons who acted on behalf of "the workers' and peasants' revolutionary government." They were escorted away by Soviet soldiers carrying machine guns. I again called the Soviet embassy to tell the ambassador that the president wanted to go by automobile to the city to see for himself what was going on. The ambassador promised to ask General Pavlovsky, commander of allied troops. Meanwhile, the president's staff and his military office were preparing the cars. There was no call yet from the ambassador, so the assistants called again and two hours later he stated that General Pavlovsky would consult with Marshal Grechko in Moscow . . . .

Until recently, there was little known about what was happening in the Soviet embassy at the time of the invasion and its aftermath. In May 1992, Poland gave to the new Czechoslovakian government a secret document that had been sent coded from Masurov to Kosygin in the Kremlin. K. T. Masurov was a member of the Political Bureau of the CPSU Central Committee, the First Deputy of the Council of Ministers of the USSR. He was stationed in the embassy and had the power to make decisions as necessary and inform Moscow. We do not know how this classified document came into the hands of the Poles. It is one of the first reports sent from Prague to Moscow immediately after the city was occupied by Soviet troops. We will quote some excerpts of the message with the permission of the Commission of the Academy of Science of Czechoslovakia:

At the meeting, they were speaking about a group asking for help. . . . They stated that during the first night they would obtain fifty signatures and they would be able to acquire the signatures of a majority of the members of the Presidium. Deputy Chairman Strougal refused to sign. By nightfall they had obtained eighteen signatures after which they stopped in their attempt. They thought that in the morning with the troops present that they would receive other necessary signatures.*

Under leftist pressure the landings took place at night. They got in touch with Soviet leadership and an airfield was lighted as the landing place. The troops landed there went to Prague. Everything went all right. The same night Indra asked that GDR troops not be sent so it was necessary to change that plan in a thirty-minute time frame. The military action went off very well. Soviet tanks moved at night and arrived an hour and one-half earlier than planned. They were in Prague by 0600. No one welcomed the Soviet troops anywhere, but there was no protest either. This fact surprised foreign intelligence services . . . . Politically, everything looks unfavorable.

Mas[urov] and Ch[ervonenko] suggest that there should be another talk with D[ubchek] no later than the afternoon. In the evening it might be too late. Fighting may begin in Prague. What shall we do? D behaves camly. He says that we have made a great mistake.[30]

On August 22 at 11:00 A.M., Chervonenko and Pavlovsky arrived at Grad together with Czechoslovakian Minister of Defense Dsur to meet with President Svoboda. The president expressed surprise, because up to that time there had been no answer to his request to go by car to observe what was going on in Prague.

---

*This describes a group of plotters who agreed to sign the invitation for the invasion by Soviet and other troops. They were to become members of the "workers and peasants revolutionary government" that was to replace the lawful government that was overturned with the help of the foreign troops.

Pavlovsky smiled and said, "Comrade president, please understand that we are concerned for your security, and so far we have not received permission from Moscow."[31]

Svoboda said also that he was surprised by the order of Soviet General Velichko to impose commandant's hour (a kind of curfew) in Prague. This decision created tension and interfered with the night work of industrial enterprises. "It's a misunderstanding," Pavlovsky replied. "There is no such order." In fact, Velichko's order that was circulated in the city had been delivered by Czech agents to Svoboda in Grad. The document was handed to the Soviet officials. Pavlovsky read aloud:

> I request all citizens not to leave their homes except for urgent necessity from 2200 to 0500 daily. This is in the interest of the citizens themselves, especially the children and young people who should not be in streets and parks during these hours. . . . This is in effect from midnight of August 21, 1968. Until a special directive is issued, meetings and all kinds of social events are forbidden. . . . In connection with the current situation, I believe it necessary that the activities of radio and TV stations, newspapers, weeklies, and other publications should be coordinated with corresponding bodies. I address the citizens and all officials of Prague and middle Czechoslovakia with the insistent request to strictly observe the demands of this broadside. Commander of Allied Troops in Prague and Middle Czechoslovakia, Lt. Gen. (Guards) I. Velichko.

Pavlovsky smiled and said, "This is not an order. It is simply an announcement aimed at protecting the interests of the citizens." Svoboda responded that troops have occupied all the offices of constitutional bodies and under such a situation, state, government, and party officials cannot function normally. "We shall check that," promised Pavlovsky, "but I, Comrade President, taking advantage of this meeting, want to inform you that Comrade Brezhnev salutes you and hopes . . ." Not listening to the end of this statement, Svoboda asked why the Academy of Sciences had been occupied as well as Kurlov University. "It's a misunder-standing," said Pavlovsky, "but I am saying that personally, Com-rade Brezhnev salutes you."

Next, the president inquired about the arrest of Dubcek, Chernik, and Smrkovsky. The ambassador replied, "We would like to know this ourselves." Pavlovsky added, "Our army had nothing to do with this." Svoboda countered that from his information Dubcek and Smrkovsky had been taken from the headquarters building of the Central Committee of the Communist Party and Chernik from government offices in Soviet Army armored per-sonnel carriers. Who took them? Where were they taken? The So-viets promised to obtain answers.[32]

New documents that have been found recently in the archives of the Central Committee of the Communist Party of Czechoslo-vakia contain evidence that despite what has been commonly be-lieved, episodes of resistance and protest from the Soviet people against the intervention in Czechoslovakia were not at all un-common. Secret reports by the KGB, the Ministry for Protecting Public Order, the Soviet Army, and other state institutions were made to the Central Committee of the CPSU and personally to the Secretary General on this "dangerous situation." These are full of alarm because of the amount of indignation of various ele-ments of the Soviet population, particularly the intellectuals.

In considering the level of morality and decency in Soviet so-ciety at this time, we find its highest level displayed by the brave seven: K. Babitsky, L. Bogoraz, P. Litvinov, V. Feinberg, V. Delone, V. Dremlyuga, and N. Gorbanevskaya. These valiant few staged their protest at noon on August 25th in Red Square, Moscow. They sat in the most historic spot in Red Square with placards that read: HANDS OFF CZECHOSLOVAKIA and SHAME ON THE INVADERS. Only one of the seven was allowed to remain free af-ter their arrest, Natalia Gorbanevskaya. She wrote a letter to some European newspapers, a copy of which we found in the records of the CPSU Central Committee. It naturally was sur-pressed in this country. Here follow excerpts of this letter:

Almost immediately there was a whistle blowing and from
all sides state security agents in civilian clothes were running

at us. The Czechoslovakian delegation to the Kremlin was expected, the reason for the agents being there on duty. As they approached, they were shouting, "This is all the fault of the Jews. Injure these anti-Soviet elements." We were sitting together calmly and did not display any resistance. They tore our slogans from our hands.

Their beatings produced blood on Victor Feinberg's face and some of his teeth were knocked out. They beat Pavel Litvinov on the face with a heavy stick. I was holding the flag of Czechoslovakia. It was torn from my hands and was destroyed. They shouted at us: "Get out of here, you scoundrels," but we continued to sit where we were. In several minutes, some cars arrived and the other six were loaded into them. They excluded me because I had my three-month-old son with me, so I stayed in place for ten minutes longer. Later, they beat me in a car. . . . We are happy, my friends and I, that we managed to take part in that demonstration. At least for a while, we interrupted the flood of flagrant lies and timid silence. We succeeded in showing that not all the citizens of our country agreed with the law of force that was imposed on behalf of the Soviet people. We hope that the people of Czechoslovakia learned about what we did. We hope that both Czechs and Slovaks when they think of the Soviet people would not think only of the occupying forces, but also of us. This belief and hope give us strength.[33]

Sending the armed forces to Czechoslovakia created a dangerous situation in the center of Europe. The Central Committee, therefore, tried to obtain as much information as possible on what the attitudes of the people were and what could be done to put the invasion in a favorable light. This was obligatory, a kind of ritual. Those at the bottom of the hierarchy daily sought to reassure their masters that all these decisions were wise and well received by the populace. Mass meetings were held with carefully controlled speakers extolling the leadership in the Kremlin for their actions to uphold socialism. Dissidents were held up to ridicule and shouted down when they tried to speak. Dissident activity was pretty well controlled and was confined to those of the intelligensia. The facts of the invasion and subsequent actions of the Soviet Union and "fraternal" states were largely kept from the people. Individuals making public statements contrary to the policies of the government were arrested and confined.

We have examined the developments in Hungary and Czechoslovakia when Soviet troops were employed to crush the goals and aspirations of the peoples of these countries, who only wanted some freedom of decision in their own political futures. These forceful interferences in the internal affairs of these nations aroused a storm of indignation and protest all over the world. Relations with the West and particularly with the United States worsened, to the detriment of the economy of the USSR and the general welfare of the people. The next adventure similar to these did not take place for several years, but when it did, the results were catastrophic: the invasion of Afghanistan.

Chapter IX

The Afghan Syndrome

The Soviet military invasion of Afghanistan in 1979 was a great surprise, not only in the Soviet Union, but in the rest of the world. Up to that time, the professed policy of the Soviet Union toward Afghanistan was noninterference in the internal affairs of that country. We had emphasized the laudable ideas of friendship and cooperation in our dealings with the Afghans, only to throw away the advantages such a policy gained for us by a naked alternative of force for dubious reasons.

Relations between the USSR and Afghanistan have their roots in the generally advanced friendly policies of tsarist governments toward their southern neighbor. Russian authorities never permitted themselves to influence the Afghan people and government from a position of force, nor interfere unduly in their internal affairs. It was obvious that the only profitable way was to treat the Afghans justly and respect their sovereignty. Any other approach would just not work because of the love of the Afghan people for freedom. They had demonstrated this proclivity amply for all to see in their determination to oppose earlier British aggression against them. The British found to their dismay that the Afghans were a determined and resourceful foe, clearly a hard nut to crack.

We will not attempt a long history of the formation of Afghanistan because we have already accomplished this in our previous book, *The Afghan Syndrome, The Soviet Union's Vietnam,* published in 1993.[1] It is sufficient to say that Afghanistan has had a very rich culture over many centuries. It is an Islamic country, poor in many aspects but typical of other countries in the region. Its territory is rugged, mountainous, and uninviting. Its population consists of a melange of tribal peoples. The majority of Afghans are Pushtuns, about 9.5 million people. Second are the Tadzhiks, about 3 million. In addition, there are Uzbeks, Turkomen, Kirghiz, Nuristanis, Kazakhs, Baluch, and Arabs. About 90 percent of the population from age fifteen to sixty and 99 percent of the women are illiterate. Ethnic minorities are practically all illiterate. Throughout the years, the Pushtuns have had a privileged position, a situation that has triggered national disturbances and armed conflicts.

Afghanistan became unified and independent after a long fight against the rule of the great Moghuls and Safavids who had dominated the country in the sixteenth century. This occurred in 1747 after the death of the Iranian Shah Nadir and the subsequent collapse of his empire. The first centralized Afghan state can be called the Durrani (a Pushtun tribe) empire under Ahmad Shah. It persisted until 1773. His successors were less capable of preserving a centralized government and in 1818 the Durrani empire collapsed. Principalities were formed: Herat, Kanadar, Kabul, and Peshawar.

Kabul later became the center of a new reunification under Dost Muhammed (1826–1863). It was during this time that the country was subjected to the First Anglo-Afghan War, which ended with the catastrophic defeat of the British. The Second Afghan War lasted from 1878 to 1880, resulting again in British defeat. This was not an unqualified success for the Afghans, however, because the emir was forced to grant certain concessions to the British. Diplomatic relations were established through the British viceroy in India. In 1907, the British and Russians agreed to use the British government as mediator in tsarist relations with Afghanistan. At this time trade generally was with British India.

Afghanistan was an underdeveloped agrarian state with 90 percent of the population peasants and nomad herdsmen. Except for small workshops, there was almost no industry, so most manufactured goods were imported. There were no railroads or highways in the country. The main means of transportation were caravans of camels, used both internally and externally to move goods from one place to another.

The country since 1901 was an absolute monarchy under Emir Habibullah Khan. His relations with Britain were rocky. For example, he refused to recognize the Russian-British agreement of 1907 and to enter into trade agreements desired by Britain. His intransigence and the obvious fact that the country depended so much on Britain caused much dissatisfaction among many "young Afghans" who had been educated abroad, as well as among military officers, liberal landowners, and public officials. These dissidents strove for reforms in the political system that would place limits on the emir's authority, draft a constitution, and institute policies to help develop the country. The movement was influenced by the abortive revolution of 1905–1907 in Russia and revolutionary movements in India. The successful Russian revolution in 1917 that overthrew the tsar provided increased hope for the "young Afghans."

A strange development was that the emir's son, Amanullah Khan, joined the dissidents, and opposition surfaced from older members of society. Clearly Habibullah Khan's reign was in trouble. The Russian revolution changed the new government's attitudes toward Afghanistan and diplomatic delegations were sent from Moscow, but without much initial success. British presence in the surrounding countries caused consternation in the ranks of the "young Afghans" to the extent that they tried to murder the emir in 1918. This failed, with attendant repressions. They finally did assassinate Habibullah Khan on February 20, 1919.

He was replaced by Amanullah Khan, a victory for the "young Afghans." He immediately proclaimed full independence in all internal and external affairs. This produced another war with Britain that started with a massive invasion from India in May 1919. This was resisted fiercely by the Afghans, and after great losses on both sides, an armistice was signed on June 3, 1919. Between July 26 and August 8, 1919, British-Afghan talks took place in Rawalpindi, India. These ended with the signing of a preliminary peace treaty.

Soviet Russia immediately recognized the new Afghan government. Diplomatic ties were established and assistance was proffered to the new Afghan government. All treaties and accords that infringed on Afghanistani interests signed previously under tsarist governments, including the 1907 British-Russian agreement, were annulled. Amanullah Khan contacted the Russian leader, V. Lenin, expressing goodwill and asking for Russian friendship and aid.[2] Lenin reciprocated, sending a letter to Kabul in which he welcomed the intentions of the Afghans to establish friendly relations with Russia and suggested exchanging diplomatic missions.[3] Nicolay Bravin was sent to Kabul as the first Soviet diplomatic representative to Afghanistan. Bravin told the emir that the Soviets would provide many kinds of assistance, including arms, to Afghanistan. In late September 1919, an Afghan diplomatic mission went to Moscow as their part of the diplomatic exchange. The Afghan ambassador, Gen. Muhammed Wali Khan, headed the mission.

Following these exchanges of diplomats, Russian-Afghan relations improved progressively despite the fact that most Western countries did not follow the Soviet lead in recognizing the Amanullah Khan government. Nevertheless, a process of dramatic reforms began in Afghanistan in the early 1930s. These opened new paths for economic and political development. Practical steps called for legal privatization of land, reform in the tax system, and abolition of slavery and slave trading. Cottage industry was encouraged and road building was undertaken. In 1922, members of the old guard who opposed the reforms were deposed. The emir's close associates were sent into the provinces to ensure that his policies were carried out. Graft and bribery were prohibited. Much was accomplished in educating the people, and medical services were improved.

During this period, ties with the Soviets grew stronger although there was countervailing pressure from within the emir's close advisers to seek rapprochement with the British, who were trying to advance their traditional position. In the long run, these British attempts were fruitless and relations with Russia became stronger. A friendship treaty between the two countries was signed in Moscow on February 22, 1921. Financial aid to Afghanistan quickly followed. New and larger opportunities for cooperation between the two countries in economics, culture, and politics emerged.[4]

The new treaty and better relations with Russia resulted in improvements in relations between Afghanistan and other countries as well. This time period was one of rivalry between the Western powers and the new Soviet Union that naturally included the friendship between the Soviets and Afghans. Britain especially tried to interfere with these relations and in 1924 helped foment an antigovernmental rebellion in Afghanistan. This insurrection was quickly suppressed. On August 31, 1926, a new pact that called for neutrality and nonaggression between Afghanistan and the Soviet Union was signed in Paghman, near Kabul. This treaty was significant to both countries in that it formalized other accords having to do with the settlement of border disputes and other difficulties. The Soviet Union was clearly the winner in the competition for Afghanistan; Great Britain, the loser. A further manifestation to this fact was the heralded visit of Amanullah Khan to Moscow in May 1928, a historic event because this was the first visit of a head of state to the Soviet Union. The visit to Moscow was part of a tour by the emir to several European and Asian countries. Afghan importance in the world was strengthened significantly by the emir's trip.[5]

Trade between tsarist Russia and Afghanistan had been important to both countries, a fact that the new Soviet rulers recognized. In the early 1920s the volume of Soviet exports to Afghanistan was relatively small, but it increased each year and became more and more important to the northern provinces of Afghanistan. From 1925 to 1926 the structure of these exports began to change. Some new items appeared in small quantities that were not part of prerevolutionary business, such as cement, electrical and mechanical equipment, and farm machinery. Raw materials and various processed goods like hides were sent to the Soviet Union. Educational aid was provided by the Soviets, as well as various modernizations of the country such as the newly constructed telegraph line from Kushka to Herat to Kandahar to Kabul. This line, still in use today, ensured reliable communication from Kabul to major cities and to the Soviet Union and British India. From 1927 to 1928, Soviet specialists helped build a cotton processing plant and an electric power plant in Herat.

After returning home, Amanullah Khan began a series of further reforms with the aim of eliminating all remnants of feudalism from the country. Among many others, one reform was the reorganization and modernization of the army that included conscription instead of an all-volunteer force. To support this force, a special tax was assessed against all citizens. This and the impact of other reforms caused political opposition to increase against the emir. He deposed certain officials from whom he could not expect unqualified loyalty and support, but the broad organized resistance of the "young Afghans" arrayed against the emir became clear in the fall of 1928. Part of this was religious in nature, and other factions were after political power. The peasants felt the squeeze of the oppressive taxes. Finally, in November 1928, Pushtun tribes in the eastern provinces rebelled, the insurrection spreading rapidly with soldiers resisting their officers' authority. In January 1929 the emir's frontline troops were defeated and insurgent forces advanced on Kabul. Seeing no better course of action, the emir abdicated his throne. Finally, on January 15, the rebels occupied Kabul. Their leader, Bacha-i Saquo, was declared the emir three days later with the name Habibullah Khan Ghazi.

Having seized power, the new emir did his best to annul the previous reforms. The departments of Justice, Education, and Schools were closed, with judicial procedures relegated to religious courts. Industry slowed and foreign and internal trade was paralyzed with consequent price escalation. Bacha-i Saquo's regime was instantly unpopular with the people, and in November 1929 he was overthrown by an insurgent force headed by Muhammed Nadir Khan, who succeeded him as emir.

The Soviet Union did not interfere in either of the two insurrections, although the previous friendly relations between the two countries had been disrupted. After the second insurrection, relations between the two countries began to improve. The Nadir Khan government signed a trade agreement with the USSR, and during the great worldwide depression of the 1930s managed to expand trade exchanges between the two nations. Other help in the building of an infrastructure was forthcoming from the Soviet Union. Unfortunately, Soviet-Afghan relations during this period failed to achieve a stable political character. Part of this was due to the lack of stability in the internal life of the country. Another coup interrupted relations when Nadir Khan was assassinated. His son, Muhammad Zahir Shah, succeeded him. Despite all this, by 1939 the Soviet share of Afghan foreign trade had increased by twenty four percent.

In the late 1930s the international situation became very tense with Nazi Germany attempting to make inroads in Afghanistan and other adjacent countries at the expense of the Soviet Union. The Zahir Shah regime, while increasing ties with Germany and its allies, did not accede to any military-political obligations with the Nazis. After the outbreak of World War II in September 1939, Afghanistan formally declared its neutrality. German agents continued to foment trouble, trying to cause difficulties for the British in neighboring India and for the USSR in the north. Both the Soviets and the British appealed to the Afghan government to put a stop to this subversive activity. As a result, German and Italian nationals who were not part of the accredited diplomatic corps were expelled.

Afghanistan managed to escape any overt aggression from the Axis forces during World War II, although there is evidence to show that Hitler did indeed have ambitions to operate in this part of the Middle East and threaten the southern border of the USSR.

During the war the Afghans were supported by the Soviet Union as much as could be expected given the desperate straits the USSR was in all during that time. Afterward, the Soviet and Afghan governments found themselves agreeing to continue their friendly relations.

The war interfered with traditional trade and economic links, as it had with many other countries. Many of the Afghan agricultural products accumulated during the war were in warehouses. The sagging national industries were unable to cope with this surplus. Manufactured goods were in great demand, but imports of industrial machinery had stopped. Added to these problems was widespread corruption, a situation calling for democratic reform. This embraced all walks of life. The antigovernment opinions of a number of political opportunists became known through their newspapers and speeches. The groups they led either came from the "Awakened Youth" movement or formed around it. They were based largely on demands aimed at democratizing the political system and alleviating the people's low living standards. One of these factions was formed on the radical left by Nur Muhammed Taraki.

The election of the eighth National Assembly in April 1952 was the peak of the activities of the several groups opposing the government. Since none of the opposition candidates was elected as a deputy, their leaders arranged a mass demonstration in Kabul that protested the rigging of the election and the authorities' interference in the election campaign. This produced a wide-scale governmental purge against the opposition. Opposition groups were smashed and their newspapers silenced, their leaders arrested and jailed. Nur Muhammed Taraki was appointed press attaché at the Afghan embassy in Washington. We will see him again later in this story.

There were no apparent ties or contacts between the USSR and the Afghan opposition at this time, probably because relations with the existing government were considered highly important. There were various disputes concerning borders, use of water barriers, and relocation of islands that had to be reconciled. Relations with various Afghan governments continued to be friendly through the 1960s with the USSR being the chief trade partner for the Afghans.

As time went on, various different political movements came and went, but many of these had religious connotations. Political liberalization tended to weaken the powers of the Muslim theologians. Stern religious clerics had always backed the obsolete socioeconomic order, but they started to lose influence in politics. Younger religious leaders from middle-class towns began to develop the concept of a new Islam having teachings amenable to more modern life. They found that certain old Islamic dogma could be adapted to socialist doctrine; principles like justice and equality applied to both. Naturally, the older leaders resisted such reforms. The overall ideological struggle for the development of the country involved all sectors of the population.

In 1971, the economic crisis grew and widespread strikes led by the Afghanistan People's Democratic Party (PDPA) swept the country. These continued with attendant unrest through 1972. Reforms were urgently needed. On the night of July 16–17, 1973, a group of army officers headed by former premier Muhammed Daud staged a bloodless coup that deposed the king and proclaimed a republic. The Republican Central Committee became the supreme power body of the state, with most of the officers who had joined the coup becoming members of the committee.

The Soviet Union welcomed the new republic, believing that a country with a socialist orientation would be a better neighbor than a monarchy. Good bilateral relations continued with various agreements between the countries, strengthening existing ties. By the end of 1977, Soviet economic and technical assistance helped establish 115 industrial enterprises with 70 in operation and producing profits. Many Afghans were trained in technical skills in the Soviet Union.

The Daud government was determined to reform the country. It nationalized banks, introduced fixed working hours and paid leaves, improved education, and extended medical care. The most significant reform was land redistribution. This all took place during ripening social tensions which in turn put pressure on the country's foreign policy. While maintaining its economic and other ties with the USSR, Afghanistan sought to improve its relations with ruling circles of Iran and other Middle Eastern countries. Financial aid was sought from these oil-producing countries.

These overtures did not please the Soviet government. The Kremlin was even more concerned over repressions that the Daud government launched against the politicians of the left. Daud had concentrated most of the political power in his own hands, with the National Revolutionary Party (NRP) being the dominant political group. The PDPA was forced to go underground, and began to work actively to overthrow the Daud regime.

On April 27, 1978, the Afghan military produced still another coup, this from the left. President Daud was killed and his cabinet and other NRP leaders were arrested. The Revolutionary Council proclaimed the new Democratic Republic of Afghanistan (DRA), electing Nur Muhammed Taraki as chairman and prime minister. Babrak Karmal became his first deputy. The first decrees of this new government showed that they were determined to lead the country into socialism. Land reform was accelerated and a program to fight illiteracy was begun.

The people's enthusiasm for the new regime did not last long, however, largely because they did not support the DRA's program to downplay the religious institutions that were so important to the populace. The situation also deteriorated because of a lack of unity within the government. Continuous discord, executions, and arrests were similar to those perpetrated by Stalin in the Soviet Union in the 1930s. History seemed to be repeating itself.

The USSR watched in horror as the situation continued to deteriorate, meaning, of course, that the Kremlin could not control the politics of the country as it desired. Coupled to this was the fact that countries like the United States were developing interests in the region. The Kremlin viewed all this with alarm.

One thing was clear to the USSR. Afghanistan was not to be allowed to move from its socialist orientation. All possible was to be done to maintain the situation and policies in favor of the Soviet Union. Relations between the two countries had been generally cordial under both monarchial and republican governments. Never did the Soviet Union resort to military pressure to attempt to affect the overall situation between them. Despite this long history, in December 1979 Afghanistan fell victim to Soviet aggression.

Today we can speak with certainty about the responsibility of the USSR for its invasion of its southern neighbor. It is clear that the orders for military intervention were issued without considering moral norms and international law. Further, Soviet leadership took this dangerous course of action while underestimating the potential of the Afghan rebels, the Mujahidin (holy warriors). We are still paying for this gross miscalculation on the part of our then leadership. Brezhnev and his cronies erroneously assumed that Soviet soldiers would quickly suppress the rebels and at the same time strengthen the Afghan Army, permitting the Soviet troops to return to Mother Russia.

What actually occurred was that the invasion stirred up the country, letting divergent Afghan groups unite in a common endeavor against both the Soviets and the Afghan government as they announced a holy war. It thus became a holy cause for Afghans to oppose the resident Afghan government installed by the USSR. The irreconcilable opposition became a kind of state within the state. All antigovermental factions joined the war, not only against the PDPA regime, but especially against the invading Soviet strangers. Various separate opposition parties were organized. They had a common basis, however, because fundamentally they adhered strongly to the Islamic religion. One of their most influential leaders was the chief of the Islamic Party of Afghanistan (IPA), Gulbuddin Hikmatiyar.

After the April revolution, Hikmatiyar continued his pro-Islamic struggle against the new government. Soon, however, he and the new president, Amin, agreed to cease their confrontation and attempt to collaborate, with Hikmatiyar to become prime minister. Another coup intervened on December 27, and Amin was overthrown by Babrak Karmal. Amin is believed to have been killed by a Soviet Spetsnaz team cooperating with invading Soviet forces, the first of which was a paratrooper unit that landed at the Kabul airport. These were closely followed by other combined-arms units, including infantry, armor, and air assets. Gulbuddin Hikmatiyar then declared a holy war against the Karmal government.

The United States became a player in the Afghan fracas, but its initial aid to the rebel factions prior to 1979 was officially limited to humanitarian supplies such as medical equipment and medicine. This policy changed quickly, as the United States wanted to promote its influence in the area. This was especially important because of the new hostile regime established in Iran. Training camps and logistics bases were established in Pakistan to support the Mujahidin and military supplies and trainers were provided by the United States and other countries. Pakistani officers were in charge of the camps and supervised the training of the rebel troops. Many thousands of Afghan refugees were supported in these camps by various agencies of the United States and other countries.

In February 1980 the American press reported that the CIA had begun covert actions to supply the rebels with weapons. An Indian researcher, Bhabani Sen Gupta, wrote as follows:

> This was the major CIA operation since the one in Angola in 1975. The rebels fought with light field weapons of Soviet design shipped from Egypt and China. . . . Weapons were also delivered by Pakistan. It was reported that Iran also provided the rebels with numbers of weapons. Egypt announced that rebellious groups were trained in Egypt and then sent back with weapons. . . . China also sent arms by way of the Karakorum Highway.[6]

Before the Soviet invasion, the rebels were armed with outdated British rifles and Soviet AK-47 assault rifles. Afterward, they began to receive growing numbers of weapons such as 82mm mortars and 75mm recoilless guns, as well as Chinese versions of light antiaircraft weapons like the ZPY-2 and SAM-7 missiles and portable RPG-7 antitank grenade launchers from Egypt. In addition, millions of dollars worth of common items such as tents, clothing, shoes, blankets, and food were supplied. Much of American military aid was sent through other countries to the rebels because the United States could not deal directly because of moral considerations on the part of the hard-line Islamic leadership. They wanted no overt interference in the internal affairs of Afghanistan because they did not want to destroy the purity of the Islamic movement. For some reason, they did not seem to object to aid from China. And not all the Afghan resistance leaders agreed with this anti-Western stance of the fundamentalists.

As time went on, the Afghan rebel leadership became more liberal as to where they would obtain their military aid. In July 1986, President Ronald Reagan received a delegation of resistance leaders headed by B. Rabbani, who had been, with Hikmatiyar, among the most solid in their early desire to avoid the West. The delegation requested increased American aid and a supply of sophisticated air-defense weapon systems, the excellent hand-held Stinger guided missile. The delegation's requests were approved, including the Stinger. This was controversial within the American military establishment because the missile was such an effective weapon against most types of low-flying aircraft and could have been used for terrorist actions against civilian airliners. Further, the Americans feared the consequences of any of the missiles falling into Soviet hands. Therefore, this approval was extremely significant.

Combat actions in Afghanistan were extremely frustrating to the Soviet soldiers who had to operate there. The terrain and climate caused great discomfort and danger. Their fighting was against determined fanatics who were defending their homeland and were used to the geographical conditions there. This automatically put the Soviet soldiers and their officers at a grave disadvantage. It was a direct parallel to the difficulties the American armed forces had had previously in Vietnam, a lesson seemingly lost on the Soviet high command. Nothing encountered in Afghanistan by Soviet soldiers could be found within their previous experience or training. In Afghanistan they had to learn from bitter experience on a day-to-day basis in small doses, a process that necessarily took a long time.

Many soldiers were of Muslim origin, which caused divided loyalties. Initially, the Soviet government saw this as an advantage because it enabled the soldiers to establish friendly contacts with the populace. Being able to communicate with the locals was helpful, but as time went on this became a real problem with fraternization between Soviet soldiers and the Mujahidin occuring. A regular commerce began that included goods and narcotics. Eventually, individuals deserted to join the rebels. Later in the war, the bulk of the troops were non-Muslim. Whoever it was, the individual soldier was in a strange and inhospitable land far from friends, relatives, and the familiar comforts of home. Another anxiety was the fact that most of the officers and soldiers were badly trained conscripts, many of whom were not motivated to serve the country in this faraway place. We estimate that at least 90 percent of the young men who arrived at the training centers in Turkestan had not the slightest notion of how difficult military service in Afghanistan would be.

Another grave problem for these young soldiers was that in addition to their being far from home in dangerous surroundings, neither they nor their relatives in the Soviet Union could understand why they were risking their lives. Soldiers readily accept military service when they know that what they are doing is beneficial to their country. We know well the respect that soldiers' sacrifices generated in the hearts of our people during the Great Patriotic War, when the security of the nation was at stake. None of this was true in Afghanistan. For this reason it became a very hard war, similar to America's Vietnam experience.

Because they were line soldiers reacting to a guerrilla type of war, many adaptations had to be made in their normal way of operating in combat. In order to control the countryside as much as possible, outposts were established in the most difficult terrain. A division was assigned about 500 outposts along a line several hundred kilometers long. A regiment would have more than one hundred of these over 130 kilometers. The loneliness and boredom experienced in these remote sites were extremely detrimental to the morale of the soldiers who manned them. Conditions like these were kept from the Soviet media and the public. So this became a war held in secret.

Over time, training improved and different organizational structures were substituted for those units ill-suited to operations in the terrain of Afghanistan. For example, when the Fortieth Army was first assigned to Afghanistan, it was basically an armored organization, well conceived for operations on the Russian steppes or in central Germany. What was needed were light mobile formations, motorized infantry, not tank-heavy formations. So the heavy equipment was sent back home and infantry fighting vehicles, amphibious trucks, and light reconnaissance vehicles substituted for them. Tactical air landings came to be used effectively to dominate heights and block areas where enemy troops were trying to locate. Prior to this war, our European mentality had never designed training or devised plans to address this kind of mission. For months at a time, battalions and regiments had to be detached for this duty. Soldiers had to remain on dominant terrain, on heights far from each other, surrounded by the enemy. We can only imagine the personal problems they had individually and with each other. Squads of seven to twelve had to live in shelters built largely of materials at hand. They had their combat equipment and very little else.

Food, water, ammunition, firewood, and everything else the soldiers needed were delivered to them by truck or helicopter every two to four weeks. As with all soldiers, morale suffered when letters from home and loved ones came only after long delays. Detached from the realities of this service, as we are today, we wonder what they could have talked about and how they were able to exist like that for long days, weeks, months, and years. They did manage to survive and serve faithfully and accomplish the combat missions assigned them.

Since there were no railways in Afghanistan, practically all supplies for the troops and their combat operations were delivered by truck, with only a small amount by air. There were only two land routes: Termez–Kabul and Kushka–Kandahar, and these had to be protected from any rebel incursions. The enemy naturally knew this and concentrated their ambushes on these highways, both to deprive Soviet units of supplies and capture the goods for themselves. The situation was so bad that some 35 percent of the Soviet troops in Afghanistan were used to protect communications lines and outposts.

There were many parallels between this war in Afghanistan and the American experience in Vietnam. One principal similiarity was the fact that both the Viet Cong and the Afghan rebels used guerrilla tactics and strategy to pursue their war. In both cases, American and Soviet troops took a very long time to learn how to fight their opponents. The enemy's fundamental tactical principle was to avoid open actions with large Soviet regular forces, acting in small detachments that surprised their foes.

A good example of this was the Panjsher operation in April 1984. The rebels avoided defensive combat with Soviet and Afghan forces, withdrawing their troops from danger and sheltering them in the mountains. They kept small detachments in the area to ambush and reconnoiter. Soviet units eventually had to withdraw and the rebels returned safely to reoccupy their territory. In certain places their aim was to capture major administrative centers and occupy critical terrain. These operations were executed in provinces close to borders so that speedy reinforcement and retreat to safe havens were available. Set piece defensive fights occurred only in case of unexpected assaults with no possibility of retreat.

Like the Vietnamese, the Afghan rebels learned their guerrilla tactics from the teachings of Mao and the other Red Chinese leaders. They involved the entire populace in supporting them. To avoid losses from aviation and artillery, their detachments stayed dispersed, living among the local people and changing locations often.

In all cases, surprise was a principle of their operations, coupled with maneuver of independent forces. They could accomplish their missions because of their intelligence of Soviet operations planned against them. Being armed with light weapons and knowing the terrain intimately, they would mount an operation quickly and then disengage equally rapidly. They attacked Soviet troops as they were advancing to contact and most often when they were returning to base, when the Soviets were the least effective. They were adept at night fighting and infiltrating a few men into Soviet positions. They thus were able to occupy strong tactical positions and fire on awaking Soviet troops at dawn. They were also excellent snipers. For ambushes, they fully exploited the terrain, taking positions along a road at distances of about 200 meters, separated from one another by some 30 meters. When the Soviet vehicles entered the killing zone, fire was directed at vehicle drivers and commanders. Then they would fire at the trucks that carried personnel. Grenades and other antitank munitions were directed at armor escorting the convoy.

Raids were resorted to frequently with a great amount of planning used to ensure success. The rebels would gather a force of about thirty men and rehearse the proposed raid in terrain similar to the site. Usually raids were planned as night operations and had the objective of destroying ammunition, equipment, and supplies such as fuel. The men were designated as fire and maneuver elements and were well trained for their tasks. After completing their mission, the rebels would again disperse in small groups, melting into the wilderness.

As we have stated above, many Soviet troop movements and resupply operations were conducted by air. Late in the war, these air operations became more difficult to accomplish because of the presence of the American Stinger antiaircraft guided missile system. This shoulder-fired rocket was a heat seeker and was effective at relatively short ranges against both fixed- and rotary-winged aircraft. This caused the Soviet pilots to fly combat missions like strafing and bombing from altitudes that diminished their effectiveness. Logistics air missions sometimes had to be abandoned entirely, forcing troops and supplies to be moved over land with attendant danger from ambushes and delay.

We have provided an overview on the war in Afghanistan as seen from the eyes of informed observers. We watched with sorrow the approximate ten years of our involvement in that impoverished land and were appalled at the casualties incurred by our armed forces. The material above depicts the kind of enemy our troops had to face in the elusive guerrilla war waged against us. We hope the reader does not get the idea from the foregoing that Soviet arms there had no successes at all. At first this was the case, but as time went on, our commanders and planners did much better, gaining success through better tactics and training. But this was a war that we could never have won, regardless of the dedication, bravery, and skill of our forces. So what did we accomplish? What were the effects of our involvement?

Many Afghan citizens were killed or wounded, as well as many of our soldiers. Probably none of the Soviet leaders who made the decision to give military support to the People's Democratic Party of Afghanistan could have predicted the economic and moral damage their act was to inflict on the USSR itself. Some people today in our country try to justify this decision to intervene in 1979, feeling that we had to react favorably to the plea from "our Afghan class brothers" and thus prevent catastrophe. Such reasoning has prevented our leaders from becoming aware of the pain and suffering the Afghan people were experiencing. We had not learned lessons from our own history, particularly of the years of the Nazi invasion. An argument goes that if we had not entered as we did, the United States would have come there with their rockets. This idea is not sound because of the traditional Afghan desire for nonalignment. The Americans would have needed agreement on the part of the Afghans, an almost impossible situation because Afghanistan is not like Iran or Pakistan. The moment the Soviets entered the country was when the United States became involved heavily, not before.

The Afghan War placed a heavy burden on the Soviet economy and on its prestige in the world. Further, it caused the people of the USSR to mistrust their government. They became more aware of their problems because of this war. It is possible that had there been no Afghan war, there would have been no *perestroika* or *glasnost*, or such phenomena might have had to wait until the next century. Probably the first real breakthrough occurred when Mikhail Gorbachev had to tell the truth about the debacle in Afghanistan. We see the East-West rapprochement and in particular the drawing together of the Russian and American peoples as fallout of the Afghan involvement. The Soviet Union stood with the allied nations during the Persian Gulf crisis in 1991. Would that have happened without the lessons of Afghanistan? We think not.

So we can see that there were some positive results of the Afghan war, but does this mean that we condone it? Absolutely not. One of the worst effects of the war was what happened to the Soviet veterans. They were about eighteen years of age when they were thrown into the conflict. They were told that they would be fighting for the happiness of the Afghan people, but they soon realized that their opponents on the battlefield were also Afghans, ready to lay down their lives to defend their own cause. They were told that they were defending the homeland. Yet when they returned home they were ridiculed and advised to take off their medals. They fought with valor, but when they returned they were rewarded with indifference and injustice. The Afghan generation missed the time when they should have been in universities, improving themselves. For many it seems to them that the war has not ended. It followed them home, plaguing them as they sought to adjust to new lives. Let us hope that time will serve to heal the wounds of these unfortunate young men; that time will let them adjust to the modern society that is forming from the breakup of the USSR.

In the history of the Soviet Union, the Afghan War is the last military adventure out of a row of military adventures attempted by our leaders. Gradually, it is being forgotten by our and the world's people for a variety of reasons. The war was absolutely senseless; it was totally unjust; and it was hopeless. These three reasons, particularly the last one, are sufficient to erase it from the public memory. The minds of our people are being overloaded by new wars and other crises on the borders of Russia, in the old USSR territories. Because of unpredictable actions of politicians, today's bloody happenings overshadow the events of the Afghan War, even if they do not entirely wipe out all our collective memory. Can we now say that nothing else will happen? Of course not.

Ordinarily, any war is over the minute the combatants come to a peace agreement, sign the necessary documents, and the losers lay down their arms, as at the end of World War II. The winners savor the joy of victory as the defeated reflect on their bitter failure. The problem is that the Afghan War is not over yet. In this vicious war, there were no winners at the time of the Soviet pull-out, and there certainly are none now.

The Afghans were able to defend their independence at a tremendously high cost: a million casualties, expenditure of huge sums, and the ravaging of a land that still remains in ruins. The "holy war" against the infidels has developed into a civil war with brothers and previous allies fighting each other.

By comparison with the Afghans, Soviet losses were modest. The troops came to Afghanistan, fought their fight, and then withdrew, leaving chaos. But the moral damage was much more substantial. Here we do not mean the individual family tragedies where loved ones were lost. The lesson we must learn is that a shameless occupation of a neighboring country is extremely harmful and downright dangerous to any state and its citizens. Proved treachery is bound to be detrimental to the public consciousness.

From the beginning, the Afghan War was conceived in treachery because of the unilateral decision to send troops into a sovereign country, entirely contrary to international rules of civilized behavior. Added to this was the assassination of Comrade Amin, his family members, and guards. This betrayal of the Afghan people resulted in the betrayal of the Soviet people. The Soviet state was guilty of mortal sin against all who were sent to fight in Afghanistan. Today it will be difficult to find an "Afghan" veteran in Moscow or St. Petersburg who thinks that the war was just and righteous, or that the troops should not have been withdrawn. Their memories of their wounds and lost comrades, however, are sacred. The collective indifference among the population to their fate, both in Afghanistan and after their return, is and was another betrayal that is not only detrimental to them, but also to the nation itself. Even our men captured by the Afghans were betrayed. In a normal situation, their future would have been an uncompromising condition of the troops' withdrawal from the combat area. Yes, the Afghan War is not over.

We will see in Chapter X that arms exports were a real factor of Soviet policy and that the story of these belongs in this book. We will see that this is a very seductive business that may prove unfortunate in the future.

Chapter X

Arms Export—An Explosive Factor

Soviet military cooperation with other countries was not confined to the sending of military specialists, advisers, and troop units with their own weaponry and military equipment. A significant part of this cooperation was the export of arms all over the globe. Frequently this also meant the dispatch of service personnel and instructors to train the recipients in the Soviet-produced equipment. This military hardware took many forms and was used as a rule by "friendly regimes" to strengthen their power and intimidate and suppress opposition groups, as well as in combat that broke out internally or between one country and its neighbor.

During the last five years of its existence, the Soviet Union exported arms and military equipment worth nearly 56.7 billion rubles. In 1990 the monetary figure was 9.7 billion rubles. Military aid given by the Soviet Union in this same five-year period amounted to 8.5 billion rubles.[1]

This arms business conducted by the Soviet Union was not unique in the world. Many other countries have been selling arms or providing them as aid to allies free of charge. The United

States, Britain, and France immediately come to mind. They have exported arms and continue to do so, feeling that such activities are in their national interest. The difference is that these other countries have not suffered economically by these sales and grants. A big difference between the arms trade engaged in by the United States and that of the Soviet Union is that some 75 percent of U.S. arms exports go to industrially developed countries or rich states like Saudi Arabia, whereas the USSR sent its arms to the then socialist bloc countries and developing countries, receiving no advantages whatsoever from the shipments.[2] The debt owed to the Soviet government on November 1, 1991 by these states was 85.8 billion rubles. There is, of course, no prospect that this debt, or even a small part of it, will ever be paid.

The major debtor countries are those that were considered "fraternal" countries until recently. These include Cuba, which owes 15.5 billion rubles; Mongolia—9.5 billion; Vietnam—9.1 billion; Poland—4 billion; and North Korea—2.2 billion. The total debt of these and other socialist allies of the USSR comes to 43.8 billion rubles.

Developing and other countries, too, are among these debtor nations. For example, India owes 8.9 billion rubles; Syria—6.7 billion; Iraq—3.8 billion; Afghanistan—3 billion; Ethiopia—2.9 billion; Algeria—2.5 billion; Angola—2 billion; People's Democratic Republic of Yemen—1.8 billion; Libya—1.7 billion; Egypt—1.7 billion; and Nicaragua—0.9 billion. The total for these and others is 42 billion rubles. There can be no dispute that the USSR incurred tremendous lossses in these foreign trade transactions.[3]

Another grave problem connected with our military aid arose on October 2, 1990, when the army of the former German Democratic Republic ceased to exist. The government of the Federal Republic of Germany was left with the enormous problem of what to do with the Soviet-manufactured equipment and weapons sent to the former East Germany. This amounted to a staggering total of 3,032 T-72 and T-62 tanks, 5,744 armored troop carriers, 2,140 artillery pieces, 400 warplanes, 1.2 million rifles, and more than 300,000 tons of ammunition. What was united Germany to do with all this armament, particularly when the most important threat suddenly became no threat at all? To whom might it sell the 250 million cartridges for the 400,000 Kalashnikov assault rifles or the rifles themselves? To whom should it offer the 24 supersonic all-weather MiG-29 fighter-interceptors? Who would need 65 MiG-23s, 251 MiG-21s, 54 Su-22 bombers, 165 surface-to-air missiles, and one million liters of jet fuel? And there were thousands of trucks, troop carriers, jeeps, field kitchens, pontoon bridges, and other military equipage. Should all this be destroyed? If so, this would be a horribly costly undertaking. It takes about 300 man-hours to dismantle a single T-72 tank, costing about 32,000 marks. [4]

Today, a T-72 tank is worth $1.5 million on the world market and a MiG-29 can fetch $30 million. A Kalashnikov assault rifle costs $1,000 on the black market. It is selling well in Africa, Asia, and the Middle East.

The sale of both new and used Soviet-made military hardware and weaponry has commenced at reduced prices to anyone who would buy them. The well-known Makarov pistol was sold for ten marks each, field glasses for 120 marks, and a Kalashnikov for 180 marks.

All the equipment and other property of the former East Germany that had been delivered by the USSR over forty-five years was estimated to be worth about 90 million marks and was sold off in some six months time. Having made profits from the sale, the German government made a generous gesture and undertook to pay 12 billion marks to Russia and other countries of the confederation by the end of 1994. Out of this sum, 7.8 billion will be spent toward building some 380 thousand apartments (4 million square meters of living space) for a like number of former Soviet servicemen. We should probably be grateful for this, considering that many other former friends owe billions of rubles for arms delivered to them.

It is absolutely clear to us, therefore, that by taking part in other people's wars and by fighting for interests that were alien to the Soviet people, the Soviet military-industrial complex brought the country's economy to ruin. It rendered senseless the very idea of the "necessity of defense."

Perestroika and the reforms carried out under the leadership of Mikhail Gorbachev, Boris Yeltsin, and the other leaders of the independent nations are designed to switch the defense industries to the production of civilian goods. Steps have been under way in all the republics to reduce arms production and the numbers of troops under arms. Quite obviously, Russian troops will not be traveling the globe as advisers to other countries. So far, unfortunately, the conversion of production is proceeding slowly, too slowly in our opinion, because of the resistance of conservative forces in the several governments.

In April 1991 the US Secretary of Defense, Dick Cheney, visited Moscow. He met with members of the USSR Supreme Soviet and told them something unknown to them: that in 1989, the United States manufactured twelve ballistic missiles, while the Soviet Union was making 140. Nobody has disputed or disproved these figures. The ballistic missiles described by Cheney are much more expensive than the SS-20s that have been destroyed. Certain Russian citizens continue to be proud of these missiles despite the fact that there are few goods in our shops and that many families are living in poverty. Cheney also disclosed another piece of information: that Soviet scientists were working on as many as four new types of missiles. This news again elicited no comments in the country.

We know too little about how the former Soviet arms can be used today and how they were used in the past. Take Iraq, for example. Practically the entire Iraqi military establishment was equipped with Soviet arms at the time of the Gulf War. Many buildings and other installations were protected by Soviet air-defense systems such as the SAM-2, *Osa,* and *Kvadrat.* Other such systems were available. But these systems were generally ineffective against the coalition fighters and bombers. Why? In our opinion, the reason is that the Iraqis simply did not know how to use the equipment by themselves. Our technicians were not available because many were sent out of the country by their commanders, and others refused to serve the regime of Saddam Hussein. In some cases the equipment worked as designed, such as the hits on the two B-52 bombers operating at low altitudes. In all, according to our information, the coalition forces lost 68 planes and 29 helicopters, figures somewhat higher than published in the press.

Anyone who had followed events in the Persian Gulf War

would have learned quickly that the Iraqis used the Scud surface-to-surface missile (SSM). Despite counteraction on the part of the multinational forces, some of these SSMs reached targets in Israel and Saudi Arabia. It is fortunate for all concerned that the warheads did not contain chemical charges as many had feared. But the fact that the missiles, armed with conventional warheads, did hit targets, aroused apprehension, not only in Israel and Saudi Arabia but in Syria and Egypt also. It was considered possible that Egypt and Syria might retaliate if Israel took offensive actions against Iraq. But Israel, having missiles available similar to the Scud, wisely refrained from taking any action. So an escalation of the conflict was averted.

The Middle East is not the only region where longstanding disputes smolder and from time to time flare up and where opposing sides possess SSMs capable of reaching targets hundreds of kilometers away. Other of these essentially third world countries desire to obtain or develop such missiles for themselves. Some of these countries are not signatories to the Treaty on the Nonproliferation of Nuclear Weapons, causing concern to the rest of the world. This, then, is a problem whose solution calls for energetic multilateral action accompanied by appropriate arms limitation measures. The type of measure we wish to see implemented would be similar to the statement on nonproliferation signed between the Soviet Union and the United States in 1990. It stated that both sides support the aims of the control mechanism on the spread of rocket technology. It calls for all nations to observe the basic spirit of the declaration. The two countries were ready to enter into bilateral and multilateral dialogue on the subject and continue to work for more strict international control over the spread of missile and rocket technology. This could be similar to the body already in place to monitor nuclear weapons proliferation.

An analysis of the practices of developed countries in the business of arms sales shows that already there are accepted principles regarding arms deliveries. Therefore, the United States government is permitted by law to sell arms only for purposes that accord with the United Nations Charter. Similar limitations are being considered on the sale of sophisticated weapons systems to developing countries. Each year the United States president sends to Congress a detailed report on planned arms exports. For each major arms sale contract, a separate report is prepared that includes an assessment of the arms sale on the stability and other considerations of the area and disarmament negotiations in general.

Although the experience of other countries is different, the sale of Soviet arms abroad was not carried out through the USSR Defense Ministry, but through other governmental agencies. The entire income from the arms trade went into the state coffers, with no single organization gaining any benefit. In Egypt, on the other hand, profits from the business stay with the military. Clearly Russia and the United States have joint responsibilities to try to control the arms trade, in conjunction with other United Nations member states.

The Soviet leadership of the past always used weapons sales as a way of determining political advantage. Economic benefits or improvements in living standards were always of secondary value. Today, the new Russia is not involved with sales or donations of military hardware to "friendly" countries as happened before, but this does not mean that we are not beset with problems from the presence of many, many weapons in our midst. Weaponry from the Soviet period was and is at the disposal of sides in local conflicts between former republics of the old USSR, such as Armenia and Azerbijan and Georgia and Abhasia.

Georgian leader Eduard Shevardnadze stated on September 29, 1993, after Sukhumi had been occupied by Abhasian combat detachments that ". . . this operation has been planned in the Russian military headquarters and was implemented with the help of Russian weapons and the immediate participation of Russian military specialists."[5]

On the night of October 3–4, 1993, Russian archeologist Mikhail Dem'yanov was interviewed on Georgian TV after being taken prisoner in hostilities near Sukhumi. He admitted that he had been transporting weaponry to Abhasia, but not all of it had been paid for in cash; that some shipments were in the form of "aid." He mentioned leading personages in the Russian military-industrial complex as people who had coordinated these shipments. He also disclosed the fact that Russian military officers and enlisted men had participated in combat directly on the side of the Abhasians. In particular, they served as members of SAM launcher crews that had shot down Georgian aircraft. Other such Russian personnel served as pilots and tank crewmen. He added that the Pskov Airborne Division after its withdrawal left its basic load of weapons to the Abhasians gratis.[6]

For many years the Soviet Union provided arms and equipment to many countries all over the world. In no cases that are apparent to us did these shipments serve to alleviate the suffering of the peoples of these countries nor to improve their standard of living. Instead, Soviet bullets and other munitions have caused death to many thousands of people and destruction of their homes and other facilities. Furthermore, these armaments caused political instability in many places in the world as these "friendly" nations sought to influence their neighbors or even export their ideology to distant places; Cuban operations in Angola are a good example of this. As we have seen in this book, the military actions of the Soviet Union throughout the world were designed to push the cause of international socialism, with the USSR the fiddler playing the tune for all the dancers. And we have witnessed the utter destruction of the socialist system practically everywhere, with only a couple of pathetic examples like Cuba and Korea still adhering to the Marxist line. Arms shipments were a very expensive concomitant of Soviet meddling in the nations of the world that the peoples of the old union are only now facing. We do wonder a little, however, when we read reports in the August 1994 issue of *Armed Forces Journal International* that the current Russian government has agreed with Kuwait to supply this tiny country with the S-300V antitactical ballistic missile and to sell some 176 Igla-1M man-portable antiaircraft missiles to Brazil (similar to the American Stinger described in Chapter IX). Despite these indications to the contrary, as loyal Russians, we can only hope that this legacy can be assigned to the dustbin of history in short order.

Conclusion

The entire history of the Soviet Union seems to be rooted in the many wars in which it fought over the seventy years of its existence. These wars or other military actions did not differ much from the actions of the tsars when they were attempting to expand the Russian empire. The only real difference is that our Communist masters took the place of the tsars, with a similar ambition in mind. But the tsars, or actually anybody else, could not be compared to the Communist Party leaders in their craft, cunning, cruelty, and adventurism and to their huge appetite for mischief where the export of "socialist revolution" was concerned.

They adhered to the Marxist-Leninist philosophy of a "world revolution" in favor of socialism/Communism, and were fanatically striving toward this goal. This final ambition was formulated by Vladimir Ilich Lenin even before the Communists took power in Russia. In his words, they desired "the United States of the world in the form of a state structure that we associate with Socialism."[1] After the Bolsheviks took power in 1918, Lenin made some more precise declarations on the form that political arrangements would take in the future. In his report at the Eighth Congress of the Communist Party in 1919, Lenin announced that the party was determined to create the "World Soviet Republic."[2]

The essence of Lenin"s program was to unify all nations of the world into one super Soviet empire to include all colonies. These would be merged into one international hybrid of Communist humanity. To start this experiment, the Bolsheviks chose Russia, which they turned into the Union of Soviet Socialist Republics. In so doing, they attempted to transform more than one-hundred separate nationalities into one nation, later to consist of the "Soviet people."

But this was not accomplished by a single bold strike. Rather, it occurred step by step. They used deception by declaring the right of the separate nations for self-determination, but then employed force to achieve their aim. Being deceived by the Bolsheviks, many non-Russian peoples began in 1918 to assert their independence and announce that they would no longer be parts of Russia. Short-lived states were created such as Ukraine, Byelorussia, Lithuania, Latvia, Estonia, Turkestan, Tataro Bashkiria, North Caucasus, Georgia, Armenia, and Azerbijan. All these were suppressed and incorporated against their will into the USSR after bloodshed and travail. They were subordinated to the single Central Committee of the Communist Party of the Soviet Union (CPSU), which set up similar governing authorities in all the republics. Elections were held with only the single candidates proposed by the Party throughout the country, with voters able to say only "yes" or "no" to a particular slate. Under a system like this there is no wonder that any political action of the CPSU, or, more correctly, of leaders like Lenin, Stalin, or Brezhnev, was approved overwhelmingly by the dominated public.

On only one occasion did the USSR suffer from external aggression, when in 1941 it was invaded by Hitler's Nazi hordes. In all other cases the wars and other military actions were foreign, waged against foreign nations on foreign territories. And we must remember that the Soviet-German war was to a great extent provoked by Stalin and his team, as we have described elsewhere in this book. Not only did the Soviet people suffer great privation and horrible casualties, but Stalin's expansionist policy contrived to join a great portion of Western Europe to the Soviet empire and forge solid power bases in Asia. Stalin had seven million combat-ready soldiers in his army, equipped with the most modern weapons available to threaten the world with new military actions. Humanity was jeopardized in a deadly manner by this monster, especially after it had obtained nuclear weapons.

The Stalin era contained the most bloody and aggressive years in Soviet history. If Lenin created a theoretical basis for Soviet expansionism, Stalin implemented it as completely as could have been desired. In the years of Stalin's dictatorship, the Soviet empire was enlarged and expanded to threatening dimensions, even before the onset of World War II. Taking advantage of the revolution in Spain, Stalin sent great resources in armaments and men there with the hope that Spanish Communists would prevail and establish a pro-Soviet regime. The plan failed.

Next he provoked a war with little Finland, in the hope of territorial acquisition and political dominance. Regular units were employed, supported by aviation, artillery, armor, and all other kinds of military force. The Red Army was badly led and suffered enormous losses in the horrible winter conditions for which it had not been trained. It had to retreat and regroup, but eventually forced a peace treaty in which the Soviet Union gained a small part of Finnish territory.

The secret pact between the Soviet Molotov and the German Ribbentrop was a logical marriage between the two bloody dictators, Stalin and Hitler. It gave them a green light in occupying foreign territories and unleashing the terrors of the Second World War. In a few short years Hitler invaded the Soviet Union, the results of which are well known. The victorious Stalin was able to establish pro-Soviet regimes in countries like Poland, Hungary, and East Germany, setting up the Warsaw Pact. But he was not content with these gains in Europe. His neoglobalism embraced the Asian continent. The war in Korea, during which American and Soviet pilots opposed one another for the first time, was the last military exploit of the generalissimo.

Stalin's military adventures were conducted in an atmosphere of fierce terror among the peoples of the Soviet Union. Hitler is said to have exterminated some six million Jews and other "undesirables," of whom only about 300,000 were German citizens. Stalin was responsible for killing, according to the calculations of Professor I. A. Kurganov, about 66 million Soviet citizens during his bloody reign, a staggering number.[3] Again it is no wonder that one cannot speak of any protests by the Soviet public.

During the years after Stalin's death, under Khrushchev and Brezhnev, the scale of reprisals was reduced, but it was still dangerous to express one's opinion that did not coincide with the party line. Punishments included being expelled from the CPSU, losing one's job, general condemnation in the press or radio, and/or being banished to some distant region. For example, Academician Sakharov was sent to Nizhni Novgorod under special supervision for his opposition in print and speech to the despotic character of the Soviet regime and its participation in foreign wars. World Communist domination continued to be the goal of all the leaders after Stalin. Khrushchev blessed armed participation in the Middle Eastern conflicts and provoked the crisis in the Caribbean with the United States.

Brezhnev channeled lavish support to North Vietnam, sending them weapons and Soviet personnel, thus helping to expand the war between the two Vietnamese states. He obviously hoped for enforced Communist unification under the rule of Ho Chi Minh, a true Leninist and friend of the USSR. It was Brezhnev who sent the Red Army to Afghanistan, hoping seriously to expand the influence of the USSR in this part of the Middle East. A bloody ten years of hard war brought grief and destruction to Afghanistan and cost thousands of lives to both sides. In addition, it brought shame to the Soviet Union and our armed forces.

Mikhail Gorbachev was the first Soviet leader to condemn this aggression against its southern neighbor. But he still did not speak against the expansionist policy of his predecessors, their strategic goal of "saving" humanity by making a Communist world. Moreover, Gorbachev voiced his philosophy of global *perestroika,* a philosophy rather closely connected with the ideals and actions of the past. He began by expressing his historic mission in the title of his book, *Perestroika and New Thinking for our Country and the World*. He concluded the book with these words: "Today the entire world needs *perestroika* . . . qualitative changes. . . . We have embarked in this direction and call upon other peoples and nations to do the same."[4]

But here we address the fundamental question. Why should the prosperous United States and other nations of the world want to follow the example of Gorbachev's *perestroika*, which occurred to save the USSR from social and economic collapse? Gorbachev cited theoretical bases for his position. In his report devoted to the seventieth anniversary of the October revolution, he stated: "*Perestroika* is the continuation of the October revolution of 1917. . . . Today we see that humanity is not doomed to living eternally the way it lived before October 1917. . . . Socialism shows humanity the way to the future."[5]

We can only grimace at the thought that this nation that for over seventy years has been plagued by poverty is going to show the rest of humanity the "way to the future." But these were the words of the last Soviet leader of the nation and the Party. He could not give up these outdated ideas either. He does deserve credit for his policy of *glasnost* which did much good to thaw international relations. He concluded important treaties with other countries and enabled the United States and coalition forces to conclude the Gulf War successfully without Soviet interference. But he was guilty of increasing military expenditures and continuing to keep huge military contingents in the bloc countries of Eastern Europe. He is responsible for starting heated military conflicts between Azerbijan and Armenia and between Georgia and Abhasia after the collapse of the political structure of the Soviet Union.

At the time of this writing, with Boris Yeltsin in power, Russian weapons are appearing in the hands of the fighting factions in various parts of the former territories of the USSR. National, often ethnic, conflicts are tending to grow into regional wars with covert or overt participation of Russian troops possible.

This, of course, is different from the old military actions of the USSR, but Russian troops continuing to be stationed in various of the newly independent countries remains highly risky for Russian foreign policy. These same troop units are being torn apart by criminal activity such as selling government supplies on the black market, including weapons and ammunition. Today we are hearing reports of black market trade in highly dangerous commodities like weapons-grade plutonium. Russian officials deny any loss of this material, but it must come from someplace. The situation is directly connected to the heavy and difficult socioeconomic climate in Russia, with daily zigzags in legal and executive powers.

These local conflicts in the former Soviet Union, where Russian soldiers are engaged on one side or the other, are echoes of the previous policy of the rulers of the USSR. This is a heavy political burden that the people of all these countries, although liberated from the Soviet yoke, will have to bear on their shoulders for many years to come. As we write, war is still being conducted both in reality and as in a bad dream in Georgia, Nadorny, Karabash, Bosnia, and Chechnya. Having discarded the lessons of the Afghan war and other alien wars, Russian leadership has unleashed another war on the pretext of fighting the criminal element in the Republic of Chechnya. An enormous military force with artillery, armor, and air support has been engaged in bloody repression against that tiny country. This force is burning down villages and towns with the only purpose being the defeat of one man, ex-General Dudaev, who was elected president by Chechnya's citizens. Fresh blood, new victims, more tragedies. The stupidity of this war is evident. The arrogance of the political leadership is indisputable.

The good thing is that we and even prominent politicians can publicize our opinions without fear of retribution. Unlike what happened to Sakharov when he opposed the Afghan adventure, Igor Gaydar, the former prime minister now leading the party called "the Choice of Russia," has spoken clearly against the war in Chechnya, openly denouncing it. He runs no risk of being jailed or deposed by the ruling officials. Other statements like his and ours are being heard with greater frequency today. Alas, hardly anyone pays attention to them.

Direct comparisons with the past are erroneous and unjust. No one should liken the present situation with that prevailing in the 1920s and 1930s, when the Stalinist tyranny was at its height, or what went on during the cold war period of global confrontation. Today there is no iron curtain or mysterious knocks on the door at night by the KGB. Today the people of Russia and the other Eastern countries are devoted to world peace and democratic principles. We have come a long way, but still have a longer way to go. The extent of reforms in Russia, the political heir to the USSR, will guide the other former Soviet countries in their own reforms. We must be careful in governing Russia because of its geopolitical situation, its huge territory, and its vast resources, as well as its large armed forces and nuclear arms. We must ensure that it is never thrown back to dictatorship because of presently unsolved social problems.

The leaders of the major industrial countries recognize the necessity of providing aid to Russia and the other smaller members of the former Soviet Union. In the dramatic days of 1993, when President Boris Yeltsin took drastic steps to resolve the crisis between the executive and legislative branches of the government, foreign leaders saw his actions as necessary and correct. Some of the aid will be used in destroying long-range guided missiles and nuclear warheads, certainly an excellent goal toward securing world peace.

We see continued support from the United States and other industrial nations as essential in ensuring internal tranquility within the former Soviet countries as well as in the world itself. It is important, particularly, that Russia occupy a dignified position among the civilized nations of the world, becoming the leader needed in this part of Europe and Asia. That is why we must resist adventures like the war in Chechnya.

In this book we have presented the story of Soviet interference in the affairs of other, usually weaker, countries. We hope it will be useful to readers worldwide in providing a window on the past. History is useful in helping prevent unfortunate consequences in the future.

Notes

Foreword

1. Pokrovsky, M. N. (1886–1932) Soviet historian, Communist Party and state figure, Academician of the Academy of Sciences of the USSR, participant in the 1917 Revolution, after 1918 Deputy People's Commissar of Education, dean of the Communist Academy of the Institute of Red Professors.

2. M. N. Pokrovsky, *Russian History, Condensed Version* (Moscow: USSR State Printing House, 1920).

3. USSR Constitution, Politisdat, 1924, p. 3.

Chapter I

1. Archive of the Russian Federation Foreign Policy, 048/14-b, Vol. 8, p. 195.

2. *History of the Motherland*, Russian Academy of Sciences, N. 3 (1990), p. 86.

3. D. Boffa, *History of the Soviet Union*, Vol. 1 (Moscow: USSR State Publishing House), p. 446.

4. Archive of the Russian Federation Foreign Policy, 146/2, Vol. 42, p. 1.

5. R. F. Meretskov, *Serving the People, a Memoir* (Moscow: USSR State Publishing House, 1989), pp. 147–48.

6. Helmut Clotz, *Lessons of the Civil War in Spain* (Berlin: Military Publishing House, 1938), p. 11.

7. Ibid., p. 12.

8. *War and Revolution in Spain, 1936–1939*, Vol. 1 (Moscow: USSR State Printing House, 1968), p. 422.

9. Quotation from D. P. Pritziker, *Heroic Deeds of the Spanish Republic, 1936-1939* (Moscow: USSR State Printing House, 1962), p. 241.

10. Archive of the Military-Scientific Society, Central Headquarters of the Soviet Army, Vol. 36, p. 19. Grusdev was a deputy to the commander of the International Tank Regiment in 1937.

11. Central Archive of the USSR Defense Ministry, 44/A/1231, Vol. 27, p. 11.

12. Archive of the Military-Scientific Society, Vol. 36, p. 112. In

1937–38, Vetrov was deputy commander of the International Tank Regiment.

Chapter II

1. *Soviet Encyclopedic Dictionary* (Moscow: USSR State Printing House, 1987), p. 1235.

2. N. S. Khruschev, *Memoirs: Questions of History* (Moscow: State Political Publishing House, 1990), p. 100.

3. M. I. Semiryaga, *Secrets of Stalin's Diplomacy,* (Moscow: State Political Publishing House, 1992), p. 169.

4. Ibid., p. 171.

5. Soviet Foreign Policy Official Documents, Vol IV, p. 463.

6. *Izvestia,* May 24, 1939.

7. Russian State Military Archive, 42/44, Vol. 7658, p. 11.

8. Ibid., 28/1364, Vol. 16-a, p. 48.

9. Soviet Foreign Policy Official Documents, Vol. IV, pp. 494–96.

10. Minutes of meeting, Main Military Council (STAVKA), April 17, 1940, pp. 618–22.

11. Central Archive of the USSR Defense Ministry, 2/75593, Vol. 7, pp. 239–66.

12. Russian State Military History Archive, 28/1364, Vol. 16-a, p. 48.

13. Ibid, p. 50.

Chapter III

1. Minutes of the Eighteenth Congress of the CPSU, Moscow, 1939, p. 26.

2. *History of the Great Patriotic War, 1941–1945* (Moscow: USSR State Printing House, 1983), pp. 175–76.

3. Archive of the German Foreign Affairs Ministry: German-Soviet Relations, 1939–1940. U.S. State Department translation, 1948, p. 21.

4. Ibid., p. 16.

5. CPSU Central Committee Closed Papers N. 34 (1987), 3/64/675-a on 26 pages, Top Secret, K Series, Special Dossier, Vol. N 46-G9 A/2g/4-1, Soviet-German Treaty 1939. Directions on file: Must be kept in closed envelope. By direction of the General

Department of the Central Committee of the CPSU, Comrade V. I. Boldin. Do not open package without his permission.

6. Minutes, Second Congress of the People's Deputies of the USSR, December 12–14, 1989, Vol. IV, Moscow 1990, pp. 256–79, 378–381.

7. Ibid., pp. 612–14.

Chapter IV

1. USSR Central State Historic Archive, 11/87, Vol. 203, p. 7.

2. USSR Central State Archive of the October Revolution and Socialist Construction of the USSR, 12/72, Vol. 211, p. 90. T. F. Shtykov (1907–1964) was a colonel-general and USSR ambassador to North Korea.

3. Russian Foreign Affairs Ministry Archive, 245/4542, Vol. 16, pp. 86–88.

4. USSR Central State Historic Archive, p. 92.

5. Ibid., p. 93.

6. Ibid., p. 96.

7. *Soviet Military Encyclopedia* (Moscow: Military Publishing House, 1983), p. 300.

8. USSR Central State Historic Archive, p. 92.

9. USSR Central Military Historic Archive, 14/40, Vol. 116, p. 18.

10. Ibid., p. 26.

11. Ibid., p. 28.

12. USSR Military Intelligence Department (GRU) Archive, 369/6708, Vol. 5, p. 11–12.

13. Central State Archive of the Soviet Army (CSASA), 2676/6, Vol. 82, p. 16.

14. Central State Military Archive, 14/40 Vol. 116, pp. 10–11.

15. Central Archive of the USSR Defense Ministry (Report of Col. Gen. Pytor Batisky), N0124, May 15, 1950, 421/2451, Vol. 14, p. 45.

16. Russian Foreign Affairs Ministry Archive, 876/1141, Vol. 45, pp. 75–76.

17. Central Archive of the USSR Defense Ministry, 765/56745, Vol. 789, p. 56.

18. Ibid., 217/4567, Vol. 24, pp. 12–14. Directive of the Chief of the Soviet General Staff, N.456/276.

19. Ibid., 442/683351, Vol. 67, pp. 12–18. Combat Operations Report of the 17th Fighter Aviation Regiment, April 1, 1951–February 10, 1952.

20. Ibid., 564/68335, Vol. 5, pp. 41–42.

21. Ibid., 456/76897, Vol. 145, p. 67.

22. Ibid., 334/3076, Vol. 45, p. 45.

23. Ibid.

24. Ibid., 764/73421, Vol. 67, p. 45. Combat Report, Headquarters, 17th Fighter Aviation Regiment.

25. Ibid., 767/224, Vol. 67, pp. 112–17. Report, Commander, 87th Antiaircraft Artillery Division, Col. Stepan Spiridonov.

26. Ibid., 24/58777, Vol. 45, p. 114.

27. Ibid., 675/683851, Vol. 5, p. 78, Combat Report, 17th Fighter Aviation Regiment, July 18, 1951.

28. Ibid., 456/6789, Vol. 7, pp. 67–68. Combat Report, 17th Fighter Aviation Regiment, February 24, 1953.

29. Ibid., 227/456, Vol. 27, p. 78.

30. Central Archive of the USSR Defense Ministry, 245/7869, Vol. 67, pp. 34–35.

31. Ibid., 242/6547, Vol. 76, p. 17.

32. Ibid., 214/214212, Vol. 24, p. 45.

33. Central Committee CPSU Archive, 654/21426, Vol. 24, pp. 45–47.

34. V. A. Kosyrev, "Russians and Americans Fought Over Korea," (*Izvestia*, July 3, 1993).

35. Ibid.

36. Y. A. Belov, *The War in Korea, a Memoir* (Moscow: Military Publishing House, 1976), p. 21.

37. Central Archive of the USSR Defense Ministry, 684/45267, Vol. 14, p. 18.

38. Ibid., 467/4328, Vol. 6, p. 16.

39. Ibid., 864/45267, Vol. 12, p. 34.

40. Ibid., 467/4328, Vol. 6, p. 16.

41. Diary, Colonel Dortsev.

42. Ibid.

43. Minutes of speeches of South Korean war veterans, Central Headquarters of the Soviet Army meeting, August 20, 1973, p. 26.

44. Ibid., pp. 31–32.

45. Ibid., p. 44.

Chapter V

1. USSR Military Intelligence Department (GRU) Archive, 67/765, Vol. 12, p. 54.

2. Russian Foreign Affairs Ministry Archive, 526/5067, Vol. 76, p. 68.

3. Ibid. p. 24.

4. Central Committee CPSU Archive, 18/27, Vol. 45, pp. 65–67.

5. Central Archive of the USSR Defense Ministry, 654/11241, Vol. 12, p. 24.

6. Central Committee, 18/127, p. 72. This is taken from a report to the Presidium of the Central Committee, CPSU, January 12, 1956, by First Deputy Defense Minister Alexandr Vasilevsky.

7. "Vietnamese Studying at the Academy" (*Leninetz*, February 20, 1972). This is an account of Vietnamese officers' training from the newspaper of one of the training institutes.

8. School for Military Cadre, Frunze Academy (*Frunsevetz* newspaper, July 12, 1972).

9. Central Committee, 18/127, Vol. 17, p. 92.

10. Russian Foreign, 21/144, Vol. 78, p. 26.

11. Central Archive of the USSR Defense Ministry, 765/145623, Vol. 12, p. 27.

12. Ibid., 645/142667, Vol. 12, pp. 45–46.

13. Communique concerning the visit from the USSR to North Vietnam as reported in an article in the newspaper *Pravda,* January 15, 1966.

14. Central Committee, 18/127, Vol. 14, p. 53.

15. Central Archive of the USSR Defense Ministry, 265/218766, Vol. 25, p. 67.

16. Lt. Col. (Ret.) Alexei Lihovitsky, *In the Jungles of Vietnam, a Memoir,* Archive of the Military-Scientific Society, file maintained at the Central Headquarters of the Soviet Army, Vol. 9, pp. 124–25.

17. Russian Foreign, 75/2112, Vol. 45, pp. 67–77

18. Central Committee, 18/127, Vol. 21, p. 14.

19. Maj. (Ret.) Nikolai Zhuravsky, *Vietnamese Crew*, Archive of the Military-Scientific Society, Vol. 9, p. 61.

20. Central Archive of the USSR Defense Ministry, 675/142733, Vol. 84, p. 47.

21. Ibid., 215/121141, Vol. 36, p. 82.

22. Lt. Gen. Alexei Dryza, *Memoirs of Vietnam Service*, Archive of the Military-Scientific Society, Vol. 12, pp. 45–47.

23. Central Archive of the USSR Defense Ministry, 215/12112, Vol. 14, pp. 26–27.

24. Ibid., 215/223114, Vol. 26, p. 11.

25. Ibid., Vol. 27, p. 16.

26. Col. Boris Arzamastsev, *Vietnam War Duties*, Archive of the Military-Scientific Society, Vol. 12, p. 127.

27. Central Archive of the USSR Defense Ministry, 216/12112, Vol. 12, p. 67.

28. Archive of the Military Scientific Society, Vol. 12, p. 50.

29. Central Archive of the USSR Defense Ministry, 216/12112, Vol. 21, p. 78.

30. Archive of the Military-Scientific Society, Vol. 12, p. 84.

31. Central Committee, 18/127, Vol. 15, p. 28.

32. Archive of the Military-Scientific Society, Vol. 14, pp. 75–76.

33. Ibid.

34. Letters from readers, *Izvestia*, December 9, 1970.

35. Central Committee, 18/36, Vol. 36, p. 19.

36. Ibid. Brezhnev's remark was also reported in *Pravda*, January 29, 1971.

37. Central Committee, 18/36, Vol. 24, p. 11.

Chapter VI

1. *Al Abram* (Cairo newspaper), April 16, 1983.

2. Ibid. August 12, 1991.

3. *Izvestia*, May 21, 1967.

4. *Pravda*, July 1, 1967.

5. Central State Historic Archive, 21452/12, Vol. 6, pp. 78–79.

6. Russian Foreign Affairs Ministry Archive, 67542/7, Vol. 45, pp. 14–19.

7. S. Zemskov, *Special Settlers*. Based on documents of the KGB and the USSR Interior Ministry (Moscow: Sociology Research, 1990), N.12, p. 56.

8. A. Ya Kalyagin, *Along Unknown Roads* (Moscow: Military Service Publishing Company, 1992), p. 76.

9. *Son of the Motherland* (military newspaper), 1993.

10. Russian State Military Archive, 17/21, Vol. 3251, pp. 56, 87.

11. Archive of *Krasnaya Zvezda* (Red Star), the newspaper of the USSR armed forces and the new Russian nation.

12. D. Goroshko, *The Way to Freedom* (Moscow: Science Publishing Company, 1992), p. 143.

13. *Old Debts* (Russian political and business daily, *Today*), February 23, 1993.

14. Central Archive of the USSR Defense Ministry, 201/2416, Vol. 1112, p. 18.

15. Ibid., Vol. 1113, p. 14.

16. "Disinterested Help," *Pravda*, May 6, 1978.

17. Central Archive of the USSR Defense Ministry , 201/2416, Vol. 1112, p. 24.

18. Ibid., 202/3416, Vol. 2061, p. 24.

19. USSR Military Intelligence Department(GRU) Archive, 36/14, Vol. 23, p. 218.

20. Archive of the Military-Scientific Society, Vol. 11/42, p. 218.

21. Ibid., p. 114.

22. Russian Foreign Affairs, 202/3416, Vol. 2062.

23. Central Archive of the USSR Defense Ministry, 202/3416, Vol. 2062, p. 43.

24. R. E. and T. N. Dupuy, *The Harper Encyclopedia of Military History* (New York: Harper Collins, 4th Edition, 1993), p. 1534.

25. Archive of the Military-Scientific Society, Vol. 11–42, pp. 87–88.

26. *Old Debts*, loc. cit.

Chapter VII

1. Central State Military Archive, 234/1916, Vol. 17, pp. 4–12.

2. Central Committee CPSU Archive, 11/64, Vol. 112, p. 27. Stenographic record of Khrushchev's speech at the Defense Council meeting.

3. Archive of the Military-Scientific Society, shorthand record of Cuban veterans' speeches, Vol. 35, pp. 87–88.

4. Central Archive of the Defense Department, 27/1446, Vol. 11, p. 34.

5. Ibid., p. 35.

6. Ibid., p. 36.

7. Ibid., p. 37.

8. Ibid., p. 39.

9. "Fraternal Solidarity," *Na Strazhe*, p. 17, July 21, 1962.

10. Ibid.

11. Archive of Military-Scientific Society, shorthand record of the Symposium on the Caribbean Crisis, January 1989, p. 12.

12. Ibid., p. 13.

13. Ibid., p. 15.

14. Central State Military Archive, 234/1916, Vol. 11, p. 36.

15. Archive of Military-Scientific Society, shorthand record of the Symposium on the Caribbean Crisis, January 1989, p. 15.

16. Central State Military Archive, p. 37.

17. "Special Mission," *Izvestia*, July 12, 1962.

18. "Fraternal Solidarity," loc. cit.

19. Ibid.

20. Archive of Military-Scientific Society, p. 20.

21. Ibid., p. 41.

22. President John F. Kennedy's speech reported in *Pravda*, September 5, 1962.

23. Ibid., p. 14.

24. Central Archive of the USSR Defense Ministry, loc. cit.

25. Central State Historic Archive, Fund 26/18-B, Inv. 1241, File 74, pp. 10.

26. Ibid., p. 12.

27. Ibid., p. 14.

28. Ibid., p. 15.

29. Ibid., p. 20.

30. Archive of Military-Scientific Society, p. 22.

31. Central State Historic Archive, p. 15.

32. Ibid., pp. 23–25.

33. Ibid.

34. Ibid, p. 27.
35. Central State Military Archive, p. 14–15.
36. Central State Historic Archive, p. 31.

Chapter VIII

1. The CPSU designated the members of these meetings. This is the reason that there were only two of the "ruling four" of the Hungarian Labor Party present, M. Rakosi and E. Ghere. Governmental attendees were I. Nagy and A. Hegedus. Non-Party members were the chairman of the Presidium, I. Dobi, and young party and state officials R. Foeldvari, B. Salai, and I. Hidesh. Soviet ambassador E. Kiselev was also present.

2. A. Hegedus, *Atortenelm es a Hatalom Igezeteben*, (Budapest: Historia, 1988), pp. 197–203.

3. Ibid.

4. M. A. Suslov and A. I. Mikoyan were both CPSU Politburo members and close associates of both Stalin and Khrushchev.

5. Rajk's situation was far more complicated, coinciding with Stalin's anti-Yugoslav plan. As part of this, Rakosi requested Soviet advisers, so Gen. F. Belkin of the KGB and others were sent to Budapest. Rakosi conducted the investigation himself, using fantasy and imagination during the trial. He sent a draft of the sentence to Moscow, where some corrections were made and sent back to him. Then a game started. A former Politburo member, Z. Vash, recalled that Rakosi in a telephone conversation asked Stalin if Rajk should be executed. Stalin avoided a direct answer. Vas Z. Betilott, *Konyvem* (Budapest: Historia, 1990), p. 75.

6. Russian Foreign Policy Archive, 059/36/8, Vol. 43, pp. 22–29.

7. *New Times* (Budapest: Historia, 1992), N. 2, pp. 197–203.

8. Russian Foreign, 059/36/8, Vol. 45, pp. 75.

9. Ch. Gati, *Magyarorszog a Kreml Arnyekaban* (Budapest: Historia, 1990), p. 141.

10. *Az 1956-os Magyar Forradolm* (Budapest: Historia, 1991), p. 61.

11. B. Yi Zhelitsky, *Hungary in 1956. Evolution of Estimates of Hungarian Historians* (Budapest: Historia, Modern History, 1992), N. 3.

12. Ibid. p. 76.

13. *Az 1956-os,* Op. Cit., p. 63–64.

14. Russian Foreign, 059/36/8, Vol. 45, p. 140.

15. Ibid., Vol. 42, p. 29.

16. Ibid., European Section, Vol. 110, p. 31, Dossier 49, pp. 21–22.

17. V. Micunovic, *Moskauer Tagebuch, 1956-1958* (Stuttgart, 1982), p. 199.

18. Central State Military Archive, Vol. 11, p. 34.

19. V. L. Musatov, "Janos Kadar and the Time of Reform in Hungary," *Modern History Magazine,* N. 3, 1990, p. 23.

20. *Mozgo Vilag,* 1992, N. 3, p. 55.

21. Central State Military Archive, 654/11241, Vol. 12, p. 70.

22. Gati, Op. Cit., p. 141.

23. *Az 1956,* p. 61.

24. Russian Foreign, 059/36, Vol. 45, p. 134–138.

25. Ibid.

26. Multunk, Op. Cit., 1990, N. 4, p. 159–180.

27. Zhelitsky, p. 52.

28. B. Radionev, "Not To Be Justified," *Izvestia,* December 26, 1991.

29. Ibid.

30. Ibid.

31. Ibid.

32. Ibid.

33. Ibid.

Chapter IX

1. Oleg Sarin and Lev Dvoretsky, *The Afghan Syndrome, the Soviet Union's Vietnam* (Novato, CA: Presidio Press, 1993).

2. USSR Foreign Policy Documents, 1917–1980, Edition 4, Vols. 1–6, p. 175.

3. Ibid., p. 204.

4. USSR Foreign Policy Papers, Vol. 4, pp. 94–95.

5. Ibid., Vol. 10, p. 388.

6. B.S. Gupta, *The Afghan Syndrome: How to Live With Soviet Power* (Delhi: Politica, 1982), p. 42.

Chapter X

1. Central State Historic Archive, 26/18-b, List 1241, Vol. 74, pp. 10–14.

2. *Krasnaya Zvezda* (Red Star), "Disinterested Cooperation," December 17, 1991.

3. Ibid.

4. V. Kiselev, *Conversion of Defense Industry* (Moscow: Military Service Publishing House, 1991), p. 16.

5. *Old Debts*, loc. cit.

6. Ibid.

Conclusion

1. V. I. Lenin, *Complete Works*, 3rd Edition (Moscow; USSR State Printing Office), Vol. 18, p. 232.

2. Minutes, Eighth Congress of the Russian Communist Party, p. 101.

3. A. Avtorhanov, *Kremlin Empire* (Vilnius: *Pravda*, 1990), p. 200.

4. M.S. Gorbachev, *Perestroika and New Thinking for Our Country and the World* (Moscow: News, 1987), p. 52.

5. *Pravda*, November 3, 1987.

Index